Pl
S
F

JEW MADE IN ENGLAND

Jew Made in England

ANTHONY BLOND

TIMEWELL
PRESS

First published in Great Britain in 2004 by
Timewell Press Limited
63 Kensington Gardens Square, London W2 4DG

ISBN 1 85725 200 4

Typeset by Antony Gray
Printed and bound in Great Britain by
Biddles Ltd, King's Lynn

for AJITH
who thought of the title

&

IN MEMORIAM
PETEY SUSMAN
who thought of Ajith

ACKNOWLEDGEMENT
Andreas Campomar

CONTENTS

PART FOUR

Life of Bi

PART FIVE

Multimedia

PART SIX

Laura

PART SEVEN

Un Promeneur Anglais en France

Obituary

Anthony Blond died of a brain tumour at his holiday home in Galle, Sri Lanka, on 23 January, aged ninety-two.

The sixties of the last century were the high tide of Anthony Blond's career, a time when he followed and led many currents. Blond published the first novels of over seventy writers, of whom a few, including Isabel Colegate and Simon Raven, survived that decade; he also introduced the prose works of Jean Genet to the English public. His imprint, now long extinct, will best be remembered for *Small is Beautiful* by E. F. Schumacher, whose title, which has now passed into the language, he claimed to have invented.

He was proud to have been the first to recognise the talents of people as diverse as Tom Stoppard and Jennifer Paterson, and was an early director of *Private Eye*, whose bank account he guaranteed. He was better at initiating projects – a literary agency in Japan, a radio station in Manchester – than pursuing them. Although his career was flawed by intemperance, volatility and quarrels, this did not prevent his acquiring a large and, on the whole, affectionate acquaintance among all sorts and conditions of men and women.

Anthony Bernard Blond was born in 1928 into a Manchester Jewish family of the *haute bourgeoisie*. His mother was a Nahum, member of an established Sephardim family in that city. His father, Neville Blond, was founder of the Royal Court Theatre and a cousin of Harold Laski.

He was educated at Eton, where he was unpopular but academically inclined, and was awarded an exhibition to New College, Oxford in 1945. Before going up to Oxford, he served as a conscript in the Royal Artillery, and was commissioned in 1948. At

Oxford, he registered as a conscientious objector, resisting the Z call up, which signified the left-wing and pacifist views he retained throughout his life.

After coming down from Oxford, he spent the obligatory three months in the family firm in Manchester, suppliers of underwear to Marks & Spencer. He realised early on that he was not cut out for life as a captain of industry and moved to London. He started a literary agency with Isabel Colegate, whose novel was his first publication in 1958, in which year he began publishing on his own account.

He fought Chester unsuccessfully in the Labour interest in the General Election of 1964 but was subsequently elected to the National Council of Civil Liberties; however, he lacked the patience and the persistence for a political career. He was once asked by a stranger at a booksellers' conference whether he had once stood for Chester. With his customary panache, Blond answered, 'Yes. Were you one of the 17,432 who voted for me?' To which the stranger replied, 'No, I was one of the 22,318 who did not!' He wanted the palm without the dust.

After a bout of teaching in Doncaster, he started a textbook imprint, Blond Educational, directed towards the secondary-modern schools of the sixties. This imprint was an instant success – though he lived to regret the effect of expressionism on the minds of children, then the current *Zeitgeist* – and this enabled him to sell his business to CBS, in 1969. After the inevitable disagreement – Blond, volatile and quarrelsome, was never a satisfactory employee – he started up again, with Desmond Briggs as his partner.

When this venture failed, Blond was absorbed by Harlech TV, where he published his second mould-breaking book, *The New Science of Life* by Rupert Sheldrake. In a management buy-out Blond began again with an imprint called Muller, Blond & White. Not surprisingly this enterprise went bankrupt in 1988, having published a lavish volume on the Sistine Chapel, on every copy of which the company contrived to lose money.

Although an energetic spotter of talent, Blond lacked the discipline and temperance to make a good businessman, and was, according to his friends, trusting and gullible. He was now bereft, having regarded an imprint as a form of self-expression.

Blond attempted to secure work through his extensive network of contacts in what he liked to call 'the publishing game'. No one wanted to know: and Blond was quoted as saying, 'None of my best friends are Jews.' Nevertheless, he was taken up, out of charity, by the Palestinian Arab Naim Attallah, as a consultant to his firm, Quartet.

Having always lived, as a New York writer commented, 'high on the *gratin*', he was delighted to be appointed restaurant critic for *Vogue*, where he worked for two years. He was helped in this office by his partner Laura Hesketh, daughter of Colonel Roger and Lady Mary Hesketh, whom he married, spectacularly, in their house in Sri Lanka in 1981.

Blond had been married previously to Charlotte, daughter of John and Isobel Strachey, whom he divorced in 1960. His private life had not been all that private: on the birth of his natural son Aaron, by the author Cressida Lindsay, a young man, Andrew McCall, many years his junior, joined his household and stayed for fourteen years.

In 1989, Blond and his wife moved to France with their adopted Sri Lankan son, Ajith. Their first act was to buy a village house in the commune of Blond and a plot in the cemetery. Laura Blond subsequently bought a large seventeenth-century townhouse in the nearby town of Bellac, where Blond passed, in unaccustomed serenity, the last years of his life.

Although more a sentimental than a practising Jew, his conversion to Judaism developed through study and reflection. He was encouraged by Abraham Levy, the rabbi at the Congregation of Spanish and Portuguese Jews, whose brief and often cutting sermons at the Bevis Marks and Maida Vale synagogues had drawn him to the religion in which he had been born but not grown up. He taught himself to read Hebrew and was said to recite without an English accent.

Blond often argued, if he could find anyone to listen, against the wisdom of the *kashruth*, considering it a deliberate political device, provoking more dispute than satisfaction and accounting for a coronary disease endemic to Jews. He renounced his belief in Zionism and feared the dominance of the North American Ashkenazi element in Israel. He developed a keen interest in Jewish law, but could not stomach the Pentateuch. Nevertheless, he was happier attending an orthodox Jewish synagogue service than any other.

He wrote two books on publishing, which were accepted texts in their day, a novel, *Family Business*, and *Blond's Roman Emperors*, marred, said *The Times Literary Supplement*, by 'simple howlers'. A slapdash attitude to essential detail was one of his more unfortunate traits. He also wrote *Mes Carnets d'un Promeneur Anglais en France*, about his first eight years living in that country. He leaves a widow, Laura, and two sons, Aaron and Ajith.

26 January 2020

PART ONE

Family Business

CHAPTER ONE

My Father

My father sat in a gilt chair, smoking a cigar and contemplating the Renoir of a little girl with fair hair and blue eyes. The effect was dramatic because the illuminated painting was the only light in the large Portman Square drawing-room. He was dressed, in white tie and tails, for a Pilgrims' dinner at the Mansion House, the Order of St Michael and St George around his neck and the ribbon of the Légion d'honneur discreetly in his buttonhole. He started when I entered the room, as if interrupted from a reverie; but I knew, and he knew that I knew, that this *mise-en-scène*, with himself as the centre-piece, had been deliberately arranged.

When he died, the obituary editor of *The Times* told me how surprised he was – as were my brother and I – by the number of encomia for someone who was not an eminent public figure. Was this noble, generous, considerate and honourable man really our father?

At a reunion of the Guinea Pig Club* – for the burned airmen rehabilitated by his only true friend, Sir Archie McIndoe – the grateful lads burst unprompted into 'For He's a Jolly Good Fellow', whereupon my father, who had paid for the occasion, stumped over to where we were cowering by the bar and declared: 'As a matter of fact, I am!' He was, too. He was also a terrible liar.†

* These gatherings were arranged by the club's welfare officer, Flight Lieutenant Edward Blacksell, RAF. 'Blackie' became the headmaster of a secondary school in Barnstable and, together with Ronald Duncan (poet, playwright and an illegitimate son of a maharajah, so it was said), started the Taw and Torridge Festival. They approached my father to head up a new kind of theatre company to sponsor aspiring playwrights. My father insisted on a theatre: hence the Royal Court Theatre in Sloane Square and the English Stage Company's first hit *Look Back in Anger* in 1956.

† In 1885, in an address to members of the Reform Club, of which he had

Quite often my father's lies were so transparent that, barely concealing reality, they did little damage. He lied on principle. Mainly, I imagine, *en famille*; otherwise how could he have sustained so many positions of trust in a long and well-chronicled career? He lied like other people play tennis, as if it were for relaxation. He never resented being challenged or accused: he would simply emit a little sigh of resignation and compassion, like a prophet rejected in his own country by his kith and kin. Like a prophet, he spoke of what should have happened or what he would like to have happened.

Yet he was physically brave – to which his Great War medals attest – and could when aroused deploy his moral courage effectively. He was in awe of his brother-in-law, Simon Marks,* whose decision in family matters was absolute. Simon had a sister called Matilda, known as 'Tilly', whose wealth and simplicity – the first very real, the second imagined – made her, so the family had decided, a prey to adventurers. Tilly was a novelist's dream. She was the original of the lady in the Somerset Maugham story, whose eyes, said the gigolo, 'make the Mediterranean look like pea soup'. Simon had bottled her up in a home for some years, where, of course, having nothing to spend her money on, her fortune, an inherited block of Marks & Spencer shares, grew. She was released from her cocoon by a formidable lady called Hilda Brighten, who organised her parties for her.†

Carl Brisson, the famous Danish cabaret star, now came on to the scene and, as Noël Coward would have said, 'proposed marriage'. Needless to say, he was promptly dispatched. When, many years later, Tilly wanted to marry an impoverished former ballet dancer, Terence Kennedy, Simon, and consequently the rest of the family, set their faces against the union. Alone, my father protested, and

---

been made an honorary member, Gladstone said Queen Elizabeth lied when she had to; Cromwell lied for reasons of state; but Charles I was a terrible liar.

* Only his wife Miriam Marks was not.

† She also organised parties for the entire cast of the latest musical at the Savoy.

convinced Simon that he was behaving in an unnecessarily unkind way to an old lady who did not want to die a spinster. Moreover, her life would be made sunny – all being well in these things – by the love of a goodish man.

Tilly enjoyed years of married life, in a *ménage à trois*, tended and indulged, petted and cared for by an intelligent, charming and witty husband and his boyfriend. When she was safely dead and buried, my father, as her executor, trotted round to see the widower.

Since she had come out, Tilly had been a determined buyer of *objets d'art*, which were mainly French, albeit from the most expensive dealers near Berkeley Square where she lived. When the Louvre enquired as to whether she might sell her *guéridon*, she coolly replied: 'Can I buy yours?' But paying over the top in the thirties had proved a brilliant investment in the seventies; and Tilly's possessions were many, exotic and, without exception, very valuable. She was 'seriously rich'. I remember their new Italian butler screeching down the telephone to a friend, 'Ecco e due Rolls!'

There is nothing the rich like more than more money; they tend to have few friends because they suspect the poor and envy those even richer. My father was no exception: he reverenced money and its power. 'Money talks,' he often said; and he enjoyed this conversation more than any other. He worshipped money, equating it with holiness.* Needless to say my father's report on his interview with the widower was awaited with keen interest. It was known that Terence was to be the principal but not necessarily the sole beneficiary. I remember coveting some eighteenth-century paintings on glass of the Seasons, for which I was punished. I received nothing.

My father reported that he had told Terence, 'I don't want anything for myself, but I would like you to think of doing something for my boys.'

---

* In the fifties, I remember Charles Clore coming to tea in his Cadillac, and my father gurgling over him as if he were Baal.

This language, coupled with this sentiment – for his indifference, in later life, to our welfare was almost regal – was so uncharacteristic that I blurted out, 'Daddy, you didn't say that!'

'No,' replied my father, 'I did not.'

Yet it was not always thus. Earlier voyages taken with my father were full of sunshine. I resembled him physically and I think that we admired each other. My happiest childhood moment was when we set off to join the rest of the family for a holiday in Criccieth, where Lloyd George had set up his legal practice. We went in my mother's open Hudson Terraplane, a black and yellow monster, with bright red leather seats. The car was open and I had a two-pound bar of Cadbury's motoring chocolate on my eight-year-old lap. It was a wonderful holiday: we caught eight mackerel in an hour and I saw my first film, *The Firefly*, with Jeanette MacDonald and Allan Jones. It was very hot, like all childhood holidays, but none the less we ate roast beef and Yorkshire pudding every day for lunch, followed by roly-poly or baked jam roll. Years later my mother remarked that my father had bribed the chef. He liked that kind of thing.

My father was socially adept and very bonhomous. On the subject of how to conduct oneself when attending a banquet, he gave me a piece of advice I have never forgotten: 'Anthony, seek out the wine waiter and give him a ten-shilling note. First, you'll get enough to drink; and secondly, people will think that that fellow must be someone important.'

My father had been brought up in an almost totally Jewish part of Manchester, Cheetham Hill, where his uncle on his mother's side, Nathan Laski, was the magistrate, the chief Jew and an autocrat. Winston Churchill occasionally stayed with Nathan at Smedley House, where he would dandle Nathan's son, Harold,* on his knee.

My father had attended Manchester Grammar School, like Simon Marks and Israel Sieff, who later became hereditary and

---

* Harold Laski became a political theorist and chairman of the British Labour Party (1945–6).

life peers respectively. But unlike them he had succeeded in entering a smart regiment and, thereby, English society; so that by the time my mother was twenty-six, and open to offers of marriage, he seemed an appropriate match. Simon Marks had previously forbidden him, on account of his reputation, to marry his youngest sister, Elaine, who eventually became my step-mother. This was probably due to Simon's jealousy of my father's military prowess. Simon spent the war cleaning up after horses in Oldham barracks, or was it Bolton, until seconded to become the assistant to Chaim Weizmann.*

*　　*　　*

Greenbank House, whence we had set off on that summer's day, was just in Bowdon, which was superior to Altrincham, the last station on the first electric railway to Manchester. My father turned his back on his upbringing in the Jewish enclaves of Cheetham Hill, Higher Broughton and Didsbury: so there was nothing Jewish about our upbringing in *Judenrein* Bowdon. He arranged, at the behest of my mother, for my brother and me to be sent away, aged eight, to a preparatory school in Thanet.

My mother's father, Victor (Diddles) Nahum, was a rich Sephardic Jew from Tripoli, Libya, who didn't have much English but managed to refer to my father, who had relatively little money, as 'that damn German'.† As soon as she could, my mother moved her gallant new husband away from the 'ghetto', as she put it, to the more salubrious pastures of North Cheshire, to Bowdon, which was, just before the Great War, the most highly rated borough in the kingdom. It was filled with des res and was to be the first place in the north of England to hit half a million for a flat – a penthouse on the top of a Victorian mansion, overlooking the Cheshire plain. As a child, I would certainly have had tea at that house, owned by a Bakerjian, Zochonis or Bigio, or some other non-Jewish cotton magnate.

---

*　First president of Israel.
†　This has the strict meaning in Hebrew of *Ashkenazi.*

Up and until my own military service, my feelings towards my father were those of a dutiful and loving son, and his to me of a distantly indulgent and fairly proud papa. Having been a reserved and inhibited child, I soon discovered at Oxford the joys of drink, people, parties, fancy waistcoats, foreign travel and falling in love – mostly with young men – *and* the need for money to support these activities. At the same time I began to encounter and create those huge waves of emotion which have followed me about ever since; the most dominant and most menacing of these was – until the day he died, when I keened uncontrollably for hours – clearly labelled 'Daddy'.

*   *   *

The author of *My Secret Life*, a sexual confession now in the British Library, originally of one million words, which I nearly published, tells how he asked the question at a private dinner at his club: 'If anyone has *not* seduced the parlour-maid on the dining-room table while waiting for his wife to dress for a party, would he please raise his hand.' Nobody, he said, did. Transfer this Victorian scenario to the boss checking the factory floor after the workers had gone home in the twenties in Manchester.

It is, shall we say, a hot summer's evening. He notices the cutter, an attractive girl, finishing off a bolt of cloth on the cutting-room table: and we have the first act in the drama of what became a *Sunday Express* headline story. It can't have been that unusual: the proportion of women to men in those CMT (Cut-Measure-Trim) factories was perhaps a hundred to one. My father was attractive and randy, and the lady was willing. In the fullness of time a paternity suit was brought against him, and he had to pay thirty bob a week to the mother, whose name was Wilson. She must have been a good and intelligent woman, for she seldom complained or demanded extra money from him. When times were very bad, however, she travelled to the back door of Greenbank House and asked for my mother, who always gave her five pounds, never mentioning the matter to my father or anyone else.

In those days, between the wars, my father, who would have

liked to have stayed on in the army as a Horse Guards officer, had he had the money, rose early to be on parade at Blond Brothers. There he worked with his younger brother, Horace, who looked like a character from *Der Stürmer*. Before the war my father took four thousand a year out of the business: enough for a cook, a chauffeur, a parlour-maid, a nanny at three pounds a week, a gardener and a gardener's boy at ten shillings a week. The latter's duties consisted, said my father, of turning round the tortoise when it reached the gate at the end of the drive, where I saw Churchill pass on the morning after the Blitz on Manchester. My brother, Peter, remembers an elderly forewoman recounting the ups and downs of Blond Brothers and concluding with the words: 'And then, ma luv, your dad went bust!'

Fortunately, for my father and his brother, they were bailed out by my maternal grandmother, Elise Nahum. But it was the advent of war, which was to save so many industries, that allowed the business to prosper under the cunning guidance of Uncle Horace. He invented a lucrative sideline in Sammy Scarves, one of which I sent to each of the assistant masters at my preparatory school on their birthdays. (I was that sort of little boy.)

In the fifties, Blond Brothers sold out to Emu Wool, whose logo was an ostrich in the form of a ball of wool pierced by a pair of knitting needles. My father, having recently returned from a successful spell as a commercial ambassador* to New York, now became chairman. His reign was disastrous. His major function now was to buy the raw material from Australia at the right price; and yet he managed to get it wrong year after year. Nevertheless, as chairman, he saw that dividends were passed constantly (this being the only office he managed to get right), much to the amusement of my friend Alan Clark.

In the end, bad judgement led to my father's eventual dismissal from the board of directors.

---

* He had been appointed in 1948, as a Jew with some savvy, by Harold Wilson – at a time when traders were tearing out *Made in Britain* labels from their cashmere sweaters.

'Should I go, Peter,' he said to my brother.

'Yes, Daddy, you must go.'

So my father pottered back to Orchard Court, where he had a stroke.

Summoned by my stepmother, Elaine, I rang the business section of *The Times* with an announcement to the effect that '*Mr Neville Blond CMG, OBE has resigned as chairman of Emu Wool in order better to attend to his duties as chairman of the Royal Court Theatre and other charitable obligations. He will, however, be available for consultation . . .* ' et cetera. This was printed verbatim and, the event being of no great import, no other version appeared. Elaine suggested that as my father had led an interesting life, an autobiography was in order. And would I find a writer?

I arranged the autobiography to be ghost-written by a journalist called Warwick Charlton, who had edited the Eighth Army newspaper for Montgomery, and whose book rights in the building of a replica of the *Mayflower* I had handled as an agent.

At first all went well. Warwick went down to my father's house in Sussex and was met at the station. They toured the farm, prodded the latest prize bull, an Aberdeen Angus, sold to my father by the astute Lord Lovat, enjoyed lunch, a cigar, then cognac shipped specially from France by his chum Eugène Buhan. Warwick listened to my father's fabulous tales and recorded them all, concluding with one in particular. Towards the end of the Great War, my father, now Major Blond, had taken girls out from the *Folies Bergère* who would apply plaster of Paris to their nipples in order to keep them in good shape. One morning he woke up barely able to breathe . . .

When, on the following Monday, Warwick read the story back, my father denied it. He was, Warwick told him, such a terrible liar that he gave up. My father pursued the errant scribe in vain, demanding that he either return or repay the advance of five hundred pounds. He wanted my advice. Wishing foolishly to sound the tough guy, I said, 'Sue him.' Even more foolishly, my father did.

Warwick Charlton fought back. His first salvo took the shape of a cartoon in the *Sunday Express* based on the Wilson relationship;

then, when the solicitors did not relent, Bang! across six columns of page two went the headline, 'The Strange Story of Mr Blond and Sergeant Kenneally VC'.

Ms Wilson's child had grown into a fine young man, the spitting image, as is often God's joke with bastards, of his father, both tall and brave. In 1942, Gunner Wilson RA had met Lance-Corporal John Patrick Kenneally, 1st Battalion Irish Guards, in the NAAFI at Crewe station on his way to North Africa. Both were discontented with their lot: Wilson was raring to get at the enemy; Kenneally did not want to die for somebody else's King and Country. So, after much warm NAAFI beer they exchanged AB 64s, Parts I and II, their military identity cards. They became each other. With millions of men at arms, nobody much noticed at Woolwich.

What happened to my half-brother is best described by Citation No. 2722925:

The magnificent gallantry of this non-commissioned officer on these two occasions under heavy fire, his unfailing vigilance, and remarkable accuracy were responsible for saving many valuable lives during days and nights in the forward positions. His actions also played a considerable part in holding these positions and this influenced the whole course of the battle. His rapid appreciation of the situation, his initiative and his extraordinary gallantry in attacking single-handed a massed body of the enemy and breaking up an attack on two occasions, was an achievement that can seldom have been equalled. His courage in fighting all day when wounded was an inspiration to all ranks.

Not everyone discovers a half-brother with a VC, so I arranged to meet him at the Waldorf in the Aldwych, on the grounds, I suppose, that unusual encounters need usual settings. He was breathtakingly like my father was as a cavalry officer in the Great War. He ordered two large whiskies and told the waiter, with a wave of the hand, to keep the change. I now understood how he had won the VC.

After the war my half-brother told me that he had gone to see my father at the Ministry of Supply. 'The old man was very polite,' he said. 'He gave me a fiver.' More than twenty years later he called again on my father who was not so polite, nor so generous.

He lived in Warwick and his business was selling cars. I'm happy to say they were new cars, and I would have bought one from him without hesitation. Business was bad and he wanted to emigrate to Australia. I offered to plead his cause *au près de* Papa, who received me, with my stepmother (like Mrs Proudie) very much in attendance. I was blamed for everything and when I mumbled that they might give him something out of what they might be giving me, they both shouted in chorus, 'What makes you think that *you're* getting anything?' I laughed at the time and when I told Flora Solomon* indignantly of their intransigence – 'and they have Monet on the walls!' – she laughed too. Their generation was less tolerant than ours of bastards; and, though they might not have admitted to being affected, the attitude of Judaism is particularly savage where illegitimate children are concerned.†

My father was often irritable, mean, spiteful and plain 'ornery', as the Americans say; but I don't believe I have ever met anyone with more charm. He loved laughing. Tales of human folly, especially mine, entertained him enormously. I once went to an auction of office equipment: Nicholas Luard's magazine *Scene* had gone extravagantly bust, despite having published the first article about the Beatles and having employed Tom Stoppard as dramatic critic. I was in pursuit of the latest intercom equipment for my new publishing premises in Doughty Street. I was very excited by my winning bid – a bargain, I thought – until I was handed an aluminium hat-stand. My father seethed like a happy kettle for hours. That is how I have always wanted to remember him.

*   *   *

My father was an artist at the ingenious wound. One Christmas – the season designed for such sport – we found ourselves unexpectedly

---

* She was hired by Simon Marks at a dinner party to introduce 'welfare' into Marks & Spencer. Her son, Peter Benenson, founded Amnesty.

† They are called *mamsers* and, strictly, though the rule is never enforced, they and their children and their children's children are not allowed to attend synagogue.

and uneasily in the same room in the family home at Gotwick
Manor, a sort of instant Manderley ('one day, my boy, this will be
yours') on the outskirts of East Grinstead. It was always filled with
guests: props to complement the décor, mouths for the mounds of
splendid food, and hands for the games of bridge, canasta and gin
rummy. We were both sitting on the sofa in the games-room
waiting for something to happen when a woman entered, and I
could see how relieved my father was at not having to talk to me.
She was the widow of a fashionable dentist, who had been the lover
of Elaine's older sister Becky,* a Frau Reichsmarschallin of a lady
who had founded the Women's International Zionist Organisation.
She had also lived for years in Palestine, in a large house with the
only butler in the state of Israel, bullying its fledgling politicians.

The widow advanced bearing a Christmas gift for my father. A
pair of enamel ashtrays in the Ming style, from Messrs Spink,
emerged from the expensive wrapping paper.

'Are they genuine?' he asked.

I observed that the Mings did not smoke.

'Have I given you a Christmas present, Anthony?'

'Not yet, Daddy,' I answered.

'Well then,' he said, 'you can take these.' And he stumped
cheerfully out of the room, having executed, as shooters say, a
perfect left and right.

As an artist in insult, he was himself vulnerable. Once I gave him
a pair of inexpensive, as Elaine would have said, woolly Greek
slippers, which would have been too small for a child of ten. Months
later he complained almost tearfully, 'I couldn't even get them on!'

'Oh dear,' said I, 'I must have bought the wrong size.'

*   *   *

When he was dying in 1970, attended by a host of the Queen's
physicians, I met Lord Evans coming out of his bedroom and asked
if he could perhaps give him some LSD.

---

*   Both Becky and her husband Israel, Lord Sieff, were famous for their
    infidelities.

'I wish I could,' replied that honest and honourable man.

I had the year before sold my publishing business to CBS, when it was à *la mode* for American firms to buy British publishing companies. It was the corporate policy to acquaint the vendors of the often-erratic purchases of Bill Paley, the founder of CBS, with each other. So I met Goddard Lieberson, the pioneer of the vinyl LP, and was given all the works of Beethoven in a lovely boxed set. And when Charles Schultz, whom Paley had also bought, came to London, I was given a man-sized Snoopy, which I knew would delight my father. He had a sense of the sentimental and the absurd, qualities alien to Elaine, who could sit through tear-jerkers like *The King and I* dry-eyed. I think, to be fair, she must have had a deficiency in her tear-ducts. She banished the over-sized Snoopy from the flat, saying did I realise he was dying and he wasn't a baby. Then my father was himself banished to an intensive-care ward, where I went to pay my last respects. He was festooned with the paraphernalia the medical profession impose on the dying and so doped up that he could not recognise anybody. I thought how dreadful that his last sight of a human face would be that of a perfectly friendly and competent, but alien, Australian nurse. 'Couldn't he be allowed to die in his own bed?' No, that was too untidy.

I kissed him goodbye.

At the memorial service in the Liberal Synagogue, opposite Lords, I sat next to Elaine and we listened to the rabbi's – by appointment to Marks & Spencer – fatuous and sycophantic address. 'He has gone to a place even more beautiful than his own lovely home in East Grinstead . . . ' It was for sentences like these that S. J. Perelman invented the expression 'wrist shrinking'. But had he? I don't believe the angels would have considered my father *that* qualified.

Later on, a medium I attended told me a crowd of people had messages for me – the most insistent, who kept tugging at her sleeve, being my old nanny. 'Is my father around?' I asked. She had difficulty in finding him and all he said, when asked about his feelings towards me, was: 'It was six of one and half a dozen of the other.' Now that sounded like my Daddy.

CHAPTER TWO

My Mother

She was born Eileen Rebecca, named after her paternal grand-mother, but chose to be known as 'Reba'. A bright child who wrote poetry, she attended that school in Didsbury which was always top of the league for girls' scholarships to Oxford, and indeed gained a place. Nevertheless, she was not allowed to take it up by her parents, who were fearful of alien – i.e. non-Jewish – influence.

Perhaps it was this stricture, coupled with the fashionable anti-Semitism of the thirties, which shaped my mother's profound distaste for Judaism and its practitioners. This anti-Semitism, which lasted the whole of her long life, even extended to a refusal to utter the words 'Israel' or 'Hebrew', which became 'Palestine' and, unbelievably, 'Palestinian'. She later brought Peter and me up as if we were Gentiles, which meant I was not allowed to be bar mitzvahed.*

My mother's younger brother, Jack, was allowed to go to Oxford and went up to Merton, and it was through him that she met and fell in love with one of his friends, Richard Henry Anstruther Morris-Marsham.† But in the meantime another marriage had been arranged. She was not in love with my father but admired him as a soldier; he also made her laugh. My parents had a tolerably happy time between the wars, until he left for the Second World War and for the generous embrace – she was very rich – of Elaine Marks, his first cousin's wife and the youngest sister of Simon Marks.

My mother was easily consoled, and, as the mistress of a large

---

* I went to College Chapel at Eton which I enjoyed, and was very nearly confirmed by the Visitor, the Bishop of Lincoln.

† My mother was only able to marry him forty years later.

house with a spectacular drawing-room where even the books were sprayed white, had quite a giddy war on her alimony of fifteen hundred pounds a year. She drove round England picking up antiques and staying in police stations when the hotels were full, and she was briefly a munitions worker beneath the House of Lords.

As a child, I did not see much of my mother. My birth had been difficult and occurred not long after the death from melancholy of her beloved sister, Phyllis, who was only twenty. Besides, she preferred my younger brother Peter,* who had golden hair, blue eyes, a sweet temper and curvature of the spine, all of which merited attention; whereas I was a somewhat surly, argumentative little boy, happy with my books and my electric trains at the top of the house.

Whilst my mother loved my brother, she regarded me as a dangerous extension of my father, who bullied my little brother Peter. She called him 'Pookle' or 'Pookins' and instructed the nanny, should Mr Blond enter the nursery, to remove the child instantly upstairs, out of harm's way. Peter grew up to be an adequate shot, a competent yachtsman and even a racing driver at Le Mans. None of these accomplishments removed him from the reach of my mother's tongue, which, when she felt in the mood, was a formidable lash. Once she addressed him as follows: 'You started off in the rag trade; you went in for second-hand cars; and now you're an estate agent – how low can you go!'†

I learned to respect my mother. I once boasted that I had deceived a bus conductor about my age to pay a lower fare. She hit

---

* He was christened Peter Robin to emphasise his gentility, neither name being capable of being Judaised – unlike Anthony/Avrom and Bernard/Baruch.

† This is technically correct. Peter was indeed, for most of his business life, a supplier to Marks & Spencer – with factories in Wigan, Skelmersdale, Cape Town and Malta – to the tune, some twenty years ago, of fourteen million pounds. He then joined Sotheby's and ran its vintage-car sales – Ferraris and so forth. At the time of our mother's outburst he had just acquired his office in Sloane Street and was in charge of the London end of Sotheby's International Realty.

me so hard that I didn't tell another lie until I denied signing a beer chit 'Benito Mussolini' at Eton, for which I was 'eight tanned'. An ambivalent experience, since I had once been 'fagged round' to the captain of the eights, who beat me in spite of the fact that a year or two before he had received me naked in his room.* These two episodes put me off lying for life.

But, of course, I loved her. When she complained of her debts – much pink gin was consumed by her admirers in the big white room, where Peter and I played Noël Coward when everyone was away – I sold my Trix for forty pounds and gave her the money. 'A drop in the ocean!' complained our nanny and her mother, 'Aunty', both of whom never failed to disapprove of my mother's lifestyle.

In 1944, my mother sold Greenbank House for very little money; gallingly, it was subsequently converted into eight flats, and later a pair of bankers' villas popped up where the tennis-court had been. When Peter visited the place, the tenant whose flat had been the big white room remarked: 'Oh, how are the mighty fallen!'

After we moved, my mother coveted the 'Old Forge' – a house at the end of an isolated Victorian village on the edge of the Blackmore Forest in Hampshire, near Liphook, whose post-mistress wrote *Lark Rise to Candleford* – and so did I. My major influence at that time was not André Gide or Stendhal or Schiller, whose entire works my contemporary Tom Bridges,† with whom my father constantly and unfavourably compared me, had read in the holidays, but Beverley Nichols. I drooled over *Down the Garden Path* and *A Thatched Roof*, and dreamed of lupins and a meadow divided by a little stream – the Old Forge, in fact. I even asked my father to give my mother the eight thousand pounds she needed and, sweetly, he did.

During my last half at Eton, which I didn't like and which didn't

---

* He is now a Lord Lieutenant.
† Later Lord Bridges GCMG, head of the Diplomatic Service, and a favourite of George Brown when he was Foreign Minister.

like me, I thought of nothing else. My only two friends, a Yorkshire squire and Peter Swinnerton-Dyer,* had left. I had been denied the headship of my house and had not made the sixth form, so I paid off m'tutor, bought a driving licence from the post office for five bob and a 1928 DT Rudge motorcycle for twenty-five pounds and set off in third gear, because I knew no other, to lunch at the Caprice with my father. At one point he left the table to make a telephone call and when I left the Rudge was not there. My father had had it removed.

I crossed the street to 12 Arlington Street, where I spent my time dialling TIM, the speaking clock, and playing Tchaikovsky's Piano Concerto No. 1 in B flat minor. The boundaries of my London life were walking down St James's to see my mother in her mews flat opposite St James's Palace and back up again to see my father in Arlington House. So the summons for a medical in Goodge Street – where on earth was that? – came as a relief. From that moment on, whether on leave from the Army or down from Oxford, until my first marriage, and while living with Andrew McCall, until married to Laura, I spent weekends evenly between my mother's and my stepmother and father's country establishments, finding the contrast both marked and agreeable. Thank God, I often thought, for the pleasures of a broken home!

When my mother bought the Old Forge, where she played the merry rural divorcee, keeping hens and reminding herself to shut them in at night by placing an egg in the middle of the carpet, my stepmother left Saint Hill† and settled into Gotwick Manor. Our wicked cousin Philip Laski called it 'Gotrichquick Manor': stock-broker Tudor, but convincing, with bothies for gardeners, a petrol pump which worked, a farm and woodlands, two tennis-courts, a kidney-shaped swimming-pool with fully equipped bar, and, later, a stream which could be switched on from inside the house. We

---

*   He later became Vice-Chancellor of Cambridge.
†   The house was subsequently purchased by L. Ron Hubbard for his Scientology sect.

were never less than sixteen for lunch and dinner, served by the infamous butler Ripley, and his colleague Gibbons, snatched by Elaine from the Carlyon Bay Hotel.

The guests were the usual troupe, enlivened by cameo appearances of the odd celebrity, like Hermione Gingold (a dirty woman, said Elaine, who left lipstick marks in the bath), Sir Hartley Shawcross QC, a new neighbour who was inveigled into coming by Fleur Cowles (socially more adept), plastic surgeons from Archie McIndoe's hospital, officials from the Board of Trade, where my father worked, and, when he became first chairman of the Royal Court, darling George Devine and Robin Fox.* Fifty-six souls depended, my father once calculated, on this establishment, all of them, like the farm Bentley, tax deductible.

My mother's familiars were different: an architect, a wine-merchant, a printer by appointment to Barclays Bank, a French photographer who remarked, 'L'art de décorer, c'est par les espaces' (which certainly did not apply to my mother, who crammed every surface with delicious tat), and an import/export agent, fashionable in times when foreign travel was tricky, who arrived in her tiny sitting-room one morning with the announcement: 'Reba, disaster! The servants have all left!'

Neither rich nor poor, troubled by infidelities on every side, to which my mother listened patiently, and laced with alcohol, the coterie was the stuff from which Iris Murdoch's novels are woven. All were amused and amusing, save for the Army major who suffered from regressive memory and was wont to remark: 'I knew him so well I've completely forgotten his name,' or, 'I've been there so many times I no longer remember where it is!'

*   *   *

My mother's second marriage, to the love of her life, was totally happy and fulfilled. Richard Morris-Marsham was a tall, courteous, establishment figure – there has been a Marsham nicknamed 'Slug' at Eton for generations – and devoted to her. They slept in the

---

* Father of the actors James and Edward, and the producer Robert.

same bed until he was taken to hospital to die and, even then, she followed him, taking the room next to his. He had regular habits: writing to his mother every Sunday, recording his bridge sessions and his consumption of 'gin and French',* and, best of all, allowing my mother to redecorate the Taylor Walker pubs in his charge, in East Anglia, with fishing nets and coloured glass balls. Sham, as my stepfather liked to be known, hated abroad and would only holiday in Northern Cyprus where he could count on bridge with his own kind, gin and French, and reliable English food. They would picnic in the mountains behind Girne, oblivious to the bullets whistling past.

Sham lived at Spilfeathers, formerly a coaching inn, in the village of Fryerning, near Ingatestone, where my brother and I occasionally spent the weekend. (This was before the Essex man, when soft-faced people lived in Essex.) The air was very Saxon; indeed the local nob, though you would not have thought it, was a Mr Disney of the oldest common family in England. He often told me that when he went to Piccadilly Circus, he was always recognised by the flower-sellers and the shoeshine boys. Mr Disney, a large eupeptic gentleman, was mostly drunk, a condition to which a man with an uninterrupted male line of a thousand years was surely entitled. He once broke his leg, falling out of his car in the garage.

Down the rolling English country road lived the Miles family, in a house I called 'Blue Gates' (because it had blue gates; it also had a tennis-court, a paddock, and maybe, or maybe not, a swimming-pool). The father was Major Miles, a dyspeptic little man, who often sizzled with rage. He had married a cool, mother-of-pearl lady, the granddaughter, it was said, and particularly by her, of Edward VII by a parlour maid. Their daughter Sarah grew up – rather quickly – went to RADA and began an affair with Willy Fox,† with whom she was later to perform in *The Servant*. When Willy went to Kenya for his national service I succeeded him in

---

* He once worked out that he had consumed 4,600 gallons.
† He later changed his forename to James.

Sarah's affections. She says in her autobiography that I drove her round in a Bentley and spoilt her rotten. I do hope I did.

She had a blazing talent. I saw her in a RADA production of Pirandello's *Six Characters in Search of an Author* and was moved to the bowels. I telephoned every producer I knew to say so, but with no result. Once in Harriet Crittall's tiny flat, where I had arranged for her to stay, she delivered to me alone, in front of an electric fire, the ' . . . thou be Dauphin . . . ' speech from *Joan of Arc*. I cried.

My brother, meanwhile, had given up driving Jaguar XKs at Le Mans on the recommendation of my mother, and not before time, because otherwise he might now be dead. In its stead, he purchased a slow, safe, comfy, Dutch steel-built motor yacht, which he drove to Cherbourg for long weekends.

Of course, I had to borrow it. Returning one moonlit night up the Beaulieu River, I mixed up port and starboard, and guided the yacht on to a bank where we stuck for the night. The first thing I noticed in the morning was the face of a cow peering through the cabin window. We were now parked in a field and there was nothing to do but wait for the river to return and pick us up. In spite of the shamingly un-nautical angle of the boat, Sarah paced up and down the deck, declaiming her latest part. After enough of this, we began the most natural and enjoyable activity known to man- and womankind, and when that was over Sarah remarked, 'Willy used to stay in me for *hours.*'

It was seventeen years later I found my riposte. I bumped into Sarah outside the Plaza Hotel in New York and said to her, 'You have to remember that at the time Willy was unemployed!'

*   *   *

Stephen Potter, inventor of 'one-upmanship', which he practised with irritating assiduity outside, as it were, office hours, and his wife Heather Jenner, who started the first marriage bureau – for lonely officers in Ceylon, where her papa was GOC – were frequent visitors to Sham's house. So when the husbands died the widows decided to team up. My mother's amateur talent for matchmaking and Heather's professionalism made them a formidable pair.

Marriages burst out all over. Sham's first wife was found a partner with a large yacht, whose company he preferred to hers; but never mind, there was no provision for service after sale.

Invited by my brother to his house in Chesapeake Bay, they were persuaded, after a few days, to take a cultural tour of Virginia. Peter, with difficulty, found a hire car with a manual gearbox, on which Heather had insisted, and sent them off with marked maps for such high spots as Williamsburg. They were reluctant, however, to venture off the Interstate Highway and cruised up and down, stopping overnight in large motels. In the morning the car would never start. Peter found out why.

American cars, though larger than their European counterparts, have only six- as opposed to twelve-volt batteries, which tire easily. They are also equipped with illuminated vanity mirrors in the rear seats. Every night before making their entrance to the motel, the ladies would repair their faces in the mirrors, and every night they failed to turn off the lights. Every morning they found the battery was flat. My mother would then telephone the sheriff from a phone booth, where he advertised his availability to travellers in distress, and would wait for his arrival to start their car. They met a lot of charming sheriffs.

*   *   *

A few years ago, my mother, then aged ninety-four, invited Laura and me to stay with her in a hotel in Northern Cyprus, which belonged to the sister of local mogul and international financier, Asil Nadir. I, therefore, negotiated an invite to tea *chez* Nadir for the three of us. When we arrived, armed guards tumbled out of a blacked-out Mercedes and ordered me to the back of the house where our little hired car could be inspected for explosives. At the sight of my mother, white haired and with walking sticks, radiant with good will and asking for help to mount the steps, they turned into grandchildren and their machine-guns wilted into asparagus. We entered a tall long building, full of lilies, which had once been a stable for camels, and were greeted by an elegant and pretty girl who told us that Mr Nadir knew of our arrival and would be along in a moment. After a bit he made his entrance, looking like a prince in exile, in cashmere, white shirt, casually knotted tie and well-tailored trousers. His teeth, the product, his secretary told me, of much agony from a dentist near Harrods, were equally manicured. He suggested a glass of champagne. It was, of course, Dom Perignon; it was also unchilled, which I thought meant it was not his usual welcome, not having been kept, handily, in the fridge.

We chatted easily about his turbulent affairs, whereupon my mother interrupted to remark, in her clear cool voice, 'Antone,* I can't understand why everyone says this chap is a cad, he seems perfectly charming to me!' One of the benefits of being over ninety, she explained to me, is that one can say anything one likes. She knocked over a glass of champagne which was instantly replaced and, after more chat, emitted a mouse-like squeak. That means, I told Nadir, that she is hungry and wants to go home. He was instantly apologetic, the guards were summoned and mother was carted down the steps to the car. We drove back through the lemon groves and loofah trees to the hotel.

*　　*　　*

At the age of eighty-six, my mother became a Christian, formally, in the parish church of Bramshott, where one of her two funeral services took place. She was worried, apparently, that I would find out, which I only did after her death.

She needn't have worried. Even after I discovered and began to practise my Judaism, I remained what the distinguished publisher Peter Mayer terms a 'church-crawling Jew'.† The pomp, the circumstance, the music, the ritual, the décor, the architecture of the Church of England – and even the gossip‡ – alone of all

---

* Her name for me.
† I have sought out the litany at Christ Church, Oxford and Bury St Edmunds, and attended the chapels peculiar of the Tower of London, St James's Palace and Westminster Abbey in pursuit of the old prayer book; I even published the *Good Church Guide* on the subject, which appeared in a Penguin edition.
‡ What Isaiah Berlin, referring to the works of César Franck, called the 'organ-loft salacity' of the Church of England.

Christian sects, attracted me – the religion not at all. Indeed, I found the idea that God should arrange for his son to be conceived by a woman and grow up to be sacrificed, to save mankind, absurd. I found the notion that anyone should drink blood in remembrance of anything nauseating and the concept of original sin ridiculous. I have never had a problem with Jesus of Nazareth as a prophet, a preacher and even as a worker of miracles; I believe him when he said that he came not to destroy the law, but to fulfil it. (My rabbi maintains that the only difference between Christianity and Judaism is the bit about turning the other cheek.)

I had always hoped my mother would understand my kind of Judaism, though I fear, as was the case with other facets of my lifestyle, she never did. Although I did not inherit her distaste for all things Jewish, from her I have extravagance, joy in new acquaintance, trust in one and all, a delight in interfering in the affairs of others, the espousal of unpopular causes and the illusion that I know how to cook.

CHAPTER THREE

Elaine Blond

'Outside British Rail, the most unpleasant woman I have ever met.' These words about my stepmother, Elaine, came not from me but from John Osborne. He is equally disparaging about her in both volumes of his autobiography. He had to see her sometimes because she was the wife of my father, first chairman and founder of the Royal Court Theatre. Indeed, without her, *Look Back in Anger* might never have been performed, for without her backing there would not have been a Royal Court Theatre. My father often boasted that he gave Osborne his first cheque for fifty pounds in 1956.* My father never made a decision without Elaine's knowledge, consent and approval, and his (i.e. her) funding of the project depended entirely on this.

She was, as Marcus, Lord Sieff said in his address at her memorial service, 'a difficult woman'. I liked her much more than I disliked her, for she was never dull. She also loved my father from the moment she set eyes on him as a little girl during the Great War until the moment he died.

When he died I inherited his watch, which I gave to his butler, his signet ring and a revolver, which my stepsister, then very much in charge, insisted be handed over to the East Grinstead police. When Elaine died I inherited nothing, but her daughter Simone let me take his portrait, painted in Arras in 1917, and his framed medals. Entitled *The Young Fella*, by a war artist who had turned up to paint the general who was not there, it shows my father, at twenty-two years of age, as a major in the Horse Guards, handsome with his crisp little moustache.

After the war he had his medals painted on to his tunic, including

* 'No, Anthony, only twenty-five,' said Osborne.

the Croix de Guerre, the Légion d'honneur and, as I thought, the Mons Star. I later had this solecism pedantically and, I must admit, bitchily, painted out by my friend Christopher Mason in the most delicate fashion. When I showed the portrait and the eight medals to a general several years ago, he said that he would have worn the Mons Star when the portrait was painted. It was a good one, he added. Sorry, Daddy.

Elaine fell for this dashing figure on sight, put his photograph above her bed and determined to marry him. She had to wait. Her brother, Simon Marks, would not allow the match to my father. Some said it was because of his reputation as a roué; others said that Simon was jealous of my father's war record. And since the sisters, though individually powerful, obeyed Simon in every respect, that for the moment was that. Elaine was therefore packed off to marry Norman Laski, my father's cousin, to whom he was best man.

My father's maternal uncles Nathan and Noah traded as Laski and Laski, India merchants, and took the steamer every year to Bombay, where they sold their cotton goods. Elaine went to India on her honeymoon. She loathed it – the dirt, the flies, the poverty.

In light of the marriage, Norman was made personnel director of Marks & Spencer. He was a blubbering ass. He had been sent to the Jewish house at Clifton and then to St John's College, Oxford, whose colours he constantly affected in the form of ties, cufflinks and blazers. His lachrymation was much appreciated at funerals of Marks & Spencer branch managers, which it was his duty, and possibly pleasure, to attend. At a party my father once broke a soda siphon on his head and nobody complained. He was that sort of man.

By 1940 my father had left home, joined the RAF and also joined Elaine; or rather she moved into Arlington House, opposite the Blond Brothers' flat, almost immediately. Norman was shunted out happily to a grand flat behind Park Lane, while my father and Elaine lived together.

By Norman, Elaine had had two daughters: Anne, an extrovert, who liked the boys and became a petty officer in the Wrens, and Simone, called after her uncle Simon Marks, reserved, a prefect at Cheltenham Ladies College, later a chairman of the London

Conservatives and finally a dame of the British Empire. My brother and I moved into that family: Anne gave me my first gin and orange and I was later to be best man at her marriage to David Susman.*

Simone married first a Winnipeg doctor of dangerous charm: he was a homosexual and a brilliant composer of musicals. Albert Kaplan, for that was his name, used her money to put one on with Jack Hylton, but of course it failed — rich amateurs are always dished by the system. He did, however, invest heavily in *Tom Jones*, through his friend Tony Richardson. I loved Albert. He diagnosed my first dose of clap acquired when I lost my virginity — in a heterosexual encounter.

Elaine, autocratic, intelligent and learned as a child — I have never seen my father or my brother with a book — was also reasonable and just; except where her own interests were concerned, and when these were crossed she became a demon. Her Zionism and her concern for Jews were paramount, though her compassion for Archie's Guinea Pig Club members came a good second. One year Albert Kaplan refused to attend the Blue Ball for the Women's Zionist Organisation at the Grosvenor House. I tried to reason with him but he had had enough of her tyranny and was obstinate too. Soon enough his number was up — neither because of his sexual tastes nor because of his refusal to attend Zionist functions. Elaine had already decided he had to go. A tearful Simone told me she thought her mother was the wickedest woman in the world. Maybe. But she was also very practical.

Simone then married an un-articled clerk, Christopher Prendergast, in the office of solicitors acting for the husband she was divorcing. My brother was best man at that wedding.

Albert died of an overdose, self-administered, partially over a dinner with April Ashley, who had failed to notice he was only eating pills. Nobody seemed to care about his death. He had

---

* Heir to the Woolworth chain in South Africa into which Marks & Spencer had bought — merger as well as marriage — but happy on both accounts.

always claimed to be orthodox, though traces of his observance were so discreet as to be invisible; nevertheless, I rang the Great Synagogue and told them he had committed suicide. They only asked, 'Was he a Jew? If so, we will bury him.' Only the simplest coffin was allowed, but the ceremony was solemn. A contingent of Winnipeg relations had flown in, humble and suspicious – Simone said they thought *we* had taken his money! – and sat glowering and overflowing in a Daimler hire car outside my house, refusing to enter. At the funeral, mourners included relations, lovers (male and female), some theatrical friends, a gaggle of exotically-got-up male prostitutes and Simone (quite giggly). I processed seven times round the coffin which lay on a handsome pram-like affair which would have made a nice jardinière. Then each of the men took a spade, put some earth into Albert's open grave and washed his hands. The tarts were very brave about getting their suede bootees covered with mud. There was no wake. After his death royalties from *Tom Jones* continued to trickle in, but where they ended up I never did find out.

*   *   *

During the war Elaine rented Saint Hill. Out of 'k of h' ('kindness of heart' – a phrase of my father's) and naked calculation, at which she was adept, Elaine turned part of this enormous house over to the Guinea Pigs, who were being treated for burns at the nearby Queen Victoria Hospital.* Since many of the patients were American and Canadian volunteer pilots, this gesture brought its compensations: throughout the war we never lacked for Hershey bars, cans of meatballs in tomato sauce and that most coveted of wartime rarities – for which women would sell their souls and, more to the point, their bodies – nylon stockings.

Saint Hill was both grand, and, being Jewish, luxurious, though it was a little too hot for a wartime boarding schoolboy. At first, the scent of the lilies made me queasy, but I soon grew accustomed (perhaps too soon?) to the butlers (one of whom, Ripley, had been

---

* Now home to the Blond McIndoe Centre.

in service with Mrs Flora Solomon),* the parlour maids, the gardens and the gardeners, the stables and the two bay horses (which, when taken to London, we used to ride in Rotten Row). It was in the ballroom that Anne danced with young men who had two holes where there should have been eyes, another two where there should have been a nose, a slit for a mouth and no ears. She was truly an angel.

Elaine, who was loyal to her servants, took Ripley to Gotwick Manor at the beginning of the end of the war when he would announce, in his sepulchral voice, the presence, overhead, of flying bombs. I suspect that Ripley, Rose (Elaine's personal maid) and nanny Boustead, who had known Elaine since her marriage to Norman, thought of my father and his sons as interlopers. I remember Rose's glee on seeing me from an upper window at Gotwick being chased by a bull – or was it a cow?

Elaine had acquired this *équipe* together with a mansion called Melbury House in Kensington (now God knows how many flats), a Rolls-Royce, a mass of gilt furniture and a swathe of Impressionists; one of which, a Monet, my brother sold more than fifty years later for £3,300,000 at Sotheby's. My brother was both lucky and clever with his Monet, one of thirteen of a bent poplar (which he put up for auction on the back of the televised sale of the art collection of British Rail). Bravo, Pookins!

*   *   *

At a stroke, when Marks & Spencer went public in 1926, Elaine and her three sisters became instant millionaires. This was at a time when there weren't so many of them, and a million was a million. She did not, to her credit, change her friends, though through her charitable 'work' she acquired a lot of nobby acquaintances. Socially she was quite shy, even naïve, not as apt as her sister-in-law, Miriam Marks, at what New Yorkers call 'upper-crusting'. She

---

* When W. H. Auden was a tutor to Mrs Solomon's son, it was Ripley who informed her, 'Mrs Solomon, I think you should know that Mr Auden is in bed with Mr Isherwood.' Ripley was not a jolly fellow.

spent a lot on clothes with Hartnell, Molyneux, Creed, Digby Morton and Hardy Amies, but not as much as 'Baby' Steinberg, Isaac Wolfson's sister, who had her nose done and dressed in Paris.

From my schooldays, through my time in the Army, when Elaine sent me a box of Lambert & Butler cigarettes and a parcel of Marks & Spencer sandwiches every week, to when I was married, I spent more time with her than with my mother. I lived with her at 49 Grosvenor Square, an address I had to declare, with near fatal results, in front of the whole platoon when I joined up. ('I s'pose your effin' valet cleans yer effin' shoes then?' 'No, the chauffeur does that.' I was very green.)

There may not be a book called *The Joys of Divorce*, but there being no disagreement about 'access' to the children when my father and mother divorced, Peter and I ricocheted easily for more than twenty years between their households. We neither spent enough time to be bored by either, nor to bore them. Though my mother did marry Sham, life was more fun with Elaine.

In 1948, I tried to offer my services as a gunner officer to the nascent State of Israel, and was sensibly foiled by Elaine who thought I would do more harm than good. She was probably right. It was therefore arranged that I escort my stepsister, Anne, to New York, where my father had been sent as an unpaid commercial ambassador by Harold Wilson, then president of the Board of Trade. We travelled first-class on the *Queen Elizabeth* where I grew fed up with caviare and *foie gras*, and getting skewed on Bloody Marys. After the war, food was scarce and dull in England, worse, some said, than during the war, so I was shaken by the mounds of uneaten *filets de boeuf* thrown overboard. Couldn't they have kept pigs in the bowels of the boat like they did on the *Mayflower*?*

On arrival, we were met at Pier 86 by a pair of substantial figures from the '21' Club (bouncers I dare say), my father having become buddies with the owners, Jack Kriendler and Charlie Berns. They stormed through customs and immigration waving

* Though the Jews might have baulked.

passes and bellowing, 'Twenny one . . . twenny one . . . twenny one!' with the porters, Anne and I panting behind them. It was a significant introduction to New York. Elaine and my father lived in the Drake Hotel, East 56th Street, midtown Manhattan, then safer, sunnier and cleaner than it is now. It was also expensive and we were given a lecture on economy – Elaine did once wash my socks.

Her friends were flashy New York Jews, like Jules Stein, who owned Music Corporation of America (MCA). She soon found some poorer relations who lived in Queens, as well as some hangers-on, like Foxy, mother of Stephen Sondheim, who was then a student. As in London, we went out every night, pounding the parquet at El Morocco after first nights at the theatre. As Elaine had announced that I was highbrow, I was taken to *Fidelio* at the (old) Metropolitan Opera House – Elaine liked the ballet – and sat in agony in the '21' box, while Jack and Charlie smoked cigars and talked throughout the performance. They didn't care. They were New York.

*   *   *

The cruise of the Greek Islands was a typical cameo of family life with Elaine. Uncle Horace had managed to sell Blond Brothers and Sammy Scarves to Emu Wool. My father – fair's fair – took the bulk of the money in cash and my brother and I were given shares. Accordingly, at the moment of the sale, he suddenly had money; and so he bought the only boring landscape Gauguin ever painted, for twenty thousand pounds, and decided to take us all on a cruise of the Greek Islands.

He rented for a month an elderly motor torpedo-boat, belonging to Earl Beatty and luxuriously converted into a private yacht, with a French chef and crew, and provisioned with wines and victuals from a ship's chandler in Cannes. It wasn't the grandest boat on the Croisette, but it wasn't bad either. My brother went for the first fortnight and I for the second. Together, Elaine thought, we might form too much of a cabal. On my stint, there was a Czech called Jan Gerke, who had known Kafka and had been invited because he had a smattering of Greek, and Robin Fox and his wife Angela. Robin Fox had become a friend of the family because he worked for the London end of Jules Stein's business, representing such artists as Frank Sinatra. He was an elegant, witty fellow with a fondness for the eccentricities – he would never have used the word 'vulgarities' – of the Jewish rich.

On this trip my father remarked, 'I believe Anthony is down to his last hundred thousand' (all from Elaine, of course), and asked me what I would do for a living if I could not afford to be a publisher. 'An advertising agent,' I answered. Well! Some of my blurbs, like that for *The Carpetbaggers* – 'the men he broke and the women he made' – may still be in use; and I did invent the title *Small is Beautiful* for E. F. Schumacher's essays on economics. Or did I? My *quondam* partner Desmond Briggs has also claimed it. It emerged at the end of a bottle of sherry in Doughty Street during a session with 'Fritzipoo' as we called him. I would settle for half each.

Robin was, however, on my side and taught me to water-ski. He also, after I had reported on a lunch with Sir Allen Lane, who was then (pre-*Lady Chatterley*) looking for a respectable buyer, said, 'Go on, Neville, buy the boy Penguin!' During our cruise, Marks & Spencer had a rights issue and he worked out exactly how much richer Elaine had become on our holiday. It was a comforting sum but it did not stop her insisting that I help her check the physical stock of liquor we had on board against the list Lord Beatty had provided. It was an exhausting business, conducted on a hot Greek afternoon; and the fact that the discrepancies were minor did not improve Elaine's mood.

For she was a bad tempered and critical lady who spoke her mind immediately a thought entered it and to whomever happened to be present. Much of her animus was directed at my father, but it stuck no longer than the water on the back of a duck.

One morning at the breakfast table at Gotwick, where the day's cabaret began when she attended in her hostess's gown, after opening a pile of bills she shouted at him at the other end of the table: 'Neville, don't you pay for anything? I thought you were supposed to help with the garden.'

For once my father stirred. He looked up from his paper and bade me ring the bell. Enter West, the butler. The tension mounts.

NEVILLE: West, what happened yesterday?

WEST: Yesterday, sir?

NEVILLE: (*impatiently*) Yes. You went into East Grinstead and I gave you some money, didn't I?

WEST: Yes, sir.

NEVILLE: What for?

WEST: Some tobacco, sir.

NEVILLE: (*triumphantly banging the table*) There, pay for me own baccy, don't I?

Collapse, as they used to say in old *Punch* cartoons, of stout party.

CHAPTER FOUR

The Nahums

Il Duce, in his open Hispano-Suiza, his left hand raised in an imperial gesture of farewell, leaning backwards so that he could not quite see the bowed figure, in top hat and tails, of cousin Halfallah Nahum, head of the family in Tripoli, whom he had just raised to the dignity of Commendatore, is one of my favourite pictures in the album of my mother. She was supposed to marry Halfallah's brother Shalom, but refused because she did not want to live in Tripoli, where the Nahums had been since the nineteenth century. The family had originally emigrated from Pisa to the Ottoman territory and had put themselves under the protection of the Dutch.*

By the thirties they had prospered enough – they had had the time – for Halfallah to become the leader of the Jewish community, with fingers in many couscous; especially the export of esparto grass, the basis of fine writing-paper. Other Nahums had migrated to Manchester, where cousin Alphonse had become a tycoon, lending money to the French government through Barclays Bank and building up Golden Mills, which manufactured the cheap coverings for furniture made by firms such as Times Furnishing.†

The children of Alphonse and Marie Nahum (née De Picciotto from Aleppo), who supported Chaim Weitzmann in those early days in Manchester, were brilliant but doomed. In 1936, their

---

* Zionists often choose to forget that at the beginning of what they call the Common Era, more Jews lived outside Palestine than inside it.
† Jews in Russia were not allowed to be landowners. Nevertheless, they could deal in timber: hence the Jacobsons of Times Furnishing, the Lebuses, and Tom Meyers who fired from his board both Harold Wilson and his friend Lord Kagan, who had been in timber in his native Lithuania.

son Ephraim, known as 'Ram', arrived at Pembroke College, Cambridge; he had gone up straight from Clifton, with an exhibition in physics, and immediately plunged himself into university politics. He started an anti-fascist league and sent tons of sausages to the Republicans in Spain.

His twin passions were socialism and splitting the atom. After graduating *summa cum laude* with a double first, he became president of the University Socialists and an atomic scientist at the cyclotron bit of the Cavendish Laboratory. Although he was exempted from military service on account of this work, a stray bomb killed him in July 1942. Undergraduates wept. He had been a generous boy.

Every national newspaper carried an obituary and *Nature* ran a third leader about his brief but brilliant career. His parents received letters of condolence from both the beautiful and the good (of the left), including Harry Pollitt, at that time general secretary of the Communist Party, D. N. Pritt QC and Harold Laski.

Another Nahum, cousin Ruth, was victim of another bomb, though perhaps the smartest of the war, which fell on the Café de Paris, where she was dancing. Her partner was blown up in her arms. I remember going to see her in Didsbury: she was languid, lovely and grieving, on a sofa.

Danny Nahum, the second son and black sheep of the family, and, surprise, surprise, my friend, inherited Golden Mills and blued it. In the war, he had turned up at the Savoy *en simple matelot* and asked for a suite. The desk said that other ranks were not allowed in the hotel. He replied, 'Tell the manager that I am Prince Nahum.' He got his suite.

Extravagance, not business, was his *métier*. Once I supplied him a personal assistant – Winchester and New College. He told me his new assistant was the only one who had not tried to blackmail him. He believed in his star, which, in the end, fizzled out in a private room (on the National Health) at University College Hospital.

Twenty years before, pursued by both the French and British police for tax evasion, he had telephoned me from Cannes, where he had married the daughter of the owner of the Bar Nautique in the old port, to ask how he could put his newly born son down for Eton. I gasped. The lad is now an OE and something, I hear, in the City.

*   *   *

But it was my mother's father, Victor 'Diddles' Nahum, uncle to Halfallah, who in the late nineteenth century decided to move to Manchester. Without a single word of English, he let it be known that he needed a local bride, adding that a dowry, for he was rich, was not essential. A young lady was found, Elise Israel, from a professional family of Manchester Jews: dignified, pretty and correct. She was also, though I don't suppose 'Diddles' would have noticed, a tremendous snob and rather severe to her Irish servants.

'Diddles' and Elise, by now living in an enormous gloomy house,* had issue: Halford (after Halfallah), who played good billiards, bridge, and the piano, but became the only man, in my father's words, to lose money in the dry-cleaning business during the war; my mother; Aunt Phyllis; and, much later, the twins, Jack and Baron.

The Nahums enjoyed a stately existence in Manchester, one of the most civilised cities in Europe prior to the Great War. The family steamed off to a rented house in Grasmere or to North Wales, like so many Mancunians, for the children's holidays; but later travelled to Tripoli or the South of France, where the precocious twins cut quite a swathe with their high jinks. Both had been sent, like their more serious cousin, to the Jewish house at Clifton, then Baron to university in Geneva and Jack to Merton. Handsome, brave and dashing, they were popular with their peers and with women – especially women – and devoted to each other. Uncle Jack's pure Sephardic nose, which had been cabbaged in the boxing ring, apparently enhanced his sex appeal. As a little boy I had to punch him, at every encounter, as hard as I could in the ribs. Muscular Judaism. Indeed, he insisted to me that it was the duty of a Jew to be tougher than everybody else. I performed this routine

---

* It is now a convent with a chapel in the garden.

with so little zest, never having had a taste for hitting people (at least not men) that I fear he put me down – and nothing in my subsequent conduct changed his view – as a wet and a bookworm.

Just as my father had become accepted by the British establishment through his military prowess, so too had the twins. They both blazed through their gamesmanship: golfing, ruggering, fisticuffing and practical joking (in very un-Jewish style) their way into the heart of English society. They showed none of the characteristics attributed to Jews by Buchan, Sapper, Chesterton or Belloc, who were so much read when they were growing up.

Both went enthusiastically to war: Jack as a deputy judge advocate general in West Africa and Baron as a war photographer. One evening in 1941, when Jack was dancing with a lady at a party in Cairo (she was my informant), he suddenly stopped and said: 'Something has happened to Baron. I must get to the telephone.'

Baron, his identical twin, in Greece with the British, among them Lieutenant Philip Mountbatten, had been hit in the shoulder by shrapnel, which cost him the use of his left arm. He subsequently continued to play golf with one arm better than many people play with two.

After the war Jack became a fighting criminal barrister on the north-west circuit. I can recall two of his cases. One concerned a garage owner in Preston, accused of selling petrol on the black market, for whom he recruited as character witness the local landowner, whom he was cuckolding at the time, Sir Cuthbert de Hoghton, father of my Oxonian contemporary, Anthony. Sir Cuthbert's testimony was continually interrupted by dialogue with his rowdy dog, which he had brought to the witness stand on a short leash. The second (unsuccessful) case he referred to late one evening at a game of poker. Looking at his watch he remarked, 'In three hours' time one of my clients will swing.' It was Mrs Merrilees, who had given her husband some poisoned homemade marmalade.

*   *   *

The circumstances of our branch of the Nahums had been much reduced by the slump and the war, which had revived the fortunes of textile manufacturers such as Blond Brothers who made uniforms. Given my uncle Halford, now reduced to cleaning carpets, was no businessman, he and his brood had to be supported by my long-widowed grandmother, known as 'Nonna'. Indeed, this steely little lady, who had put the twins through university before the war from a small villa in Nice, where she played nightly the Labouchère* system at roulette, now shared with Uncle Jack her genteel house, Lindsey, Groby Road, Altrincham,† whither I bicycled to collect a few eggs during the war from posher Bowdon.

During the war Halfallah Nahum had managed to send money from Tripoli to England, but in 1948, on the establishment of the state of Israel, he was shot on his own doorstep. The Nahums now scattered, to Paris, Florence and Istanbul. My brother, patrolling the North African littoral as a National Service Officer in his RASC launch, visited Palazzo Nahum and reported it very run down.

I stayed at Lindsey, Groby Road, for six months after leaving Oxford, when I conscientiously took the electric train, the first in the world, from Altrincham to Manchester, early enough to arrive at the 'works' by eight o'clock. It wasn't much fun, but it gave me a taste of what most people do all their working lives.

*   *   *

Jack Nahum was a ladies's man – the Don Juan of the north-west circuit – and a man's man, but he wasn't a man for me. Like many

---

*   The Labouchère system, consisting of doubling up on even chances, is a slow, boring but, provided one has the patience and the difference between minimum and maximum stake is wide enough, goof-proof way of making small sums at roulette. Nonna used to go home after she had made a fiver (this was in the thirties). The *Spectator* columnist Taki relates that Captain Maxwell, less patient, lost thousands playing many tables in this way a night or so before his death.

†   Alan Clark, who at the time lived in Upper Terrace House, Hampstead, one of the grandest addresses in London, where the ashtrays were by Henry Moore and nine dukes once came to lunch, used to enjoy reciting this address as a sort of mantra.

barristers, he carried his adversarial technique into the home, accusing me for instance of murdering his dachshund when all I had done was to take the ailing animal to the vet, where it happened to expire under the knife. An insomniac, who kept a glass of whisky in a baby's-bottle warmer by his bed, he was often irritable with me, whom he felt obliged to put up and put up with. More importantly I did not share his tastes for golf, sexy women and Lancashire comics like Al Read. Jack was far funnier and was the star turn at the Thursday Club: racy fellows of a bohemian turn, who met in Baron's theatrical apartment in Kinnerton Street for blue stories and bun fights, as often or not in the presence of Baron's chum, Lieutenant Philip Mountbatten.*

Baron had become a lion of that section of London society, at that time more from Mayfair than Eaton Square, which appeared in the *Evening Standard*. His other great help, Margot Fonteyn, was his conduit to the world of ballet, which he constantly snapped; but he only ever made any real money, he told me, from photographing food and William Hill's horses.

His annual fancy-dress party in his studio in Park Lane was a national event and was on television when that medium made its appearance. One year I blacked up and went as an African prince in beads and a blanket; weaving home, I was stopped in Park Lane by a cordon of bored tarts, polite but enquiring in pidgin English – the Dorchester had not yet been taken over by genuine Nigerian chiefs – what I had under my blanket. I was rescued by a couple of police officers, equally intrigued, who escorted me to my father's flat in Portman Square.

Baron later tried to help me as a literary agent, but, foolishly fearful of being patronised, I wouldn't be helped. Nevertheless, we did sell Muffin the Mule, a creation of his friend Annette Mills, to Marks & Spencer's children's books, then master-minded by George Weidenfeld, one of whose early wives was a Sieff. The

---

* I remember the Duke of Edinburgh, in replying to a foolish remark of mine that Baron was 'mad', stated that, on the contrary, he was the sanest man he'd ever met.

only one of Baron's friends I took to was Gilbert Harding, a lonely, pious, good and scholarly man.

At Oxford I started the University Press Club and it seemed sensible and polite to ask Baron, the court photographer,* to come and talk to us. At the end of the evening he took me aside and rebuked me in an avuncular fashion for having as friends so many obvious 'pansies'. Though camp behaviour was fashionable at the time and many undergraduates with droopy hands and voices went on to be the chairman of Lloyds Bank† and that sort of thing, his judgement was accurate enough. Needless to say, he singled out Martin Stevens as the exception.

Then a rotund, eupeptic and ambitious young fellow, Martin blew up in 1986 from obesity in West Africa. He was a gay deceiver, the most intolerant and exclusive homosexual I ever met, which did not prevent him from becoming Conservative MP for Fulham and one of the top brass at the clouty Imperial Cancer Research Fund. The only woman allowed through the portals of his house in Montpelier Square, which he shared with a couple of other well-connected gentlemen of similar tastes, was, I seem to remember, Patricia Hornsby-Smith. To Baron I never let on.

*   *   *

When Nonna lay dying in Lindsey, Groby Road – medicine then allowing such a performance – the Nahums assembled: my mother, the twins (of whom she disapproved), my brother and myself. Jack and Baron played gin rummy, my mother clucked, and Peter and I moped. Proximity, for members of most families, except for those of the philoprogenitive, tolerant poor, like Dickon's in *The Secret Garden*, acts as a stripping agent, removing the varnish and politeness we present to the world, to which families, all too knowing, are indifferent.

Nonna, in control to the last, had the sense to die quickly. She

*   Baron was accompanied on visits to Buckingham Palace by his assistant, Tony Armstrong-Jones, with well-known results.
†   Sir Jeremy Morse was a very drawly youth.

left me her set of mah-jong and her complete works of Dickens, having observed, fairly enough, that I had enough money.

Uncle Jack had married, during the war, Aunt Sally, who had rather good legs and had been a manageress of the NAAFI in Cairo. But as Douglas Cavendish Fisher, Baron's sophisticated friend from the East End, himself the father of a marchioness, remarked, they were 'the legs of a manageress'.

Baron, loving of, and beloved by, many famous beauties, had never married, so it was with delight and surprise that the family (as well as the media) learned of his engagement to Sally Ann Howes, actress daughter of Bobby Howes. I remember swooning over her as the starlet in *Dead of Night*, with hundreds of other conscripts.

One weekend, at my mother's house, we were playing with the Ouija board and my mother asked, 'Will Baron marry Sally Ann?' The glass on which we all laid a finger began to judder horribly. This was not by any means a family routine, but an occasional flutter with the occult does no permanent harm, be it via Tarot, runes or psychometry. I believe in them all. My stepfather, that very correct Englishman, then entered the room and with surprising ferocity, for he was a mild man, told us to pack it up. This we did.

Baron, thinking it prudent, as he was about to marry a woman much younger than himself, decided to take out a life-insurance policy. On the advice of his friend Prince Philip, who wanted him to join the royal party for a tour of Australia, Baron went to Sister Agnes – the platonic Jewish lady friend of Edward VII, who founded the eponymous hospital – for a minor operation on his hip. He died of a heart attack during the operation.

No good reason was given for the death, a few months later, of his brother Jack, there being no medical term for a broken heart. They were fifty-one.

CHAPTER FIVE

Simon Marks

The first sniff of wealth in my life occurred in 1942, when a parcel of *Wonder Books* was delivered to Greenbank House 'with love from Elaine'. They were very new and bore elegant covers. Mine were very old and had lost their covers.

I examined the new books with both excitement and loathing, as if they had been a circus master introduced to discipline and humiliate my battered teddy bear. I asked who Elaine was. Auntie, the mother of our nanny, Miss Evans, explained that she was married to Norman Laski, my father's cousin, and was very rich. She did not say (indeed she could not have known) that Elaine had pursued my father since she was a teenager and was the youngest sister of Simon Marks. Even at the time I suspected a plot in which I would want to cooperate. It would make sense for a woman who was after a man to ingratiate herself with his children. My father must have noticed that I was obsessed with *Wonder Books* and probably said: 'Send him some new ones.' It would have been uncharacteristic of him to have asked what I *really* wanted.

In the middle of the war my father arrived in a green Rover at Eton to take me to tea with the Markses at Ascot. From him I have inherited my navigational and topographical skills: we were soon lost. But we were also lucky, for I spotted on the Ordinance Survey map our destination, 'Titlarks Farm'. Titlarks was a very unfarmy farm, lacking even a cat or a dog, but it was long on Renoirs, gilt French furniture and central heating.

Four made-up ladies, smoking cigarettes through holders and wearing more jewellery than I thought natural, comfortable or even possible, sat around an embroidered card-table playing gin rummy. One of them was a very pretty Irish lady called Eileen Goodenday. She was married to Jack, the owner of Kayser

Bondor, which made nylon stockings, as much a part of the romantic ammunition and currency of the rich as of any American army officer. I rather loved her because when I was asked by Marcus Sieff about anti-Semitism at school and replied, truthfully, that I had not heard the expression, she shot him a look meaning, 'leave the boy alone', and then called, 'Gin!'

Lolling uncomfortably on the lawn was Simon's son Michael, roughly shaven and wearing spectacles. He was in the company of a spotty girl in a shirt and trousers, who, he told me proudly, was a communist. Michael, my father later told me in the car driving back to Eton, was apt to send pianos to girls he fancied. Fortunately these objects did not always fit into the bed-sitting rooms of his inamorata. I longed to see more of this extraordinary family.

Once my father had married Elaine Marks, my brother and I were welcomed by our new stepsisters (and second cousins) into a family whose wealth and power derived from one source, Simon Marks.

At the age of eighteen Simon had inherited the family business, founded by his father Michael, with thirty-five thousand pounds in the bank (a cosy sum before the First World War) and the responsibility for four younger sisters. In an early move he took his partners to law, all the way to the Court of Appeal, and won. He behaved impeccably to the Spencers,* who drank their money away, and visited old Mrs Spencer piously in Newcastle, or wherever it was, every year of her life.

By the time I arrived on the scene – and what a scene it was – Simon had turned his four sisters into millionaires, scrupulously respecting the voting shares left to them by their father. The sisters all had enormous flats in the West End – three within a few yards of each other in Grosvenor Square – and large country houses in the Home Counties. At weekends their country houses were crammed with friends of the family, many of whom, also being their private suppliers, were interchangeable. They shared everything: antique

---

* Tom Spencer's purchase of a half-share in Michael Marks's business for three hundred pounds in 1894 had been 'the investment of the century'.

dealers, gallery owners, accountants, lawyers, doctors and even –
and especially – a masseur. When there was a wedding in the
family, the masseur always sent a gigantic piece of silver plate.

Although Marks & Spencer did not trade outside the UK, Simon
maintained agents in Paris and New York and, later, Hong Kong.
Their function was to supply the family with local goodies – of all
kinds, I suspect – and currency, then restricted for ordinary citizens.

Simon played the *Godfather* role with bravura. I was there when
he said to Norman Laski that he was a lucky man because it had
been agreed that the position on the board he had held for so long
was to be given to his son-in-law, David Susman. Simon then
walked away. He had a wicked owly face with shiny brown eyes,
like Fénelon, from which the fire poured like a torrent, and I
fancied he gave me a wink.

*   *   *

Simon used to honour his sisters by only visiting them occasionally. Miriam Sacher was the cleverest of the lot; she was also the
funniest and the kindest. For years, Andrew McCall, my permanent houseguest, and I went once a month for the weekend to her
Lutyens house near Basingstoke. I would go when there was no
shooting and when no other members of the family were present.
We were always the same lot, occasionally permed, and we rarely
saw each other elsewhere. We all had to play bridge, except for
Bumble Dawson who had other social graces. He was however
accused by Johnny Sacher, on one of those unfortunate occasions
where the two halves of Miriam's life met, of killing his young
pheasants by looking at them.

One weekend, I took my friend Bertie Hope-Davis to stay with
Miriam, and she took us to see her herd of dairy shorthorn cattle
which monotonously won the first prize at the Royal Show.
Typical of her genius, she had found the prize dairyman, a German
refugee, in what she called 'Isrul'. Entering into the spirit of things,
Bertie announced that he too had cows.

'Doncher think, Mr er . . . er, that they should be allowed to
keep their horns?'

Bertie agreed passionately: 'Absolutely, Mrs Sacher. When they cut mine off, I told them, 'Put 'em right back on again!''

*   *   *

My first confrontation with Simon Marks was in fact a collision at – or rather, after – lunch at Gotwick Manor. There we were down to eight indoor and five outdoor 'staff', as they were always called, and at a dining-table with twenty assorted relations and sycophants, Sir Simon Marks and one bolshie undergraduate – me.

The conversation had entered that self-congratulatory groove of reminiscence and eagerly gobbled-up new anecdotes about the benevolence of the business towards its employees. I suggested that this was a course only pursued because they wanted to make more money. I maintained that a contented, well-paid, warm, well-fed and well-treated shop-girl would be more conscientious, less likely to fall pregnant, more honest, diligent, nay devout, in her concern for her employers than her opposite number at, say, the Co-op. Moreover, the kindness meted out to their staff was motivated – I don't think I knew the word then – by self-interest and why not be honest about it. Flown, like Milton's sons of Belial, with insolence and wine, I volubed on until my father thought it was time to join the ladies. The men filed out leaving Simon at one end of the table and me, red-faced and panting, at the other. As Simon got up to go and passed me, he squeezed my shoulder: 'You're right, my boy, come and have lunch at the office.'

I can't have had lunch in the boardroom at Michael House more than a few times; though I always went with Michael, who appeared to need me, and his own thermos of tea, for protection. Simon noticed and started an instant legend that he only saw his son when I came to lunch.

The newly airborne State of Israel had just emerged from the chrysalis of the Jewish Agency and the ambassador was present at the first lunch I attended. In some way he, or his country, had offended Simon. The Markses had been the first supporters in England of the Zionist movement. The egregious and magical Chaim Weizmann, who only spoke Yiddish when he first arrived in

Manchester, had been introduced to Churchill by my great-uncle Nathan Laski. Moreover, the Balfour Declaration in 1917 had been concocted in the St John's Wood house of Chief Rabbi Gaster, whose daughter married Neville Laski, son of Nathan.

Not only did each member contribute deeply and zealously to the Zionist cause, which at that time seemed so noble, but Marks & Spencer was an engine generating, through it suppliers, funds for the land of Israel.

Simon would not have seen anything wrong in favouring a supplier, either Jew or Gentile, who was seen to take advertisements in the endless programmes of gala nights at the Dorchester – sometimes even Grosvenor House – or film premières or first nights. If someone's heart was in Israel then he could send in another gross. Of course, he was not the only businessman of his generation to support Zionism, but he was the foremost. He drove the beat. Isaac Wolfson and Charles Clore may even have given more, but Simon was the first to be knighted and the first and maybe the last to be given a hereditary peerage. To the Israeli ambassador, he was the most important man in England, practically a founder, with his friend and protégé Weizmann, of the Jewish State of Israel. The ambassador might even have known that in 1917 Simon Marks had been transferred by the Foreign Secretary, Arthur Balfour, from being a lowly gunner in Preston, where he held board meetings in his gunner's uniform, to being the secretary of the new Palestine Commission.

His Excellency was being talked to by the chairman as if he had been a delinquent head of department about to be sent off to manage Yeovil (the Siberia of Marks & Spencer) for his sins. Simon was a little man who reeked of power, but then so was Stalin. He didn't raise his voice when angry, which meant the ambassador had to lean forward to pick up his punishment. Finally, Simon lit up a cigar and, relapsing into Lancashire Yiddish, which he affected as an indication of benevolence, announced that he felt like having a *schtauss*. One could guess what he meant.

Of course I was flattered to be asked to lunch by Simon Marks, who certainly flattered me with little attentions. Once, when he was showing me round an exhibition of the early stall in Leeds, *circa* 1884 – 'Don't ask the price, it's a penny' – he beckoned with his finger to a middle-aged man in a suit who nearly fell in half at being indicated. The man was profuse in his gratitude when asked about his pension. 'Early retirement,' said Simon to me in explanation. 'We have a good scheme.' I then asked if pensions were transferable. 'No,' snapped Simon. I was rebuked by one of the courtiers, Jan Gerke, for walking on Simon's 'wrong', i.e. deaf, side. Gerke had been employed because he had been a lover of Simon's sister, Becky; his daughter later became a Marks & Spencer supplier – a typical scenario.

Simon asked me, when he became a peer, whether he should become Lord Marks of Ascot, or Virginia Water, where he lived. I replied that he would be criticised for being pretentious. 'Where were you born?' 'Higher Broughton.' And so it was, Lord Marks of Broughton. I don't suppose I was the only one to be consulted over this monumental decision, but it was nice to be asked. Nor did I ever become a familiar. The number of times I talked to him alone was tiny, but he was a great man and one remembers conversations with the great. I was on the fringes of the family of which he was *fons et origo*: like a king, a Bourbon rather than a Hanoverian, he ensured that each sister was a sort of Princesse de France, with an independent fortune and establishment.

Simon did not control the family through money but through his prestige as head of the business, but it must have maintained a slush fund to bail out the financially delinquent – of whom none was more spectacularly so than his brother-in-law twice over,* Israel Sieff. Israel was the opposite of Simon: a large man, looking somewhat akin to the president of a Balkan republic determined not to remain obscure, a lavish entertainer and storyteller. Everything about him, from the glasses of Chambolle-Musigny, the size of flower vases, to his libido, was overblown. With his lion's head and thundering voice, he behaved like a major prophet: a lecherous Elijah, one of whose liaisons, with Lady Scarsdale,

---

* Brother and sister having married sister and brother.

ended in a breach of promise action which cost Simon fifty thousand pounds.

Simon, on the other hand, was sparing with words: he hated paperwork and was famous for purging Marks & Spencer of tons of duplicate invoices and order forms. Israel made the speeches and Simon took the decisions. Israel was generous and ample; Simon was charitable on a grand scale but organised and sweetly devious. Once at Ascot when a race was about to start he asked me whether I would like a fiver on the winner? Why, oh why, oh why did I say no?

Israel and Simon were like the Tweedles – Dum and Dee, Box and Cox. Simon loved Israel. One of the reasons for his dispute with his partners when he inherited the business was their refusal in 1915 to allow Israel on the board. When he was whisked out of the army by Balfour to help Weizmann, Israel was already his secretary. Israel worshipped Simon and always acknowledged his mastery. They hunted together.

Flora Solomon, a grand Russian lady, who had met Simon at a dinner party, was put in charge of welfare when Simon had no answer to her question, 'What happens if one of your assistants falls pregnant?' Her father was a millionaire who had reluctantly given money to Rasputin, but had kept enough to buy the Flatiron building in New York and provide his daughter with a household and *train de maisons* in London. Flora was no ordinary employee and her selection by Simon was typical of his genius. She recalls in her autobiography how Simon and Israel, *en route* to Ascot in grey toppers and morning coats, popped their heads round her office door (two Jews who had made it) grinning like Cheshire cats. Quick as a flash she demanded a minimum wage of three pounds a week for her girls. She got it.

Aside from his business, Simon's passion was the family. Only the family had voting shares in Marks & Spencer, a situation regularly ignored by Simon, since as long as he controlled the family, he controlled the business. This was never disputed but occasionally Simon felt threatened.

One of the more memorable threats to Simon's monopoly came via his daughter Hannah, who was 'walking out', as my father would have said, with a restaurant owner called Jerry Markow. Hannah was of strong character, as bold as her father and mother, with some *audace* of her own to boot. She was a famous gambler and accustomed to winning. She had once backed a horse on the rails at Ascot, having put five thousand with each of the bookies, and watched her horse come in. *En route* to a gala in Monte Carlo in a small plane provided by Prince Rainier, she quarrelled with her fellow traveller and guest Zsa Zsa Gabor, also a Jewess. At Lyons, where they had to refuel, they both telephoned to complain about each other. Zsa Zsa was left behind.

Such a person is not likely in youthful middle age to fall for a callow fortune hunter of the John Beaver in *A Handful of Dust* variety. And Jerry Markow was not callow. He was vigorous, witty and successful, and older than Hannah. Nevertheless, Simon was swayed by the malicious tongues that lap the circles of the great and said he was a Maltese adventurer – a man of straw. He smelt danger and decided on a course of action that was utter folly: he called in the heavies. I told the story, with Jerry's permission, in my novel *Family Business* and repeated it with one slight difference.

One evening, Jerry, about to leave the small block of flats (so small that the entrance was a street door to which the tenants had the key) where he lived just off Park Lane, was approached by a man in an overcoat who had crossed the road from a parked car to ask him for a light. Jerry, scenting danger, kept his hand on the door; when the stranger lunged at him, clumsily, he opened it so that his assailant fell flat on to the marble floor of the hall. When he recovered, the villain recognised Jerry as the distinguished proprietor of a West End restaurant, in which milieu he was well known. Jerry invited the elderly and once reliable, but no longer effective, thug up to his flat for a glass of vodka and some explanations. In his right fist the man had crumpled up a box of matches to give added force to the intended blow.*

The hit man did not know who his ultimate employer had been, nor did Jerry, who is discreet, tell him. All this I learned many years

---

* In my novel I turn this into a bunch of keys.

ago in the Ritz in Paris where the lovebirds, Jerry and Hannah, had
bolted and where totally by chance I met them. They pounced on
me like eager exiles, knowing that at least I was running no risk by
being seen in their company; for it could have been dangerous for
a member of the family to appear to be on their side. Like all
dictators, Simon demanded absolute loyalty.

Jerry, who was much better equipped for battle in this area,
decided to turn the tables on Simon. Every morning when Simon
left his flat in Grosvenor Square he could not avoid seeing two
men in the front seat of a Humber watching him from the other
side of the square; and every evening when he left the office
(Simon never went out to lunch) the same two men in the same
car were on the other side of Baker Street. If he went to the theatre
they were there; when he left the Savoy after dinner they were
there. And so on, day after day, night after night. It was probably
Miriam who brought this ridiculous matter to an end.

The next time I saw Jerry was at a party at Orchard Court given
by my stepmother. The door was opened and there he was, arm
in arm with Simon Marks. When the butler approached Simon
to offer him a drink, it was Jerry who said: 'Whisky and water,
without ice.'

When Simon was buried, in the Jewish Cemetery at Golders
Green, his son Michael keened. He howled like a dog. The rest of
the family and the inner courtiers stood around in their expensive
clothes, silent and aghast as if the soundtrack had gone wrong; but
I was proud of Michael for behaving like a son and Jew. (When my
own father died I made such a noise the neighbours nearly called
the police.) A generation later, through my wife Laura's friendship
with the second Simon Marks and his wife Marion, I was happy to
be the godfather of the third Michael Marks.

When Simon died in 1964, the business did not just survive – it
boomed. Simon considered it his mission to clothe cheaply,
warmly and durably. Simon did not want to sell food: it was
too messy. Israel Sieff, who was later followed by Teddy Sieff,
succeeded him as chairman. The latter was a saint and his successor,
Marcus Sieff, Simon's nephew, was not; but he did turn Marks

& Spencer into the most successful purveyor of cooked and uncooked food in the United Kingdom. The family still stuck in there (for a while) but no longer control the business. Simon Susman, son of David and my second cousin once removed, used to buy the fish, which must have made him the biggest fishmonger in England.

PART TWO

Blond Educational

CHAPTER SIX

Wellesley House

Bowdon may have been, in 1913, the highest rated borough in the kingdom, but it was only nine miles from Manchester. My mother's cousin, Alphonse Nahum, the founder of the Golden Mill, which made all that nasty cheap upholstery, referred to us as his 'bluddy Cheshire cuzzens'; and I believe my mother was afraid lest I grew up like him – common and very rich. So when I came back one afternoon from my local school, where I was very happy, and said something about a 'yaller brick road',* my mother was not best pleased. Anyway, I did not pronounce the word 'yellow' with the silvery finesse favoured by Girton gels on the BBC, who were able to manage the 'h' in 'white' and of whose diction my mother thoroughly approved. She winced and decided to send me, rising eight, to a boarding-school in the south.

Wellesley House was nearly as expensive as St Peter's Court, its neighbour on the Isle of Thanet, where the brother of a fashionable Harley Street paediatrician in the nineteenth century had started a boarding-school. Wellesley House was boxed by flint walls and smelled of Brussels sprouts. The institution was designed to prepare boys to pass their common entrance into a public school – two misnomers – and Eton was the favourite. The headmaster, a wizened old man with round spectacles, beat me for putting something on top of my Bible, and again for calling a boy who had called me 'a Jewish pig', 'a Christian pig'. That's the kind of place it was – a sadistic greenswarded hell.

Although the school had a high academic and social standing, the victuals served would have been recognised by Oliver Twist. This department was arranged by Miss Audrey, who took a fancy

---

* Is this a solecism? Did the song appear years later?

to me and, placing me to her right at lunch, allowed me to eat the tops of her two lightly boiled eggs. She also ate salad on which she sprinkled sugar from a silver sifter and finished her meal with bananas and cream. That these two simple dishes still fill me with gooey delight has to be the memory of their contrast with Miss Audrey's tawdry catering for poor little rich boys, who used to tear into laundry baskets full of stale-bought stale bread and dripping.

I wasn't altogether miserable. My best friends were Nicky Mavroleon, whose parents had presented the school with one of their boats and whom I never saw later, and the Hon. 'Mitty' Bowyer. I was once commanded to judge between the beauty of two older boys, both naked – for some the stuff of which dreams are made – so I can't have been *that* unpopular.

When war was declared we banged the tops of our desks in jingoistic frenzy; and I remember looking at the map of the world, a quarter of it coloured pink, and thinking how could we possibly lose? The parents of some of my contemporaries, like Milo Cripps, Alan Clark and Edward Montagu, clearly thought we might and sent them off to Canada. My father, on the other hand, was a pillar of the British Legion, a patriot and a Jew, and would not hear of it. (I fancy Simon Marks may have issued a ukase on the subject.) For us a special train was hired and the school decamped to Loch Rannoch, in Perthshire, leaving the heavily powdered Miss Audrey, who had as the French say 'du monde au balcon', to the mercy of the German shells from across the Channel.

At Loch Rannoch, we were installed in three lodges on the shores of the lake belonging to a Suffolk brewer named Cobbold, whose son was at the school. My lodge was Talladh-A-Bheithe (pronounced 'Tullavay'), and I was one of twenty-eight boys presided over by W. G. Williamson for what were about to be the happiest years of my life.

*   *   *

'Billy' Williamson was a magic man. We were so fond of him that when he lost his cool and beat every one of us on the bare bottom, I think we hoped he enjoyed it. Some spoilsports spotted that he never beat Cobbold. (Boys are quite as slanderous as their elders.) His perpetual goal was that boys should shine in common entrance, if need be beyond their abilities. Unfortunately, on arrival at their public schools, certain boys were occasionally demoted to a lower form, rumbled, with Bill's magic no longer present to sustain them. His savage spelling bees taught us how to write correctly 'antediluvian', 'independent', and because we also learned Greek, 'diarrhoea', 'psychic' and 'rhythm'. We knew the true meaning of 'decimate', never intentionally split an infinitive and could recite the names and dates of the kings and queens of England from William the Conqueror (1066–1087) to George V, which was then as far as they went. Under him – or as Etonians say 'up' to him – learning became fun. He invented a wonderfully irregular verb that I can still recite, viz.:

> sago / riso / sesesemolina / tetapioca epeekfreen
> σάγῶ, ῥίσω, σεσέσεμολήυα, τετάπιοκά, ἐπηκφρην

He married the mother of the most intelligent child in the school who was found in tears after an examination. When asked was it too difficult, he replied, choking back his rage, 'No, too easy.'

Loch Rannoch's shores were too precipitous to allow grounds for football or cricket, the only two English pastimes for which I have never had any sympathy.* Instead we built dams, stalked, fished, thundered down snow-laden slopes in our 'galleons'† and fought each other with staves. I excelled at these activities as much as I de-celled – if there is such a word, and if not then why not? – at team games, which cost me dear at placid, meadowed Eton, where adventure was never in and team spirit never out. We also invented our own pleasures, which included concerts at which I imitated Hitler. After one such successful performance I took a bath – then a rare privilege – and was caught in it peeing voluptuously by a boy who delivered a lecture I have never

---

* It was only when Laura and I invited the South African Test cricketers to our house in Sri Lanka that the mysteries of the game were explained to me.
† Sheets of corrugated iron.

forgotten: that I must not think that applause entitled me to behave badly.

We were only small boys, but our characters are etched gigantically in my memory. The boy who reprimanded me may only have been twelve years old, but his rebuke affected me as if it had been delivered by a magistrate. A sort of Attic freedom blew round those shores of Loch Rannoch, with Billy Williamson harnessing the gods of the wind. We were taught the Bible so well that I won the divinity prize in my first half at Eton; even so our morality and discipline derived more from fifth-century Athens than from Victorian England. For instance, it was decided that Blond *ma* was too fat, and, put to the vote by Billy, it was decreed that I should go for runs. I puffed cheerfully along that shingled shore.

I shared a room with Heathcote and Birley at the top of the lodge, and the idea that we would ever be separated in life was unthinkable. Heathcote wept easily and Birley was stern. We all agreed that Lloyd was the nicest boy at Talladh-A-Bheithe, because he was so fair and so considerate, and that there was something creepy about Mr H. who taught us maths. Mr Strachan, on the other hand, who alas could only stay for a few months before joining up, was quite marvellous. We were right about Mr H., who interfered with the boys and one morning just wasn't there.

(Whatever happens to those assistant masters at preparatory schools who can't keep their hands to themselves? I suppose they stay on the carousel, swapping their mounts until they fall, clutching a Simon Raven novel, into oblivion.)

Half a century later, I saw a photograph of Mr Strachan in the financial pages. The eighteen-year-old god had become the jowly chairman of Ben Line, on one of whose boats, the *Ben Cruachan*, I had travelled, as assistant librarian, from Osaka to Colombo. I wrote to him in praise of a senior employee, whom he had abruptly sacked. He did not reply. Ben Line was not known to be a considerate employer. The *Ben Cruachan* had broken her back in the Pacific and had been told to maintain radio silence, as the owners feared a rescue and consequent costs. A rival Edinburgh tycoon once told me that Strachan had been allocated shares in the company by the family when he became chairman: but only on the condition that they could be repurchased at the same price when he retired.

My first sexual trauma was the sight of the private parts of a boy I shall call Bristow. They were developed and he reported that he could emit a sticky white fluid, and that the sensation was extremely agreeable. I was horrified and disbelieving, as I was to be when a well-meaning friend of my mother tried to explain to me the facts of life. In view of my subsequent behaviour – described as 'rackety' by my solicitor when a libel action was in the air – it may seem odd that my childhood, adolescence and indeed early man- hood were entirely chaste. In fact, I passed through five years at a public school, two years in the Army and three years at Oxford as a virgin, without any form of sexual experience with anyone of either sex. I was not ignorant: indeed, having read Hirschfeld's *Sexual Anomalies and Perversions* at an early age, I was quite *instruit*. I was just terrified, and my natural persistence in chastity might very well have come from the sight of Bristow's private parts.

Billy Williamson, who might have helped because he would have been trusted, did not enlighten us on the subject. It might have been the only aspect of human behaviour of which he was himself unsure. He was in love, as teachers have to be (without being practising pederasts) if they are to keep sane, with the concept of the 'boy' – and with some specimens more than others.

Like all magic men Billy was a storyteller: he fed our fantasies with a hero, who was like himself, only he had a Bentley. He was also very partial to potted shrimp* sandwiches and would stock up with this item before setting out on a mission.

After the war Billy set up his own school in the Ashdown Forest, which was instantly successful. He accepted twenty years later, without demur, my ward, whom I had snatched, full of nits and ignorance, from the upper room of a café in Tangier. But that is another story. I was pleased too that Billy got his Bentley.

---

*　Potted shrimp, along with bitter beer in a silver tankard and the sound of church bells, is all of England I miss now that I live in France.

CHAPTER SEVEN

Eton

I was a Jew at Eton. That wasn't the trouble though – the trouble was me. I arrived from my prep school, which I quickly learned to call my 'private', a sunny, happy, popular boy and left four years later surly and withdrawn.

I made a propitious start. My first term, or 'half', in the summer of 1941, was literally strawberries and cream: I was terribly popular. I had a bicycle and a wireless in my room and was not immediately told that possession of both was against the rules. The bicycle was one thing, but I resented 'm'tutor', who thought I was spoilt and should be trodden down like young wheat (his phrase), removing the wireless which was battery-powered and to which I listened with ear-phones.

As new boys we had to learn, within three weeks, the initials of the other twenty-five housemasters, their location and that of other crucial venues like Barnes' Pool, Lower and Upper Sixpenny, the Drawing Schools (the word 'Art' was forbidden), Tap, where the older boys could drink beer, and so on. We did. We were beaten if we did not. Eton was run on fear and terror. Some of the boys were really rather dim. I remember one called Gilpin, whose family had been to Eton for centuries and who had difficulty in remembering anything. He suffered.

We also learned the potent and memorable Eton argot, e.g.:

'sock me a banger' – give me a sausage sandwich
'spout me the construe' – tell me tomorrow's lesson
'oil up to m'dame' – suck up to matron
'keen' – trying too hard, pejorative (as in the injunction of
    Talleyrand, so popular with the British upper-classes,
    '*Surtout pas trop de zèle!*')

'oik' – member of the lower classes, also *oikish* (from the Greek
   oikos – inhabitant)
'scug' – a boy with no athletic colours.

I began as a 'dry bob', playing cricket in the summer half, but
then transferred to the river as a wet bob. We had a very good baby
four, which I coxed, being the smallest, and we did rather well in
practices. I, however, completely lost my nerve during the final
competition and coxed m'tutor's star baby crew on to a raft. We
lost the cup, the only cup we were likely to win as a bad wet-bob
house. As a result I became very unpopular and nobody spoke to
me for three years.

My second mistake was to win m'tutor's tennis, that sport then
being considered wet. I was rather good, well good enough to
win five bob as the best player in the house. Not that it did me any
favours. For these and other trifling reasons, I was bullied by three
boys whom I will not forget or forgive even on my deathbed. My
fagmasters, however, Canning, Reeves and Tyrrell, were all kind
to me. Tyrrell had a moustache and smoked a pipe; Reeves, a
beautiful young man and an excellent shot, was killed with
Canning at Caen.

Tea in our rooms after school or games was the only decent
meal because we ourselves – or our fags – cooked it. Some boys
were sent pheasants by their parents, and I wondered how people
could kill such beautiful creatures. I was more familiar with the
homely grouse.

Eton, sixty years ago, was not the caring, innovative school I am
assured it has now become. The Gilpins of this world are excluded
and there are many more Jews, Negroes and Arabs. There were
only nine Jews at that time: we were Goldblatt, Haskell, Montagu,
the Rossiter twins, Sebag-Montefiore, Vos, and Blond *ma* and
Blond *mi*. If the truth be told there was little in the way of anti-
Semitism, except of course in orthodox Christian views of the
crucifixion and exchanges such as:

'Sir, why do people dislike the Jews?'
'Because, Blond, they killed Christ.'

I do remember that nobody liked Vos. On VE Day, he had to barricade himself inside a lavatory to escape the attentions of an incensed mob. But this had more to do with his genius for making himself disliked than with any inherent anti-Semitism. I suppose it was really a case of anti-Vosism.

When I first arrived at Eton the bright young 'beaks' had gone to the war, so I was fortunate in being tutored, one to one, by two refugees: in German by one who occasionally called himself Baron Velleman von Simunich and broadcast in Schweizerdeutsch on the BBC, and who was sacked by the headmaster for wearing a scarlet cloak at 'chambers', the mid-morning congregation for beaks; and in French by Jean Bony, who would only speak French, and who would become an authority on the history of medieval architecture, with a chair at Berkeley. Bony could date any church or gargoyle in the Buckinghamshire countryside. There was also a wonderful beak that went by the name of Baron Marochetti; he liked to take boys up to London in his vast Hispano-Suiza. Needless to say he didn't last very long. The majority of beaks, however, were a shower.

There were some good moments, but I only regularly found pleasure in the daily services in College Chapel, in the occasional summer afternoon on the river in a 'dodger' with Mitty Bowyer, and in the school library. The school librarian was a Mr Cattley, whom Wilfred Blunt described kissing each of his boys goodnight when he was a house tutor. He didn't know me very well, but once gently pushed into my view a copy of *Horizon*, a glimpse into another world. 'You might like this, Blond,' he said. And I did: I loved it. Until I read Connolly, I hadn't recognised the sensuality of life.

*   *   *

During my time at Eton, I only had two encounters with the headmaster, Claude Aurelius Elliott. A cold creature, clad in tight-fitting soutane, he was not even liked, his niece Betty Radice once told me, by his family. When selected as 'Head Man', his predecessor, C. A. Alington, had walked out of his room in the

Provost's Lodging. None of this, of course, did I know when I invited him to attend the performance of a play by Molière which I had directed. At the curtain, I asked him if he would care to send a message to the cast: 'Congratulate them on my behalf, but I thought that Welby wore too much pink.' I had cast Welby in the woman's role because he was petite and only slightly freckled.

From *Who's Who* I gather that he is now in his seventies, the seventh baronet, father of three sons and a daughter, and, from the reticence of the entries over the years, conclude that he has lived, like his ancestors, the life of a Lincolnshire squire. Not having spoken to him for more than fifty years, I decide that I should ring him up. He confirms that after a spell in the City as an accountant he became a 'backwoods' baronet; was 5' 8½" tall (an inch taller than me); was a grandfather several times over; and took an interest in the affairs of the county. He remembered well his role in *Le Médecin Malgré Lui*, and added that Betty Rowe, the wife of his tutor, had been so excited that she insisted he wear a lot of her jewellery, which cannot have pleased the Head Man.

I met Mr Elliott again when he signed, in Latin, my leaving book: Gray's poems bound in vellum with the school crest in gilt, an item that figured as five guineas on my last bill. He asked me if I had enjoyed my time at Eton, and when I said no, looked so pained that I reassured him that it must have been my fault. This explanation satisfied him and he moved on to the next school leaver.

So, what was the point of the place? At the battle of Mons, where my father gained his eponymous medal, his commanding officer, a man called Ackroyd, insisted that if he should ever have sons they should go to Eton. This he would arrange, so that my brother's and my presence there, for which through birth, wealth or intelligence we were not inevitably destined, was through my father's military prowess. Over the centuries Eton, founded by that 'poor key-cold figure of a holy king' Henry VI, for seventy scholars, of whom a third should be cripples, had developed into a greenhouse for the growth of boys designed to be men of power; and the evidence is that it has worked. Regard the roster of Prime Ministers, from Canning to Macmillan, and Foreign Secretaries, most recently Carrington and Hurd; and they have not always been drawn from the Tory Party, for has not one of the most significant Labour backbenchers of recent years been father of the house Tam Dalyell, an Old Etonian baronet?

Successful Etonians learned the joys of privilege and practised natural authority without let or hindrance: witness the self-electing and self-perpetuating ruling clique, the Eton Society – 'Pop'. These golden youths* wore braided morning coats, exotic waistcoats and could sport calceolaria in their buttonholes. Members of Pop could fag any boy anywhere in the street, organise much feared beatings in their own clubrooms, where the only complaint was from the cleaner who begged for more ashtrays. Of course, they could not all, however well fancied, become Prime Ministers.†

Occasionally a hiccup derailed their climb to the heights. When my brother arrived at Eton, he found himself in the same house as one Jeremy Thorpe. Together they made a musical pair – Peter played the oboe and Jeremy was a talented violinist – and were protected by their dame, a cottage loaf of a lady with family connections to the Harrovian poet Byron.

Jeremy manoeuvred – he had planned his career from the day he arrived at Eton – himself into Pop. Peter lost sight of him until thirty-two years later when the telephone rang in his Belgravia home. Jeremy was a born politician in the Etonian mould: eloquent, witty, persuasive and never known to forget a name or a place; but he proved to be short on the principles that should clothe that profession. Nothing, he considered, should impede his progress, so that, there being no glory in post-war Army service, it was to be dodged. Flat feet, homosexuality and incontinence were the options. The first was manifestly inapplicable, the second politically incorrect, so Jeremy literally peed himself out of the Army and was

---

* I particularly admired Ian Gilmour, whose mother was a Cadogan and who married a daughter of the Duke of Buccleuch, and the portly young Sir Edward Boyle, both surely destined to rule England.

† Gilmour suffered as one of Mrs Thatcher's wets and Boyle backed out as a minister to run a provincial university.

honourably discharged. As leader of the Liberal Party he nearly fixed a coalition with Heath, but nemesis struck when it was alleged that he had tried to have his troublesome male lover exterminated like a dog. During the trial Jeremy came to have tea with Peter 'in the plucky Hillman', performed his famous imitations and left.

'Whatever did he want?' I asked.

'Money?' suggested Peter.

At this time, when these accusations were all over the *Evening Standard*, our friend Tony Lincoln, a High Court judge, came to dinner and said that Jeremy Thorpe would be acquitted because a British court would prefer to believe him rather than his accusers. He was right. *Floreat Etona*. I fear it is still the school for rulers.

*　　*　　*

Concerning Edward Bulwer Lytton, whom he had encountered as a schoolboy at Harrow, and whom he later made Viceroy of India, Disraeli said, 'I gave him half a crown, now I give him a whole crown.'

As night fell on 8 May 1945 – VE Day – many of the older boys were drunk and in a violent mood. Alcohol can be found in most places on earth – whisky is served in the gents' cloakrooms prior to diplomatic receptions in Islamabad – and Eton was no exception. A mob of us stormed into the private side of Mr Lyttelton's house, baying for 'Bloody Bill', a hated house tutor who beat excessively his own boys and who, we were told, was dining with Mr L. Clad. In cap and gown, a grand figure appeared at the top of the double staircase, contemplated the yelling boys and spoke. 'I understand you are looking for my guest Mr Marsden. He has gone home to bed and I suggest you do likewise. Goodnight, gentlemen.' He then withdrew.

Silence. Then a voice cried out: 'Let's go and see the king!' This melodramatic intervention took the fancy of the crowd and we rushed out shouting: 'To the castle . . . to the castle!' Those who made the three miles would have been too fagged out to cause much trouble. Whoever thought of that one deserved to become a viceroy.

CHAPTER EIGHT

The Army

The Captain

Gunner Blond finally made it to OCTU (Officer Cadet Training Unit) at Mons Barracks in Aldershot in late 1947. The commandant who set the tone for this horrible place (suicides were not unknown) was a full colonel and an even-fuller-paid-up shit. He was also possibly a sadist and certainly a roaring snob. I remember the words of his opening address: 'Gentlemen, we are not unreasonable here. If you wish to race your yacht at Cowes or go home for the Eton and Harrow match, you may.' I hadn't got a yacht at that time, but I did go home for the Eton and Harrow match.

The regime at Mons was designed to break the spirit of cheerful individuals and the back of anybody else. The war, we always said, must have been nicer. The fear of being Returned to Unit (RTUd) was savagely played on by the staff, and it was this that made some boys hang themselves. None was more skilful at this ploy than our platoon commander, Captain Weiss of the Royal Scots.

He was elegant to the point of effeminacy and would, if he had been in charge of a group of navvies, have been subject to wolf whistles as he winnowed down the aisle of our lecture room every morning, cradling a miniature dachshund in his soft, perfectly manicured left hand and trailing, as if it were a mink coat, a walking stick in his right. He had perfect epicene olive skin and velvety brown eyes; he never smiled. He was predictably very brave and had a longer row of medal ribbons than the other officers of his age, which could not have been more than twenty-something. He was reputed to have thrown himself on top of a live hand-grenade, which had been accidentally dropped, to protect his men: it had not exploded.

He was *very* cool and we only once saw him lose it (both

expressions not yet current). On one exercise we had to direct a section of men by shouting – I suppose the noise of battle can be quite distracting. In our platoon was a cadet from Jordan: a small, undistinguished, pox-marked young man with a ratty little moustache. When his turn came, he ascended the hillock, opened his mouth and spoke in what we presumed was his normal voice. Captain Weiss shouted at him to shout. Still no audible sound. Captain Weiss yelled at him to yell. Still the volume remained resolutely down. Angrily, Captain Weiss summoned him back to base with the unmistakably military gesture of placing his open hand upon his head.

'Why won't you obey orders?'

'In my country,' said the Jordanian quietly, 'it is rude to shout.'

A strange lesson from an unlikely source. Captain Weiss's pretty puppy face went puce with rage. 'Arrest this man!' he screamed. The sergeant and the corporal were prompt to obey. They grabbed his beret, with the white potential-officer's disc pinned behind his badge, and snapping, 'Left-right-left-right-left-right,' frog-marched him across the blasted Aldershot Heath back to the barracks. We later learned that the Arab was not only a prince but also a commissioned officer in his own army. Moreover, he would not move from his cell until such time as Captain Weiss came to apologise. For a little while he became a sort of hero. It was the first Arab-Jewish encounter I had ever witnessed.

One of Captain Weiss's little games was to torture me. On parade he would examine me like a surgeon about to operate and only cease when he had found a smidgeon of green blanco on my elbow, which justified confining me to barracks. On the other hand, on the assault course where my friend, Officer Cadet Goldfar, was having problems heaving me over some obstacles – we were both swearing at each other – it was Goldfar who was RTU'd and not I.

The final interview, when each cadet is told whether he has passed and can now proceed to a sort of finishing school for potential officers, went as follows:

CAPTAIN WEISS: Blond, you are idle on parade and more often than not dirty.

BLOND: (*stiffly at attention*) Sir!

CAPTAIN WEISS: You have shown absolutely no officer-like qualities during your time at Mons.

BLOND: Sir!

CAPTAIN WEISS: You are incompetent.

BLOND: Sir!

CAPTAIN WEISS: If you have any ideas in your head, they are not military ones.

BLOND: Sir!

CAPTAIN WEISS: You are quite good with the bazooka.*

BLOND: (*blushing with joy and resisting the impulse to embrace Captain Weiss*) Sir!

CAPTAIN WEISS: And I am recommending you for a commission. Dismiss!

I saluted and, as I about-turned, I heard him say quite clearly, 'Alle yiddische Kinder.'†

The Colonel

The Colonel disliked me on sight. He was neither old nor was he distinguished in any way, and neither was the regiment he commanded at Sheerness (nicknamed 'Sheernasty' by my mother). We were in charge of a huge gun plonked in the middle of the Medway, where, rumour had it, the gunners ran around naked. But I never saw them or a fully clad gun. There was nothing to do. On my first day as orderly officer – a duty I was allocated more often than was fair – I noticed in Standing Orders that I had to turn out the fire picket. I tried to do this but they were in that part of Prince Louis of Battenburg's headquarters used as a cinema. As the bumf dictated, I put them on a charge – only to be rebuked for conduct unbecoming a gunner officer. After that I gave up.

---

* This was a sort of catapult that propelled a grenade; I alone in the platoon had hit a target.

† 'All Jewish children [must stick together].'

My contemporaries at school, who walked 'up the hill' to Victoria Barracks and marched down again three months later as Guards officers, had fed me with tales of how one behaved in the mess. The commanding officer had to be addressed as 'Colonel Roger' and we did not stand up when he entered the room. I did not succeed in introducing this code to the inner sanctum of the officers' mess at Sheerness.

One Whit Bank Holiday, I was made orderly officer and my duty was to sit at the adjutant's desk and keep an eye on the red telephone, which, so was said, was directly connected to the War Office and could ring at any moment and order us to fire our gun. My commanding officer entered the room and I stood up, attempting to conceal my reading matter, a copy of *Vogue*. 'Couldn't you find anything more suitable?' he asked me and then stomped out. He was probably irritated because there was no one around to push his awful little boat off the mud. He returned several hours later to find me genuinely deep in *King's Regulations* (I have always had an appetite for anything in print). He thought I was teasing him and remarked: 'Blond, you have the worst report of any officer ever sent to me. I can't understand how they ever gave you a commission.' I never did tell him.

The Major

Now here was a man after my own heart. First of all, he was never there. The two of us had been entrusted with the task of setting up the administration for a Territorial camp near Thetford. At any moment the Nissen huts would fill up with part-time soldiers on their fortnight's refresher course, and, in anticipation of this, a training unit of officers, sergeant instructors, bombardiers and a few gunners would be installed under what the Army called 'field conditions'. We quickly made ourselves as comfortable as possible; and there were enough of us to generate sufficient swill to excite the appetites of the local farmers.

England in 1948 was not the gastronomic cornucopia it has become. Rationing was still severe, rendered bitterer by the fact that we had won the war. We were not hungry, but we had nothing nice to eat. Regulations decreed – I was learning how all-embracing they were – that a dustbin full of swill from the other ranks' canteen could not be sold to farmers for more than 1/6d. I now promoted myself from mess secretary to mess president and sold the priceless pigswill to a farmer who, in return, sold me ham, eggs, butter, cream, chickens and, it being Norfolk, duck. By tacit agreement with my fellow officers it was understood that mess bills, which under field conditions were not to exceed a nominal sum, should be settled each week in cash; and that no accounts were to be kept. The bills rocketed, but so did our *train de vie*, and with it unexpected visits from officers of field rank from Eastern Command who had heard of the pleasures of our table.

I was quite happy and so was the major. He was busy, with the help of a couple of gunners, covering the floor of his house in Kent with Army linoleum. The Territorials never showed. One week-end, the major turned up in pursuit of petrol, which, like everything else, was rationed. He had a perfectly simple plan. The ordnance depot next door was full of the stuff. All we needed to do was to borrow a couple of three-tonners and steal it in the middle of the night. To avoid suspicion we would disguise ourselves as gunners. My job was to pretend to break down by the guard house, revving the engine violently, while the major slithered into camp with his plucky wire-cutters and hose in order to siphon off the petrol. It was a moonlit night and I was in the middle of my stalling operation, when, during an interstice of the engine's revolutions, I distinctly heard an owl hoot. It was a pre-arranged alarm signal and I shoved the vehicle into gear and bolted. It emerged that the Ordnance Corps had not been quite as drunk or as sleepy as we had been promised in the pub. I don't know quite how many King's Regulations the major and I broke that night, but for officers to disguise themselves as other ranks must have been worth quite a few months in the glasshouse. I might have sworn youth and susceptibility, but then some other major would have sworn about the high quality of my cuisine, and then the lid would have been off the swill bins.

Months later, when I was at New College, I received a formal letter from the major asking for the accounts during my reign as mess secretary/temporary acting president. I was limbering up for registration as a conscientious objector – my only military success – designated class A1 – and I fear I replied somewhat curtly. Still he was a man after my own heart.

CHAPTER NINE

Oxford

My father wanted me to go to King's, Cambridge because he knew the bursar, R. F. Kahn, who was big in government counsels. But I loved the antechapel* at New College, with its memorial to the three young German noblemen and freshmen –

IN MEMORY OF THE MEN OF THIS COLLEGE WHO COMING FROM A FOREIGN LAND ENTERED INTO THE INHERITANCE OF THIS PLACE & RETURNING FOUGHT & DIED FOR THEIR COUNTRY IN THE WAR 1914–1919

– which made me cry.† So I wrote on my form of preference, 'New College, New College, New College'. They must have liked that, for I got an Exhibition in History. So there I was, bowling down the Henley Road‡ on my brand new BSA 250cc motorbike to matriculate in the class of '48, feeling like an emperor, until I fell off. (I had been riding too fast: the engine overheated and the pistons suddenly stuck. Had I pressed the valve actuating lift . . . but I didn't know where, or what, it was.)

Learning that I was to be a pupil in philosophy of Mr Stuart Hampshire of All Souls, and knowing nothing of either tutor or subject, I rushed round to the rooms of Isaiah Berlin. I ignored his sported oak, found him in bed and complained. (It was not that early in the morning.) I actually said, 'Mr Berlin, sir, I am not

* The antechapel was later adorned by Epstein's *Lazarus*. Warden Smith was an unlikely friend of Epstein and insisted on a piece of sculpture being commissioned rather than a portrait. The domestic bursar commented: 'I wish they'd stick to paintings – they stack better.'
† Erected in 1930 to three German members of the college: Prinz Wolrad-Friedrich zu Waldeck-Pyrmont, Freiherr Wilhelm von Sell and Erwin Beit von Speyer.
‡ In the nineteenth century, surely one of the most beautiful in the world.

satisfied with my tutor;' at which he turned round to look at me and, in that wonderfully orotund voice, replied, 'Déjà?' The dialogue was quickly converted into my opening, 'I'm Blond,' and his replying, 'Patently false!' – which, as they say, went round Oxford. When I went to matriculate in a pale-grey summer suit – very unsubfusc – that I had bought at Bonwit Teller in New York, Isaiah covered me with his gown and my reputation began. (Not as a scholar, for although the class of '48 was subsequently billed as a brilliant generation, we were not swots.)

Indeed, I failed two successive examinations under the patient tutelage of Stuart Hampshire and the view was taken, granted his eminence, that there must have been something wrong with the papers. I was not even rusticated, having convinced Warden Smith that I had no home to be rusticated to.* Thus, I was temporarily deprived of my Exhibition and was entrusted to David Ogg, who had a personal hatred of Louis XIV, to whom he referred, through clenched teeth, as 'Lewis the forrrteenth.' When I recall the amount of attention poured over my thankless head by these august academics, I shiver with guilt.

*   *   *

The class of '48, an expression first made known to me by Michael Codron, who belonged to it, was the first not to have fought in the Second World War. Our predecessors wore suede shoes and duffle coats and pushed babies down the High Street. We were younger and so much smarter; and though, of course, we had been conscripted, only a few of us had heard a shot fired in anger. We were, therefore, entitled to our ex-serviceman's grant of about three hundred pounds per annum. Being honest or stupid – or both – I declared that I had some money from my father and didn't take the grant. But three hundred pounds was then enough, believe it or not, to live on.

---

* Just before the interview with the Warden, after a year of drunken behaviour, I checked his publications in the college library. He had indeed written a monograph on Kant, and a fellow academic had inserted in the copy of a review from *Mind* – 'the work of a literate donkey'.

At Oxford at any given time perhaps ten per cent of the university population (some four thousand in 1948) think they are *it*. We were absolutely sure we were *it*, and the colleges we tolerated and were members of were Christ Church, New College and Magdalen, in that particular order. Some were at Merton, though we didn't know anybody from St Edmund's Hall or St John's or Evelyn Waugh's *quondam* college, Hertford, or even Wadham, except for the Warden, Maurice Bowra, who was considered absolutely OK.

Oxford custom was to live the first year in college and then move out to lodgings elsewhere. There was no lodging house more bizarre than that at 167 Walton Street, run by a Swiss lady known as 'Maxi'. The top floor was occupied by Donald, whose real name was David Duck, and his friend Martin Jones. They dressed entirely in black, in which colour their apartment was also painted, and boasted among their furnishings a coffin containing a skeleton. Martin Jones killed himself over thirty years ago and David Duck currently lives in Lisbon. Below them lived Toby Rowe, not an undergraduate but a Jewish antique dealer and nightclub owner. He had the first queer club in London called the Rockingham in Archer Street and used to fling scent at sailors.

Another room was inhabited by Rocky Woodford, a Rhodesian. Milo Cripps lived there for a year, and played cards regularly with Digby Neave and David Clark; these two were known as 'Digby Sheffield-Naïve' and 'David Shark'. John Aspinall was also a constant visitor, playing cards and making about seven quid a week in this connection. Another character was 'Bouncer' Quennell, whose father owned a chemist's shop in Piccadilly Arcade and was known by John Pollock as the 'Ancient Mariner' because 'he stoppeth one of three' (cheques). On the ground floor of this household lived Jocelyn Baines, with his mistress Marion Wriothesley, whose daughter later married David Tennant Sr. He, Jocelyn, was a superior figure, but yet another suicide. Baron Peebles von Friesen and his mistress, the manageress of the Oxford Playhouse, were also around. Peebles had an old Rolls-Royce with a Ford engine.

*   *   *

Oxford portraits

Memorialists (or is it memoirists?) like to point out that many from their acquaintanceship have moved up in the world, but not too many linger on the failed human beings in their lives. Perhaps failure is contagious. A doctor in Montpelier Square, when I asked what he did for the poor, replied, 'I find if you do too much you tend to join their ranks.' My rabbi in Maida Vale positively forbade his wife to go visiting in Shepherd's Bush (this at a time when some poor people could be found in that part of London), because he couldn't bear her coming home in tears, night after night.

My contemporaries are either dead, drunk, in Parliament or chairmen of various successful or not altogether successful public enterprises. The successful ones are, of course, the ones I no longer see. Nevertheless, during my three years at New College, which were the next happiest of my life, I contracted friendships and expanded an acquaintance which has endured for more than fifty years.

So as not to dwell on failure and cause offence, here is a glimpse of a few of my Oxford contemporaries, some of whom have moved up, down or even across.

Peter Fison

A man of violent expostulation, a judge of his fellows, with a gossip column in *Cherwell* – permanently in the second league to *Isis*, the other undergraduate magazine – to support his views. He once described my rooms in 19 Longwall as 'off-white, off-smart'. He fancied himself as a *bon viveur*, and Michael Rutherston, who drew just like Max Beerbohm, cartooned him rejecting a bottle of wine at the Randolph Hotel. He was proud of his friendship with Lord Snow, who became one of the trustees of Padworth College, a boarding establishment Fison started, when he went down, for the delinquent daughters of diplomats *en poste* in London. He offered Michael Molian employment as 'unpaid maniciple'. Jennifer Paterson became the cook and her recipe for keeping the girls happy, granted the modest budget, was to feed them on huge tins of jam washed down with cider. I later melded him with

Prince Rupert Loewenstein for the character of 'Ferty' in my novel *Family Business*. Peter Fison died young, as did Michael Rutherston, of a broken heart.

Michael Molian

An elf-like figure with a deep voice and an imposing delivery, he was considered the brightest of us all – so it was thought unimaginative of the university to award him only a third-class degree. He was devoted equally to soldiers and sailors, and once compared his indecision at Waterloo (station), as to whether he should take the train to Aldershot or Portsmouth, to that of Newman, hesitating between turning his horse's head towards Oxford or Cambridge. He became an interpreter at UNESCO in Paris and once wrote me a bread-and-butter letter containing an exquisite pun, viz.:

> I returned to find that my office had been moved to a part of the building overlooking, as I fear I am unable to do, the playing fields of the Ecole Militaire.

Milo Cripps

Patron to both Peter Fison and Michael Molian, he had been to Ampleforth (thence Corpus) and had that visible sense of right and wrong peculiar, I have noticed, to English Catholics. His deep rooms in the quad of Corpus were well furnished with liquor and healthy young men, who looked as if they had just escaped for the day – or night – from captaining the second XI. He once spent the whole of a lunch I was giving for my stepsister Simone Laski in my off-smart rooms under the table. The next day I received a flower with a note, on which was written the single word: 'Miz'.

Milo's uncle was Sir Stafford Cripps, then Chancellor of the Exchequer, whose watchword was 'austerity'; but Milo took his tune more from his mother Violet, a great beauty, rider to hounds, toast of White's and a Duchess of Westminster. I went to her large corner house in South Audley Street – part of her settlement no doubt – for the occasional glass of wine (champagne). She always called me 'Mr Blond', considering perhaps that, as a Jew, I had no

Christian name; she would also tell me that Milo had once saved someone from drowning. Certainly, he has always been gallant in attending to my needs and to those of our friends, however unworthy.

Jimmy Goldsmith

The first time I saw Jimmy Goldsmith was on the stairs of that infamous house at 167 Walton Street. He was there, I think, playing chemmy. He had come from Eton in a hired Daimler, having won handsomely on a Yankee at Windsor.

In the late forties and early fifties, petrol was rationed and cars were few and far between among undergraduates. My stepsister Anne had kindly lent me her Standard 8 open tourer, so one spring vacation Oliver Carson, my constant companion and co-editor of a magazine I had started called *Harlequin*, set off from London to drive to Portofino with Jimmy Goldsmith in the back. The car, because of our journalistic connections, of which we were deeply proud, sported a far too large sign with the word PRESS on it. I remember driving in past the OUT sign of the Carlton, Cannes, of which Jimmy's father, Major Frank Goldsmith, a former liberal MP, was the director. We stayed in the chambermaids' rooms and were screeched at by them in the morning.

Arriving at Portofino for the first time, I smelt orange blossom and felt the tug at the heart familiar to all northern Europeans, exemplified in the lines of Goethe:

> Kennst du das Land, wo die Zitronen blühn,
> Im dunkeln Laub die Gold-Orangen glühn,*

We stayed the night in a hotel next to the water's edge in that enchanting and unspoiled town. In the morning Jimmy had gone on to Venice, where there were more fun and games, women and more games. There was an electric quality about Jimmy aged

---

*   Know you the land, where the lemon trees bloom,
       In the foliage the golden oranges glow.
                                        Wilhelm Meisters Lehrjahre (1795)

sixteen – as I dare say there had been about Jimmy aged six. His preoccupations seemed to be sex, gambling and the outrageous: by which I mean he enjoyed sensation in any form and from any source. Both he and his elder brother Teddy, whether in Paris, London or Cannes, spoke in accents neither English nor French, and had the manners of high-powered hoteliers.

John Aspinall

One hot day in the summer of '51, two undergraduates, dressed unaccountably in severe grey overcoats, which they refused to remove, appeared at Schools for their degree examinations. They both said in turn that they felt giddy, and nearly fainted. The elderly invigilator, who was one of the many retired dons brought in to earn a few coppers, swiftly advised them to retire to their lodgings until their illness passed. They tottered off and, as soon as they were out of the invigilator's sight, they nipped round the corner into a hired Daimler and drove to Ascot for the Gold Cup. The bond which united John Aspinall and Ian Maxwell Scott was a passion for gambling.

Aspinall alone influenced the gambling laws in England and Wales by the particular climate he created. In the fifties, when gambling was illegal, he ran a small game of poker in the Ritz when the going was good. When it was not so good, he ran it in the Green Park Hotel. I remember once whilst we were playing – I always seemed to lose – Maxwell Scott's voice could be heard screaming for money from Piccadilly. Aspinall walked over to the window, detached a ten-shilling note from his wallet and let it float down in the air. A busker, assuming it was for him, muttered, 'Thank you, sir,' and reached out his hands, not knowing it was intended for an eager young man with a nose like a greyhound who snatched it and ran down the street.

Although loyal to his friends, Aspinall did not like being crossed by them. Inadvertently, I became not so much an enemy as a friend for whom the sun no longer shone. When my father and stepmother were in New York, my brother and I decided to give an enormous party in their comfortable stockbroker Tudor home outside East Grinstead. We had permission of sorts, but not the kind of permission needed to accommodate John Aspinall. We received buckets of friends and drink and girls and even, I remember, my uncle Jack. Aspinall ran a *vingt-et-un* game at which everyone seemed to win. I remember Uncle Jack saying to me with pleasure that he had won forty pounds. When the chemmy kit was brought out at about one o'clock in the morning my stepmother's treacherous shit of a butler, Ripley, threatened to ring up New York. As he was stone deaf, I'm not sure whether he would have been capable of such a deed; all the same I made the decision to put a stop to the party and confiscated the cards. More cards were produced. More confiscation. Finally, in an atmosphere of ill will, everyone left sounding curses.

Of course, what I had failed to realise at the time was that I had ruined Aspinall's first big attempt to gain himself a reputation. I think he lost about four hundred pounds that night, which must have set his operations back by quite a few months.

The last time I saw Aspinall was at the funeral of *un âme damné*. Aspinall arrived in a stretch limo wearing a black silk suit, which he obviously only wore on such occasions: an albino mafia leader surrounded by henchmen.

'Ah, Anthony, you look like a successful Jewish businessman of Libyan extraction,' he said. The first observation was not too accurate, but the second was precise. My mother's family came from Tripoli, something I must have told him some forty years before.

John Pollock

John Pollock was tall, willowy, and I suppose some would have thought beautiful. He had won, at the age of seventeen, an open scholarship to Balliol, but he was already showing signs of dereliction, abetted by drink. He was a kind of official genius *manqué*, neurotic to such an extent that he would not go to any tutorial. He found this modest obligation too demanding and would take the train to London to avoid it.

A friend of both Jimmy Goldsmith and John Aspinall, he later became another denizen and member of their chemmy school. He suffered equally from lack of funds: an orphan, he expected daily, as though it were the Jewish Messiah, a legacy, but, like the Messiah, it never came. After a desolate career,* which included stays in various asylums, he ended up supported by his brother in a large chilly house in Belgravia. He was only allowed a pound a day to buy a pint in the Horse and Groom, the pub in the nearby mews.

One day, Jimmy Goldsmith was early for a rendezvous in Wilton Place with Edward Heath so he dropped into the nearest pub, a move he had not made for many a moon. 'Ah, Jimmy,' stuttered John Pollock, drugged and shaky, fondling his solitary pint, 'could you possibly lend me a fiver?'

Jimmy (one of the richest men in the world) excoriated John (one of the poorest) for asking for so little, and harangued him on the decline in the value of money since the late forties. I am unsure whether, in the end, any money changed hands.

Peter G.

A young man with whom I was in love. I am not being discreet: I have forgotten his name. When I saw him my knees turned to jelly, and when he once touched me, on the shoulder, I nearly fainted. He was keen on art, so I used to buy him Phaidons and lay them humbly on the floor just inside his rooms. My great friend, Michael Briggs, who never forgets anybody, told me he saw him years ago in St James's Park, dressed as a tramp. Perhaps he was a tramp.

Sir Anthony de Hoghton

An absolutely monstrous albino who specialised in bad behaviour: peeing in the letter-boxes in Christ Church, throwing soup in the faces of waiters and writing blasphemous poems. One of them opened: 'God is in his garage, cranking up his Bentley.' I refused to publish it in my magazine *Harlequin* – I have always been *that* sort

---

* I published three novels of his, including *They Wouldn't Stop Talking*.

of a coward – but Mark Boxer, up at Cambridge, was not and was sent down for it.

Anthony knew twentieth-century French literature and became a buddy of Enid Starkie. Together they would troll round the bars of Oxford: she clad (only) in a fur coat and he carrying a leather bag from Swaine & Adeney, containing a tin of *foie gras* and a bottle of brandy, in case he felt peckish.

When he inherited the family seat, Hoghton Towers, a grand Elizabethan house near Preston, which looked like the set from *The Hound of the Baskervilles*, he blued the money on wine, young men and Caribbean cruises until he was derelict and destitute. My future father-in-law, though of course I did not know it, was his trustee and resigned in despair after Anthony, with a view to selling it, had attempted unsuccessfully to evacuate – he tried to cut it in half – the famous table on which King James had knighted the loin. Jeffrey Simmons, a publisher and a mutual friend, gave a fat and grizzled beggar sixpence in Sloane Square and realised a hundred yards later that it had been Anthony de Hoghton.

James Cameron

He was de Hoghton's Boswell and *cicisbeo*. Together they wafted down the High like a pair of fluttering galleons on an aft wind. James was Australian, which accent he overlaid with a richly emphatic voice one can only call 'camp'. He admired de Hoghton's arrogance and self-concern, particularly the story of Anthony's not lingering to say goodbye when embarking on a cruise ship because he was in a hurry to have a word with the pastry chef.

He had a taste for what was known as 'rough trade', which was his undoing, and divided the desirables into DIS (Desert Island Stuff) and RDIS (Remote Desert Island Stuff). He became a very successful advertising agent, specialising in market research. I remember his advising Jimmy Goldsmith not to try and sell the French shaving foam, because so many of them cut open toothpaste tubes with a razor to extract the last scraping. He was murdered one hot summer night in his little house in Islington. As

I was in his diary and address book, two policeman called at my office in Doughty Street* to interview me. Their questioning was intense and frightening.

'Mr Blond, are you a member of the Wig and Pen Club?'†

'No, but I have been there. It's rather boring.'

One of them wrote down my response.

'Do you know the Caledonian Club?'

'No, er . . . I mean yes.' (I was beginning to get rather frightened and had imagined at first that they might be referring to some low queer dive patronised by James.) 'You mean the one in Belgravia? *That* really is boring.' (Uneasy laugh from AB.)

'Did you often see Mr Cameron?'

'Not really, the last time he saw me he crossed over to the other side of the road.'

'Oh?'

'He owed me twenty-five pounds and, though I knew he earned a lot of money, he didn't seem to want to pay it back.'

They both looked mistrustful and hostile, and I was beginning to feel that it might be easier to confess to the murder than endure their questions (which explains why the wrong people are so often hanged). I pressed on the intercom to summon Desmond Briggs, whose arrival with pipe and spectacles reassured the police as much as it did me. To Desmond, who was a Justice of the Peace in Wiltshire, they confided that James Cameron had been shot in the head through a pillow, and the neighbours had only noticed something was wrong when his body had started to decompose. The two policemen thought he had been a victim of extortion: that someone he had picked up had tried to get money out of him – more money – and that he had refused. The defence would be that James had been making unnatural advances, but this would no longer wash. They'd get him, they said.

---

*   Now the offices of the *Spectator*.
†   Rumoured by Warwick Charlton to be one of the few buildings to have escaped the Fire of London.

CHAPTER TEN

V. E. R. Blunt

Conscription into the Army was an agreeable shock for me. Although, as far as material comfort was concerned, it was in contrast to the flat in Grosvenor Square where I had been lodging with my father and stepmother, the comradely and unsuspicious atmosphere of a General Training Corps, or 'spider', was a welcome change from the competitiveness of an Eton house, where the boys were literally locked up every night into, or – in my case – out of little cliques.

In the Army, I immediately discovered I had a capacity for making friends with young men from all walks of life. Williams and I had nothing in common except our affection. He was a hairy, randy, sibling of three equally large rugger-playing brothers who lived with their parents in a house in Harley Street. The whole family was in the medical profession, and I remember his mother injecting the Christmas cake with brandy from her hypodermic syringe – nice to watch. I kept up with the Williamses, so that when I was at Oxford looking for something to do in the vacations they introduced me to Mr Blunt, a businessman, who, they said, needed an assistant.

V. E. R. Blunt was an unlikely man. He was an imposing figure, a cross between Humpty Dumpty and a brigadier, who had rowed hard in his youth. He always wore a dark-blue pinstriped suit, waistcoat with a gold fob, a red carnation and a trilby, and carried an umbrella. The whole was topped-up with a bristly white moustache, a ruddy complexion and blue eyes. With his sonorous Balliol voice, he was the picture of a well-established businessman in the lucrative and then fashionable (because one could go abroad and a get a decent meal) import-export trade. He was not the blimp he looked, being affable, witty, courteous and not at all well-bred.

He owned a magazine called *Sailplane and Glider*, and offered me the post of acting editor at an emolument of five pounds per week. He had a small dusty office behind the Strand with no secretary but a lot of telephones. Milk was delivered daily for the endless cups of tea, which it was one of my duties to prepare. My employer was always short of what he called 'change' for the milkman, the window-cleaner (then a necessity in London), and for a round of drinks or a taxi fare. This deficiency was but a symptom, I soon understood, of an almost complete absence of money.

Mass employment and low interest rates, shortages, quotas and regulations were the staples of the British economy in the late forties and business failures were few. Even book publishers prospered if they could but find the paper. It amazed and finally irritated me that Blunt and Partners – I never saw *them* – could not and would not flourish, though we were in the business of importing scrap metal, which had produced England's first post-war millionaire, George Dawson, who now lived in the South of France. Europe and North Africa were littered with the debris of armies, which could have been turned into steel by the hungry blast furnaces of Scunthorpe and South Wales.

While I copy-edited the queasy-making experiences of *Sailplane and Glider*, Mr Blunt would compose telegrams to dubious Arabs in Benghazi about bills of lading, certificates of quality and tonnages, whether fob (free on board) or cif (cost, insurance and freight). These putative deals in scrap-iron were on a grand enough scale to keep my employer on a permanent high, but something always misfired and the deal would collapse. The back-to-back credit (*dos à dos*) fell over . . . the completion-bond guarantee never even began . . . Mr Blunt had to return to the bread-and-butter business of selling china in the East End through his friend Colonel Karnibad, an immaculate Pole with an eyeglass and one well-pressed shiny brown suit. These transactions, for reasons I did not then comprehend, always seemed to occur in the dead of night. I once, however, sold a parcel of sixteen-ounce tins of Irish ham to my local grocer, Jacksons of Piccadilly. Being Irish, of course, they only weighed fifteen and a half ounces – but Jacksons didn't mind. They were lucky to have them.

In the intervals between these desperate and expensive cablegrams to Benghazi – they were long and frequent – my employer would reminisce. I think he paid me, when he paid me, to listen. And the more he talked the more I admired him, for Mr Blunt was not so much a self-made man as a self-invented one. The vaguely Leander tie, the definitive Oxford accent and the old-world gallantry with which he handled the ladies, especially my mother, who I think saw through him, were all made up. He told me that as a little boy in the back streets of – *I think* – Belfast, his job was to watch out for coppers while gin was being distilled in the family bathtub. Yet he did make it to Balliol and thence to the favours of great ladies. (He must have been a very handsome young man.) One of them was Claire Booth. Had I not heard her play *Love is a Verb*? No, I hadn't, nor was it listed among her works. 'Verb,' he repeated, 'Vernon Ernest Rowland Blunt!' And he triumphantly slapped his knee.

The Blunt family home was a large, ramshackle house with an untended and brambly garden. He had a beautiful young wife, three angelic children and a cat. I feared for them, but they were so cheerful, happy and loving, like the characters in a play by J. M. Barrie, that I was sure all would end well in the last act. It didn't. Daddy went to gaol. But first an interlude when something went well.

Blunt and Partners' chronic negative cash flow never impeded expeditions, by the senior partners, to the Continent. Like many a careful spender he was good on treats, and I accompanied him on one such trip to the Ruhr in pursuit of miles of steel tubing. We returned empty-handed: the tubes being a crucial millimetre or so too thick or too thin.

He was away on one of these expeditions when I noticed that a scrap-iron deal simmering in Tunisia seemed to be giving off a positive glow. Blunt and Partners were suddenly in between a willing seller, an honest wog, a willing buyer and a helpful official at the British Iron and Steel Corporation. Each agreed the other's terms and there was no question of a back-to-back credit (thank God), because there was no need for any such complication: we were, as Nye Bevan said, in a position to make easy money just by standing in the tide of supply and demand. There was, however, the little matter of the completion-bond guarantee. I telephoned the nice man at the British Iron and Steel Corporation and asked for an appointment. He examined the documents and remarked that they looked satisfactory. He then looked at me, a rather immature twenty-two-year-old, and said, 'Mr Blond, do you know what a completion-bond guarantee *is*?' I blushed. 'Perhaps, then,' he said, 'you will allow me to arrange it for you.' He did. Blunt and Partners made several thousand pounds of which, much later, Vernon Ernest Rowland Blunt sent me fifty.

*   *   *

Mr Blunt and Colonel Karnibad were prosecuted under a Board of Trade regulation for conspiracy to sell china, destined for export, on the home market. When the case was heard that particular regulation had been rescinded, but it was, as they say in Lancashire, 'hard butties', for, as the legal saw goes, *Nullum tempus aut locus occurrit regi.** Mr Blunt went down, but Colonel Karnibad was acquitted. The latter had stood rigidly to attention in his shiny suit and, affecting not fully to understand English, had answered every question by saying firmly and respectfully, 'Sir!' The judge knew a gallant Pole when he saw one, and he also – oh dear, oh dear for Mr Blunt, who had elected to defend himself – recognised a barrack-room lawyer.

The gaol at Weymouth is a grim building, designed for and built by Napoleonic prisoners of war, but it was a sunny day when I drove the family down to see its head. We sat with a picnic basket on a green sward, and my former employer looked even more like a brigadier in his bulky battledress. The particular bulkiness of the blouse became clear to me when he hissed in my ear the following instructions: 'Anthony, I have in here a cat. It is just alive, but only

---

*   'Time never runs against the Crown.'

just, because the prisoners are, I fear, brutes. They are always trying to strangle it with a lavatory chain. Any moment now,' he looked over his shoulder, 'the guard will turn round and walk the other way. When I give you the signal open the picnic basket and when the cat's inside, shut it.' I froze. He then gave me the signal and in a flash a bundle of living rage and claw was incarcerated in a safer place. After some weeks of care this wild animal became a fat contented Surrey mouser.

From my two vacations working for Blunt and Partners I learned three things. First, if you don't know what's going on, say so; secondly, defend yourself, but never in a Court of Law; and thirdly, there is only one element which matters in business – luck.

When the curtain finally fell on Mr Blunt there was, after all, a happy ending. What I have described took place over fifty years ago. In the early eighties, I saw a letter from him in the *Daily Telegraph* about the international oil trade, on which he had become something of a guru. I had a glass of sherry (from a decanter) with him in a well-furnished flat off Sloane Square, which he called his *pied à terre*. And his eightieth birthday was announced in *The Times*.

PART THREE

The Publishing Game

CHAPTER ELEVEN

A False Start

In 1951, I went down from Oxford, having promised to try the family business. I did just that and lived with my uncle Jack, at Lindsey, Groby Road. Every morning, for six long months, I took the electric train to Manchester, arriving at the factory of Blond Brothers in Cheetham Hill absurdly and unnecessarily early. After a few days of eating in the canteen, I was approached in a motherly way by one of the forewomen called, I think, Flo.

'Mr Anthony, we all think you'd be much happier having smoked salmon and roast chicken with your uncle Horace upstairs.'

This arrangement suited Uncle Horace, whose life was dedicated to avoiding boredom and discomfort; indeed he enjoyed my company enough to offer me fifteen hundred a year to stay on as his lunch guest. Once a month our cousin, Mabel Laski, sister to the great Harold Laski, came to lunch. She always had to have chicken, roast potatoes and peas, and was always rude, in her flat, rasping Lancashire-Laski voice, about my aunt Rita, who was neat, pert, painted and well coiffed. Mabel was grisly and embattled like a Giles-cartoon grandma, but, as she always pointed out, quite a bit younger than Rita.

From Uncle Horace I learned that the art of business is akin to deceit, which it did not amuse me to practise (if that makes me a prig, so be it). He was a most ingenious man. He sent his suppliers a Christmas present one year of a pair of trousers, three inches long, explaining that if only they could sell him some more cloth . . . But in 1951, suddenly, no shortage of raw materials, and Marks & Spencer, who consumed mountains of underwear generated by the three hundred, mainly teenage, machinists, cancelled deliveries at the contracted price. At this time a story circulated in the *schmotter* trade of an unattended lorry being filled up with double its load, while the driver went off for his lunch.

Blond Brothers bought cotton from a spinner called Collins in Bolton, sole proprietor Marco Bakerjian, whom Horace did not want to pay in full. We drove off in his big car* through the grim streets of the industrial north-west and were welcomed in satanic Bolton with Armenian courtesy. I remember being shown round the mill, that was powered by a shiny steam engine, dated 1885, called Esmeralda. The din was terrific, but *Music While You Work* was on the loudspeaker system. I asked how the workers could possibly hear any music. In reply, the manager threw a switch and immediately a hundred heads jerked up in alarm, a fine example of the efficiency of the human ear as censor. Back in the boss's office, Uncle Horace took a Woodbine from his Cartier cigarette case and suggested that Marco sue him. Marco looked at my uncle with suspicion: litigation, it seemed, was for the Gulbenkians of this world. Horace won that round; he also defeated his own employees over the price of a cup of tea, which had increased from threepence to fourpence.

Discontent over such matters was not expressed by a trade-union official – I never saw one – but by rhythmic chanting, like 'cuppa tea fer tuppence', which penetrated to the over-heated, over-carpeted, panelled sanctum of Uncle Horace. Finally, he agreed to receive a deputation. 'You can have the tea for nothing,' he told them, 'just bring the milk.' He had it all worked out.

I left my uncles, between whom I had shuttled for six depressing months, without regret. I understood that my family's brass derived from the muck of the north-west, but did it have to be so *mucky*? The indifference of capitalists to town planning, to pollution, to diet, their thoughtless exaction of working hours† – all this created a lumpenproletariat whose pale-faced existences were only enlivened, or more accurately deadened, by two world wars. Within the terraces of slums, *bonhomie à la Coronation Street* certainly flourished;

---

* He could not drive and in a long life had only three chauffeurs.
† The three-day week in 1974 hardly diminished output.

but before the package holiday these millions had never tasted a fresh peach or felt the sun steadily on their backs.

I had become a socialist in the library at Eton on reading Greville's diaries. When attending the trial of some children, who had been condemned to death for thieving, he remarks, 'I never did see boys cry so.' The time I spent in the slums of Manchester, where I saw children playing in the streets without shoes in a world from which I had been so carefully insulated during *my* childhood, confirmed me in this view. But I did nothing about it.

When the six months were up, I was off to London – no other place would do. (Lady Rothermere, later Anne Fleming, offered me a job as a journalist but pointed out that I would have to start in Cardiff or some such; I said, No, thank you, to that too.) I went to work for a literary agent called Raymond Savage, whose sister was married to the Bishop of Lincoln, and who wanted to sell me his business, which had the rights to T. E. Lawrence's unpublished – and actually rather boring – book *The Mint*. I didn't buy it: I set up my own.

I started Anthony Blond (London) Ltd, literary agents, at 161 New Bond Street, in a back room above a bank, Churchill's Night Club and Goya smellies. We paid our landlord, who was a play agent,* three pounds per week for the privilege of a small room with a gas fire. My sole employee cum partner was Isabel Colegate, then notorious for never uttering a word. She didn't mind writing, and this is how she recorded that period in the foreword of the reissue of her first three novels, called *The Blackmailer*, *A Man of Power* and *The Great Occasion*, which I originally published between 1958 and 1963 under the Anthony Blond Ltd imprint.

> At the time I wrote *The Blackmailer* I was working in a Literary Agency called Anthony Blond (London) Limited. It consisted of Anthony Blond and me. I had contributed fifty pounds towards the initial expenses and was theoretically a partner. Thus, when

---

* He lived off ten per cent of Dodie Smith, but whether he is still around to collect his share of all those *101 Dalmatians*, I do not know.

Anthony in full flood of eloquence before a dazzled client gesticulated towards me and said, 'I'll get the girl to type the contract,' I would frown ferociously from behind my typewriter. 'Ah,' he'd have to exclaim. 'I see the girl's not in today. My partner, Miss Colegate, may be kind enough . . . .' In fact I was the typist, though I kept the accounts and wrote reader's reports, mostly explaining in detail why the typescripts concerned were quite unpublishable, falling as they did so very far below the standards set by the world's greatest literature, which in my ignorance of there being any other standards I was applying to them. My reports must have been deeply disheartening.

I married about this time and we were given a Cavalier King Charles spaniel. My bus journey from Chelsea to the office behind Barclays Bank in New Bond Street was more or less the one taken by Judith and her dog in *The Blackmailer* and by Vanessa in *A Man of Power*. When *A Man of Power* was published, John Davenport, who had given it a good review in the *Observer*, telephoned me to explain that it would have been even better if the Literary Editor hadn't cut it, and said, 'I see you know the man who longs for Paris on the top of the 22 bus . . . .' Peripherals do come in, sometimes changed or combined with others to make composites, sometimes almost complete. The man on the 22 bus in *A Man of Power* was complete as far as I knew him, so was the dog in *The Blackmailer*. The publisher who turned down that book was convinced that the character of Feliks Hansecu, the publisher in the book, was André Deutsch; I don't think he believed me when I said I'd never met him. Feliks was based as much as anything on the fantasies of office life in which we used to indulge in our little back room above the Goya Perfume shop offices with Binky asleep in front of the gas fire and Major Clare and Mr Fitch, our friendly neighbouring dramatic agents, walking through every time they went in or out of the inner room to which ours was a passage. Not only my inexperience but also my incapacitating shyness prevented me from venturing out into the commercial cut and thrust of the literary world. My bolder partner came back with the tales which no doubt provided the information for the character of Feliks.

The agency was not a success: nor was it a failure. Our landlord, Mr Fitch, knew Anthony Heckstall-Smith DSC, who introduced me to his publishers, Charles Fry and Tony Gibbs* of Allan Wingate, where I was soon installed in a small upper room that they let me paint purple.

*   *   *

The firm of Allan Wingate, a name made up by the original founder, André Deutsch, who was squeezed out by the Jesuitical machinations of the other partner and principal shareholder, Tony Gibbs, occupied a small four-storey house at 12 Beauchamp Place off Knightsbridge, now pullulating with boutiques. In different bits of the building, books were created, edited, warehoused, packed, invoiced and dispatched – a vertical set-up of the type beloved and recorded by Sir Stanley Unwin and one which could not exist today. Mr Wingate, a mythical figure, was supposed to come in on Friday and sign cheques. He didn't exist.

Allan Wingate performed every publishing function except print the books – which is not a publishing function. There was nothing wrong with the system, just the operators. On the *piano nobile*, as it were, there was just room for two desks: one large and flat on which Charles Fry – Humpty Dumpty with a head like a boiled egg – thumped his fist when he wasn't angrily polishing his shoes. Upstairs was a Catholic widow, Mrs Rowell, in charge of advertising and publicity, and the conscience of the firm. (It needed one.) Mrs Rowell was reputedly, that is to say according to Tony Gibbs, futilely in love with Charles Fry. Adjacent to her was Archie Savory, of strawberry hue, in charge of production. He was a multi-faceted artist into bondage; a theme he tried to introduce into Wingate jackets, an effect which was tolerated, because it saved money. He was married to Violet, widow of a ginger-wine-making Bibby, a lady well known in Bembridge society, who used to give monthly dinner parties for wives. Nobody knew that the

* Son of *Street of Adventure* Sir Philip.

elderly parlour maid who served at the table was in fact her husband in drag.

Allan Wingate's working capital came from punters who invested in exchange for a directorship. Needless to say, the investment never accrued. The Hon. 'Winky' Portman, beneficiary of a legacy whereby any money he earned would be doubled by the estate, was such a one. Arnold Goodman, a friend of Charles Fry and the only person to attend his funeral, administered the details of this arrangement. The directors became so numerous that Simon Harcourt-Smith – the ultimate plagiarist* – suggested that they should all march down Beauchamp Place carrying a banner, ALLAN WINGATE UNFAIR TO DIRECTORS!

After Charles Fry's suicide, Tony Gibbs decided to go into liquidation, typically while publishing a bestseller – *Exodus* by Leon Uris.

---

* He once typed out a published book and presented it as his very own work.

CHAPTER TWELVE

Chester Row to Doughty Street

The telephone rang and it was Sir Geoffrey Faber, of the eponymous duo, on the line.

'Do you agree that fifty thousand pounds is the minimum venture capital necessary to start a publishing firm?' I asked.

'Yes,' and the conversation ended. That was fifty years ago.

In fact the venture capital of Anthony Blond Ltd was a tenth of that sum and I had already blued it on my first list of twenty-one ill-assorted and unrelated titles. Fortunately, I was later saved from financial disaster by one title, *The History of Orgies*, written by a family friend, the late Burgo Partridge, whose mother, Frances, came to writing late in life. Paul Hamlyn, who watched my activities with weary compassion, sold the American rights to 'Uncle' Nat Sobel of Crown – you see I did not know about American rights. Nevertheless, my first few books were moderately successful.

Red Sky at Night (one of twelve books, it emerged, with that title), by Jo Capka DFM, at sixteen shillings, was the story of a Czech pilot whose lost eye was found and replaced by a member of his ground crew. Vanora McIndoe, daughter of Sir Archie, was the source; she also found for me, as an agent, *Boldness Be My Fame* by Richard Pape, which I sold to Paul Elek and which busted a block or two in the fifties. The first impression of *Red Sky at Night* sold out and, encouraged by the author's appearance on *This Is Your Life*,* I reprinted. Sheer folly. We got one order, for fourteen copies, from the Co-op in Romford, where our hero had settled.

On the same day in May, I published a first novel, *The Blackmailer*

---

* Since it had an audience of millions, I worked out that only one per cent needed to buy the book.

by Isabel Colegate, at thirteen and six, a shilling more than the norm, with a wraparound jacket by Ruth Sheradski. Isabel's novel had been at first accepted then rejected by Bob Knittel, an editor at Jonathan Cape. She nearly lost her baby from the disappointment. The novel contained an all too accurate portrait of our mutual friend Alan Clark, who himself had written a book, about the Stock Exchange, called *Bargains at Special Prices*. Alan had had the book withdrawn for libel of the stockbroker Edgar Astaire. We – I was beginning to relish the publisher's 'we' – printed two thousand five hundred copies of *The Blackmailer* and few came back. William Miller, an editor at Panther Books, bought the paperback rights for one hundred and fifty pounds and it was reviewed generously in the *Observer*. We published three more of Isabel's novels before she left and reissued them all in one volume on the back of her subsequent hit with *The Shooting Party*.

*   *   *

Anthony Blond Ltd consisted of myself in the back room, formerly the garden of my modest terrace house in Chester Row, with a girl who typed.* Production was in the charge of a printer's rep, by day a print salesman for Taylor, Garnett, Evans, who came in one evening a week. I reasoned it was more economical to have only one printer and trust him; moreover, I told him to make our books look more like Cape's. They didn't: they ended up looking kitsch – even by today's standards – and small. Mr Noel Ranns, for that was his name, wouldn't take any money and made the mistake of advising me not to republish *Confessions of Zeno* by Italo Svevo, solely because the costings did not work. I learnt later that if a book is strong enough it doesn't matter about the costings.

After a few books had been published and a little resonance created, I was asked to lunch at the White Tower in Percy Street, the sort of place for what would become known as a serious lunch,

---

*   In fact she was much more than that; she found and edited books such as *The Ha-Ha* by Jennifer Dawson. Esther Menell left when we moved, which was my fault entirely.

by a man I had not met named Desmond Briggs. He was working for the London end of an Australian firm called Angus & Robertson, and was understandably rather bored. Desmond was the son of a Kenyan planter and politician, and had been to Magdalene, which he told me was well known for its table. I was impressed by this provenance and liked him, but said I couldn't afford to pay him. He said that didn't matter. He joined me in the back room.

London in the fifties must have been full of young people with the same inclination, to be in publishing, and the same ability in the same circumstances to manage without being paid. We were quickly reinforced by a Miss Hazel Frame, heiress to a South African Jewish blanket manufacturer, who was to take care of publicity and advertising sales in our handbooks; and then by Mr Lyon Ben Zimra, also Jewish, from Gibraltar, who was to be the editorial polymath behind the success of Blond Educational. Miss Frame, who enjoyed making daily visits to her psychiatrist, insisted on garaging her long mink coat on our dining-room table.

*   *   *

When Desmond Briggs and I moved from the back room in Chester Row to a freehold at 56 Doughty Street, he brought with him an office manager. Miss D. M. Thornton was a commanding little lady, blind in one eye, with the gait of an admiral, who for many years managed the office – and me. Bad-tempered, bossy and snoopy, she was disliked, but feared, by everybody – except of course Desmond and myself, who cherished her.

Even then, in 1962, she was more than a certain age, having had a boyfriend during the Great War, whom she rejected after she first saw him out of uniform. Between the wars she had worked for the founder of Glaxo, then but a maker of powdered milk, who gave her some shares. Unfortunately she cashed these and forwent a fortune.

She had two friends: one an office lady who lived in Potters Bar, whither she repaired once or twice a year for a weekend; the other, Charlie, the chauffeur of Edward Heath, then Leader of the Opposition, who only spoke to Charlie to complain of the manner in which he changed gear in the official Humber. When her lady friend died, Miss Thornton announced: 'Bang go my weekends in Potters Bar.'

She was a tenant, virtually grace and favour because the rent was so low, of a capacious mews flat behind Peter Jones, distinctly capable of improvement, which she ignored. Nevertheless, the shabby dwelling was handy for Chester Row, where she would drop in, every morning, an envelope detailing my arrangements for the day. She was amused when I handed it back, unopened, on my later arrival at the office.

One year, Desmond dreamt up the 'Big Bang Book Fair' in Russell Square, and it was masterminded by Martyn Goff, a director of the National Book League. We hired Coco the Clown, who arrived at Doughty Street in an ancient London Omnibus, with a lot of children, including one of mine, drawn by two horses. I entreated Miss Thornton, whom it was difficult to cajole from her desk to brave the rain, to come and look at the spectacle. She proceeded to poke her one eye out of the door and sniffed: 'They only had one horse.'

Eventually she went potty and had to go. We discovered that she was seventy-eight and not sixty-eight, the discrepancy being partly attributable to her having been born on February 29th. She had taken to tearing up my airline tickets, resenting my departure from the office, where she now arrived at 7.30 p.m., mistaking the time of day. She had liked to arrive early to inspect the mail – everybody's mail – and in this way discovered that one of our representatives was having an affair. When I protested, she replied calmly, 'Someone in this office has to know what's going on!'

At the crunch, she refused to leave without consulting her doctor. 'She is waiting for you in the cab, Miss Thornton,' I told her. A masterstroke of planning I thought. 'I will not go without my typewriter!' So I carried it into the taxi.

The last time I visited her I found Charlie slumped, in his dark-blue chauffeur's macintosh, in front of one bar of the electric fire; Miss Thornton was stationed silently behind him. I opened four quarter-bottles of champagne I had given her ten years before.

'I'm afraid, Mr B., she hasn't long to go,' opined Charlie.

She hadn't.

I could not attend the funeral because I was in Corfu. Desmond told me it was quite a jolly affair. Miss Thornton left me one hundred pounds. We always tried to honour her death in the *Daily Telegraph*'s In Memoriam column on every February 29th.

*   *   *

Desmond, who later became '& Briggs' when the firm changed its name, was the naturally reassuring end of Anthony Blond Ltd. I had persuaded Spike Milligan to write a novel, and all we had to do was to get him to sit down and do it. This was the difficulty. Finally, Desmond wrote the story, about a village in Northern Ireland which was cut in half by the border. Spike put in a few jokes like: protagonist pulls out a five-pound note from a envelope in order to pay, only to be told, 'I'm sorry, we don't take cheques, sir.' *Puckoon* sold better than anything Spike ever wrote and made a lot of money for Penguin.

After some twenty years I had become increasingly bored by the whole business: I was more occupied with a boyfriend, a novel, a house in Corfu, and then a girlfriend, Laura, who became my wife. It was while I was out in Ceylon that I received the news from Laura's sister, known as 'Smugs', that all was not well with Blond & Briggs Ltd. She was right. Desmond was busy writing a novel about me, which his agent had persuaded Tom Rosenthal of Secker and Warburg – not an old friend – to publish. I had to dismiss any thought of suing: *The Partners* inaudibly hit the stands.

When Blond & Briggs was bought by Lord Harlech, Desmond retired to Castle Combe to pursue a new career as a magistrate; though he was not at all inhibited by the presence of his partner, a cheerful and charming young man called Ian Dixon. Over the years, Desmond blossomed in his role, and Ian hobnobbed with the local nobility and bred llamas. When Desmond died, I was in hospital suffering from the granddaughter of all strokes, so I could not attend the funeral. I believe a Desmond Briggs room has been opened in the Magistrates' Court in Chippenham.

CHAPTER THIRTEEN

Books and Bookmen

Over thirty years I got to know some of my authors quite well. The subject of the seven portraits following are all dead: Anthony Heckstall-Smith of emphysema in Brighton; Humphrey Slater of malnutrition in Madrid; Burgo Partridge of a broken aorta whilst talking to my first wife Charlotte on the telephone; Simon Raven, with an unearned advance of twenty-six thousand pounds, in an East End hospital; Alan Clark of a brain tumour in his castle; Sir John Betjeman at his home in Trebetherick, where he is buried; and Graham Greene of a blood disease in Vevey, Switzerland.

Anthony Heckstall-Smith
Tony crawled out of the Aegean up to the feet of an admiral.

'That's the third ship I've had sunk under me, sir!'

'Never mind, Smith, I'll see you get something for this.'

So Lieutenant-Commander Anthony Heckstall-Smith got his DSC and gained the material for *Greek Tragedy 1941*, the story of a brave little country betrayed by its own generals and let down by a couple of our brigadiers, of whom more anon.

When the war interrupted the run of his play *Juggernaut* at the Savile Theatre, Tony joined the minesweepers of the RNVR. One of his lighter duties was to censor the sailors' letters and it was when, in pursuit of this task, he was sitting in a deckchair, smoking a cigar, one sunny afternoon in the Mediterranean that a tuft of pubic hair fell out of an unsealed envelope and was wafted overboard by the breeze. Tony remembered the sailor was called 'Ginger' by his mates. 'This is a little bit of me you may remember,' the sailor had written. Tony snatched up a bit of coconut matting, carefully replaced the errant love token, and sealed the envelope with a kiss. This is typical of the stories, vivid, indelicate and rarely repeated, which bubbled out, accompanied by gusts of wheezy laughter, over thirty years of our acquaintance. (Tony died of emphysema at the respectable age of seventy-nine in 1983.)

Tony could turn anything that happened to him into a book. After the war he lived for a time in the South of France on a small yacht and an even smaller income. Spry, witty and faintly heroic, the son of a yachting companion of George V, whom that monarch dubbed 'Bookstall-Smith' on account of his propensity for the pen, Tony moved easily in a world of cocktail parties, where the guests were trashy or grand, usually hospitable and occasionally chic. He played golf – which, of course, he pronounced 'goff' – in Cannes with the Duke of Windsor; and once when two foursomes, including Alfonso of Spain and Umberto of Italy, were holding them up, to the irritation of the Duke, he remarked, 'Yes, sir, I'm afraid that today the course is littered with ex-kings.' It was their last game together.

An insouciant former naval officer, living fairly high on the hog and with the appearance of having money, Tony caught the eye of a Hungarian couple called Gertz. Throughout his life Tony was drawn to Jews. His two most significant lovers and eventual supporters, not to speak of his last – and, believe me, loyal – publisher, were Jews; but the Gertzes were an unfortunate choice among so many.

They were a charming, gluttonous and persuasive pair of professional confidence tricksters and they took him for the lot. Tony signed a sheaf of papers without reading them too carefully, not that he would have understood them if he had. When the not-so-serious Fraud Squad came to arrest him in London he enquired after the Gertzes, whom he had not seen for some time. The Fraud Squad, then less pure of heart and clean of hand than it is now, shrugged its shoulders and sighed. The Gertzes had vanished it said.

The fruit of this episode was *Eighteen Months*, for although Lord Goddard had described Tony in court as 'more of a fool than a knave', that strange and twisted fellow couldn't not sentence the debonair former naval officer. Whatever Tony did wrong he could write about all right and Sam Campbell, editor of the *People*, commissioned him to pursue and confront the scoundrel pair. Tony unearthed both of them in a modest apartment in Jamaica, and as Madame Gertz opened the door he was overwhelmed by the aroma of a serious Hungarian goulash.

'Ah, Tony . . . ' breathed the Jewish mother, 'just in time for a spot of lunch.'

At this remark, Tony said that his accumulated rage oozed out through the soles of his espadrilles.

Sam Campbell was a crucial prop to the firm of Allan Wingate – Tony's meal ticket for whom he ghosted many titles (most of the list it seemed) – because Sam bought the serial rights. A typical Wingate book of those days was the memoirs of Puttlitz, a high-born Prussian diplomat who had defected to East Berlin, in whose queer bars (the word 'gay' had yet to be coined for *that* inclination) Tony and his publisher, Charles Fry, had a lovely romp.

It was at 12 Beauchamp Place that I first met Tony. He shared the *piano nobile* with Charles Fry and had the smaller desk, at which he sat monocled, giggling, chain-smoking, having invariably arrived every morning on the dot of quarter to eleven and parked his Phantom II Rolls in the street below. But after Tony Gibbs decided to go into liquidation, Tony was left without a publisher.

I had meanwhile started up in the back room of my house in Chester Row, so Tony became one of my regulars, along with Simon Raven, Isabel Colegate and Burgo Partridge. I think it was Hugh Thomas who dubbed me 'Blond, the spot-cash publisher', because I paid up immediately on receiving a chapter.

The system suited them. Tony was generous and improvident. (He ended up in queer street: the classic financial curtain to a lifetime of authorship, beginning with a play in 1939 and stretching through a score of books and hundreds of articles.) His first book with me, *Tobruk*, in 1959, was a success; it was translated into Portuguese, French and Dutch and was published in the United States. He was a fearless historian and his books always created a stir, not necessarily to their advantage. *Tobruk* upset the South Africans, whose conduct at the siege had been less than zealous. The British Legion did not like his view that British soldiers had enjoyed gambolling naked in the Mediterranean without their wives and sweethearts.

Greek Tragedy 1941 provoked High Court writs from a couple of brigadiers. Tony stated that they had abandoned their troops, including the Jewish Brigade, and had taken a flying-boat to go to dinner at the Gezira Club in Cairo. I was in Corfu at the time of 'service', so Desmond had to cope. He summoned his godfather and together they repaired to the Senior Naval and Military Club (where the brigadiers were also members) for a pink gin (or two), to test the water and spy out the land. Club opinion seemed to favour us and it was suggested that an approach to the general officer commanding be made. Field Marshal Lord 'Jumbo' Wilson attended Anthony Rubinstein's chambers in Gray's Inn and declared: 'The chaps were yaller; I should have had 'em shot' (or words to that effect). Yes, he would put it in writing. When he left, Rubinstein explained that when the case was eventually heard we would probably win and that our costs would be about five thousand pounds. If we considered making an apology, which was all the brigadiers were after, that would set us back fifty pounds. As only the rich and neurotic contest libel actions in England, we went quietly.

The Fleet That Faced Both Ways was *more* of a tragedy. The French Admiral Darlan, pugnacious, passionate and astute, had cosseted the French fleet throughout the many governments of the inter-war years and did not like the British. (His great-great-uncle had shot Nelson from a yard-arm at the Battle of Trafalgar.) Hitler was aware of this and the terms of the 1940 armistice were so favourable to the French fleet – it could remain intact provided it was neutral ('Defend your colonies,' advised Hitler, 'the British will be after them') – that they were not printed in *The Times*. Churchill did not trust Darlan and feared he might defect to the Germans, or maybe he needed a victory in those dark days of 1942. So the French fleet was shelled by the British when anchored in Alexandria, hours after their officers had dined together. *Perfide Albion!*

Admiral Sir Dudley Pound (whose papers Tony was later given by his widow) was in command at Gibraltar and received intelligence that what was left of the French fleet was about to steam through the Straits. He cabled the Admiralty for instructions but it had gone away for the weekend, so he telegraphed the simple message: '*Bon Voyage.*' Churchill was incensed and expelled him to the Isle of Wight.

When *The Fleet That Faced Both Ways* was published, the implacable Admiralty issued a D-notice (a device now happily abolished, through the efforts of Jonathan Aitken) to newspaper editors, signalling that any reference to the book would damage Her Majesty's Government. The only paper not to take any notice was the *Daily Mail*, whose proprietor's mistress was a friend of Tony's. I knew James Callaghan, who was the opposition spokesman for naval affairs, and I asked him to lunch with Tony at the Reform. He related that his father had served on the Royal Yacht *Britannia* and that his mother's proudest moment had been when King George V, driving through Portsmouth, had waved to her in the crowd. We hoped Mr Callaghan might be able to do something to reverse the Admiralty's decision. Tony said to me after he had left: 'Don't you see, you idiot, all he wanted was fifty quid?'

In the conception and writing of *The Consort*, neither the author nor the publisher had the slightest intention of rocking the throne. Tony was replete with anecdotes favourable to the Royal Family and I particularly remember his tale of Queen Mary's comment when F. E. Smith, then Lord Birkenhead, pissed as a newt, threw up over the dinner table on the Royal Yacht: 'I'm sorry to see that lobster does not agree with the Lord Chancellor.' Though left-wing, I am a monarchist and I always follow the Jewish prayer book in its loyal reference on the Sabbath Day; my eyes still mist over when I hear (decreasingly) the National Anthem.

The Consort was a perfectly risen meringue of a novel, with a kick in the *crème Chantilly*, and it was not thought by us to be the sort of publication which could land author and publisher in gaol for criminal libel – a fearful English law which sensible folk feel should be erased from the statute book. Yet that it was was the opinion we received from counsel. (I was given an equally potty opinion when I wanted to publish the Casement diaries.)

The consort is married to a queen who reigns over a Catholic country, which is occupied by the Germans in the last war. The chief of police, a big part, cannot possibly be English. He is a *pédé* into *petit point*, with a numbered Swiss bank account. Oh dear, no! The prime minister, playing endless games of 'cabinet reshuffle', resembles the late Harold Macmillan no more than any other incumbent of that role in the world.

So we 'privished' rather than published *The Consort*, sending out no copies for review. Barney Rosset in the United States, where the Queen's writ does not run and which the Duke of Edinburgh was about to tour, took the book for his company Grove Press, which had published *Lolita*. Stacks of *The Consort* were on display in the cities and airports on the royal route and reports were that HRH was amused.

Sadly, Tony died in Brighton – where else – from cigarettes and bad temper, and did not leave enough money for his own funeral.

Humphrey Slater

'England is separated from the Continent by an invaluable stretch of cold water.' Thus ran the opening and, as far as Humphrey Slater was concerned, closing line (for he never wrote another) of a book I had commissioned from him entitled *The Channel Tunnel*. This was 1956 and the project was very much in the air. I had convinced Tony Gibbs and Charles Fry that Humphrey Slater would be an ornament to the Allan Wingate list.

Humphrey, then in his fiftieth year, *was* an ornament. He had lived in the USSR, and been through the Spanish Civil War and several wives. One, Henrietta Jackson, was a beautiful *femme fatale*, and another was very rich. It was typical of Humphrey's style that the film rights of the only book from which he made any money, *Calypso*, were sold when he was with the rich wife. He lost it all – his earnings being subsumed in her super-tax, as it was then called.

When I met him he was poor again and very into drink. He used to send Lady Mary Rous, his minder, to Allan Wingate to collect his weekly tenner. When I enquired after the progress of the great work, she just smiled and said that Humphrey was waiting for me at the Bunch of Grapes, round the corner in Brompton Road. *En route* for lunch – a meal on which he always insisted – Humphrey popped into the pawnbroker to redeem his teeth, emerging with the gagging grin, which had enchanted all those wives and disarmed all those majors he had declined to turn into colonels, on the course they were on for that purpose, during the war. For Humphrey was a doyen of military strategy, on which he had written a couple of books. Indeed, a logistical brigadier (a veteran of the Falklands and the Persian Gulf) who once came to lunch with us in France, had only heard of him in that capacity.

During our conversation the brigadier assured me that Humphrey had invented the classical teaser – still employed, I am told – whereby an officer cadet is told to take a section of men across a stream using a log which is just a little too short for a bridge. (I failed that one in my OCTU.) 'The answer is,' said the brigadier, 'that you tie a rope to a tree that happens to be handy and swing 'em!' Humphrey's games for officers who aspired to command battalions came trickier. He told me about one of them.

Each officer is given an eight-figure map reference, and each starts from a different point; they are all told to rendezvous at the bridge over the brae which they will find there. Eventually most of them roll up – no marks for getting there – but no bridge and no brae. The conversation, said Humphrey, settling into his fifth glass of *vin ordinaire*, might go like this (he knew, because he had stood inside the hollow tree, which was actually the point of the map reference):

MAJOR A: Bloody typical. He was obviously tight when he thought of this one . . . talking of which I could use a drink if there's a pub in this God-forsaken country.*

MAJOR C: I noticed a telephone booth on the B970 a few miles back and . . .

MAJOR D: . . . and that's on the road back to camp, isn't it?

MAJOR E: We could commandeer a vehicle to get back to the camp. There *is* a war on you know.

* Scotland, of course.

MAJOR A: There'll be a telephone in the pub, and we can put the
        drinks on a chitty for refreshments while on duty . . .
    ALL: Good thinking . . . with you, Charlie . . . OK . . . let's go!

Humphrey's verdict – there being no correct strategic answer to
this problem – is that Major A has scored, because it is his
suggestion that is adopted.

The final test for the aspiring officers took place when they
thought the course was over. The evening before their departure
was a 'mess night' – military expression for a piss-up – and
Humphrey instructed the stewards, on pain of their being returned
to their much less agreeable units, that all officers should be made
totally drunk. Since battalion commanders in the field have access
to alcohol, it is crucial to know how they may react to its effect. So,
throwing up, singing hymns, passing out, weeping and making
advances to each other or to the mess waiters were all forgiven on
this special night, but picking a fight was not. An unnecessarily
aggressive colonel might be a danger to the men under his command. So Humphrey, knocking back the whisky-and-ginger-ales
without the whisky, smiles and watches his majors carefully.

After the war, Humphrey invented the 'Horse Game' which
gained devotees among the young, of which, I suppose, I was one
once. Each player is dealt a set of cards – enough, if played
shrewdly, to take his horse over the jumps and the water to the
winning post of the steeplechase. The highest card in each trick
advances the horse the most, but one must not go so far as to fall at
a jump. The skill derives from divining which cards the other
players will put up. It becomes a sort of character test, like poker,
which is both exasperating and exciting. I took the idea to W. H.
Smith who sent me to see their main supplier, Waddingtons, who
in turn said the 'Horse Game' was too near their horse game
Totopoly. Damn them.

Humphrey attended the party at 23 Knightsbridge to celebrate
my marriage to Charlotte Strachey in 1955, where I remember
him standing in line with Eddie Gathorne-Hardy – 'Je suis riche, je
suis bien né, et je veux un garçon' – and next to Miriam Marks in

her diamonds and furs. The seat of Eddie's trousers was visibly torn and he brought no present, but Humphrey, unsteady in the queue, held a little box containing a tortoise that he had bought in Harrods. Miriam was horrified: the family weren't too keen on animals.

Humphrey Slater died of malnutrition in Madrid. Twenty years or so later I was in Hamleys and noticed a recognisable version of the 'Horse Game' on sale for rather a lot of money. I doubted if his estate was benefiting, and out of respect for his memory I did not buy it.

The balance of the twelve thousand or so lines of *The Channel Tunnel* were completed by Correlli Barnett. The book did rather well, and its author even better; but it is of Humphrey that I must sing.

Burgo Partridge

The telephone rang: 'Do you want a life of Diana Dors or a history of orgies?'

It was 1958 and I had been publishing for a year or so from the back room of the house in Chester Row. My father had granted me permission to borrow five thousand pounds from my trust but I had either lost or spent it. *The History of Orgies* by Burgo Partridge saved the firm of Anthony Blond Ltd from bankruptcy. It contained the sort of soft porn that one could sell in those days: near enough to the bone for titillation, but not so sharp as to provoke authority. The wraparound jacket sported a fleshy Poussin from the National Gallery, whose courtesy in allowing the publishers to use it was acknowledged in bold writing on the jacket. I do believe this relieved the book's unashamed hedonism and cheerful sexuality of hostile attention from the Director of Prosecutions. Burgo was thus welcomed to the writing fraternity by Cyril Connolly in the *Sunday Times*, which was hardly surprising considering the amount of hot dinners that original *glittérateur* had enjoyed with the author's parents, Ralph and Frances Partridge.

The Ralph Partridges lived at Ham Spray, which was situated at the foot of the Berkshire Downs. The house had been bought by

Lytton Strachey out of the profits of *Elizabeth and Essex*, and was already famous in the fast-filling-up annals of Bloomsbury. The bedroom where Carrington had shot herself remained untouched and undusted: an odd and Dickensian practice for a couple who hated humbug and the veneration of anything or anybody, especially God. Frances was a high priestess of atheism, a topic on which I would dispute with her on the rare occasions that I dared.

I was welcomed with that sort of chilly courtesy Bloomsbury retains for dealing with unfortunate circumstances which could not be foreseen or controlled. I was to discover that this manner, from a conviction that intellectuals should think harder than they feel, informed and inhibited the expression of any emotion. When Burgo ran away from school for the umpteenth time and was collected by Frances in her car, she simply said, 'Burgo, do you want to sit in the front or the back?' I don't know his reply. He was not allowed to call his parents 'Mummy' or 'Daddy'; neither was there any physical contact between them. If primo-geniture is the curse of the land-owning classes in this country, then imprisonment of emotion has damaged the intellectuals. In her book *Memories*, Frances Partridge records her mother's dictum that one's feelings for people should never be cheapened by letting them be seen.

This is not to say that Ham Spray, where my first wife Charlotte and I frequently spent the weekend, was not fun. There was an abundance of food, wine and laughter, and Burgo was a passionate friend. He was dark, louche in aspect, powerfully built and his energy, which invested every activity, was almost manic. He had a ferocious temper, which came and went like summer lightening. He once drove a croquet ball into the air and through a window at Ham Spray, bursting into delighted giggles at this feat. He had instant, furious, unexpected views on any topic, whether it was the ingredients of a Bloody Mary, Suez (the issue of the day), Maria Callas, Rachman, naked bathing or where to have lunch. He never knew quite what to do. His private money and later on the royalties from *The History of Orgies*, which went on and on (Paul Hamlyn sold it for me in America), guaranteed him immunity from regular employment, of which he was shy and disapproving. Staring into the windows of Cecil Gee in Shaftesbury Avenue, puffing a Gauloise and wondering whether to buy a shirt – he always decided not to – he looked like one of the usual suspects.

*　　　*　　　*

Contrary to the advice of my soothsayer William King, Charlotte, Burgo and I took off for Yugoslavia in my brand new Ford Zephyr in 1956. While being driven recklessly and much too fast through Rijeka (Fiume) in a thunderstorm, the car slid on an oil slick and hit a concrete lamp-post at sixty miles an hour. I was flung out of the car, which was lucky as the steering column was forced through the driver's seat by the impact. (If seat belts had been in vogue I would not be here today.) I passed out through loss of blood from my arm, which had been ripped open by the broken steering wheel, having enjoyed the delicious, though not uncommon, I'm told, sensation of floating up a tree and watching the scene below. The crash occurred at the gates of the enormous Ospedale Civile di S. Spirito, where we were picked up by an heroic Yugoslav in a Volkswagen, who drove across a fallen tree in the thunderstorm and up the long drive to the hospital.

When I came to the next day I learnt that Charlotte was uninjured and that Burgo was well enough to have been arrested in the port while trying to find a decent place to eat. Charlotte and I were convinced that it was simply because he *looked* suspicious. Forty-eight years ago, before the advent of package holidays, which changed the face of the Mediterranean, Yugoslavia was short of food, clothes and kindness to strangers, unless, as is common among the poor, one was in distress.

Due to the prang, my broken nose had swollen so that it spread across my face and I could not open my mouth; the nurses fed me by pushing grapes between my teeth. The green Ford Zephyr had been moved to the Rijeka fire station where it was displayed with other wrecks, including a bus which had skidded on the same patch of oil. (This is not the sort of book, nor am I the sort of writer, to give advice to motorists, but I have been told that rain on overheated road surfaces can release oil.) My first visitor was a car dealer who offered me twenty-five pounds in cash for the spare parts.

Throughout the incident, which was not horrible because no bones were broken, Burgo was considerate and unnaturally calm. He had that type of temperament which flared up over tiny catastrophes, like the spilling of a glass of wine, but accepted, with the composure of a psychotic, a narrow escape from death on the highway or being arrested in a foreign port as natural events. In this respect he was quite unlike his mother, who never raised her cool Bloomsbury voice, even when told by Burgo, in response to her offer to help him furnish his flat in Old Compton Street: 'Frances, stop buggering me about!'

Frances Partridge had a considerable private reputation among her Bloomsbury friends: Gerald Brenan, Cyril Connolly, Raymond Mortimer, Desmond MacCarthy and Eddy Sackville-West; and of course among the numerous and ancient Stracheys who received me courteously as Charlotte's husband. She was a qualified botanist in charge of one square mile of England, and through her I met Dickie Chopping. He drew flowers, the covers for Ian Fleming's books and a famous one that I commissioned for David Benedictus's novel *The Fourth of June*.

Burgo had of course met Simon Raven, the first really successful novelist I published. (In ten years I published seventy first novels and it damn near finished me.) Both were eccentric, demanding, spoilt and, when necessary, charming. They charmed each other, but not sexually, as Frances sort of implies in her memoirs. Burgo was not remotely queer, and Simon was only 'half queer at Cambridge', where he married to legitimise the child he had fathered.* When Burgo and Simon went off to live in separate lodgings in Hydra, one afternoon a boy arrived at Burgo's house with a note, 'This one is an artist in buggery.' The boy was dismissed intact.

---

* The product of this union was Adam Raven, a respected artist and *quondam* baby-sitter to our son Ajith.

Nevertheless, the *Zeitgeist* in the intellectual, not to say artistic and thespian, world was, in those pre-Wolfenden Report times, pro-homosexual and, incidentally, philosemitic. (Lovely word, but I can't seem to find it in the *OED*!) Manners, speech and clothes were homosexual in tone and were dictated by queers. Everyone used the expressions 'get you' when putting someone down, and 'my dear' was the common form of address for the uncommon people we thought we were.

Ken Tynan's stuttery voice, floppy hat, velvet coat and, on occasions, painted fingernails, which enabled him to avoid national service, epitomised the dominance of the homosexual *esprit* in matters of mores. Of course, Tynan was a masochist but not gay.

Burgo was hugely relieved when he lost his virginity at Stokke, Lady Mary Campbell's house, where Charlotte and I were staying one weekend in her absence. We spent a few lovely days with her daughters Nell and Serena Dunn, going down 1,300 points doubled and vulnerable at a goulash hand of bridge. Burgo's experience with an old friend from my Oxford days, a latter-day Zuleika Dobson, with whom my two best friends had been in love, gave him a taste for this pastime.

*   *   *

David Susman was the only member of my late stepmother's family, the Markses, to have taken a benign, continual and positive interest in my welfare. His first gesture was to buy me a car in the Chinese spirit: 'If you save a man from drowning, you have to look after him for the rest of your life.' This philosophy has been the source of many treats ever since. He suggested (or did I?) that we fly to Athens to 'do Greece', and that Burgo and Simon be bidden to accompany us and share in our pleasures.

Burgo had booked us rooms in a modest but clean establishment. On day two, with a sort of self-effacing shimmy which could not provoke resentment, David announced to Burgo and Simon that he had moved to a suite in the Grande Bretagne, which had room for me too. The suite was very grand indeed and was used, I would think, by tycoons and royal persons with money. The doors could be locked and unlocked from a control in the arm of a great leather sofa, a facility that seemed to me to be the acme of luxury and pointlessness (it was many years before the invention of remote controls). From this fortress of the high and flighty, we sortied to the low life of the Plaka and to a place arranged by the head porter where the needs of four healthy young Englishmen could be assuaged.

Forty years ago, English visitors in pursuit of Greek *girls*, and in possession of one-thousand drachma notes (prior to the age of plastic), were fairly rare. The attentiveness and curiosity of the patron ended with him asking David for a chat in his office. David had been ordering bottles and bottles of retsina, whose prickly cool was infectious, in *Italian*, on the principle that in foreign parts any language works better than one's own. The patron now proceeded to give a lecture on the laziness, amateurishness, inefficiency and unsatisfactory conduct of his girls. David listened solemnly, like a Midwestern senator hearing the complaints of a farmer about his crops. He had fought in the last war and in Palestine in 1948, and was a man of the world. 'Be that as it may,' he replied, 'my friends are prepared to sample what you have on offer.' The owner looked relieved and said that the girls would be 'on the house', but if we cared to tip them then that would be our affair. David explained to me that the patron was convinced that we were Italian mobsters contemplating moving in on his territory.

In Greece, in the days before the pill and the opening up of the country to tourists, a poor village girl's only asset was her virginity. If she lost that she was an object of no value, and, whether or not she had any talent, she went to the big city, inhabited by the 'eaters' (the peasants' name for Athenians), to be a whore. They were often touchingly young.

Our lot were about eighteen years old, and we set off to a sort of 'dorm' with cubicles where the action took place. After my performance I thought how much better off I would be at the Grande Bretagne and left my gently snoozing temporary consort for that grander lodging. In the morning, furious at my desertion, she entered Burgo's room and, apparently thinking he was my brother, slapped him across the face.

Later in the day, Burgo discovered that all his money had been stolen and told us that he would pursue the matter. 'I'm going to find mine and get it back!'

'Where?' we all asked with worldly mocking laughter.

Burgo shrugged.

He did find the girl in the Plaka, and the following dialogue ensued:

BURGO: You stole my money!
  GIRL: So? You are rich and I am poor.
BURGO: I'm not that rich.
  GIRL: (*shakes her head*) No?
BURGO: Give it back to me, *please*.
  GIRL: No.
BURGO: Half?
  GIRL: Endaxi [OK].

And she returned half. They were both quite young.

We didn't see as much of Burgo after he married Henrietta, the daughter of Bunny (David) Garnett. They bought a flat in Cadogan Gardens, and Burgo discovered unsalted butter and took to dinner parties and to being greedy. He still didn't do much else. The marriage was blissful and a daughter was born.

One afternoon, whilst talking to Charlotte on the telephone, Burgo died. He was suffering from von Falkenhausen's disease and part of his aorta had flaked off and choked him. I am told that when his mother was informed she telephoned Harrods and asked them to collect her son's body, cremate him and send her the bill. And, as far as I know, what is left of Burgo remains, among the other uncollected ashes, at the top of Harrods. Frances Partridge, one of the most intelligent, witty, loyal and hospitable people I have ever met, became a well-known writer in her eighties. I liked and admired her enormously, but I never forgave her.

Simon Raven

My association, rather than friendship, with Simon Raven began with *The Establishment*. This was an invention (though disputed) of the late Henry Fairlie, which was to be the title of a volume of obviously anti-establishment essays, to be published by Anthony Blond Ltd in 1959. Originally I had asked Richard Wollheim, the smartest but not the most diligent don about town, to be editor. But either he or someone else suggested Hugh Thomas,* a Cambridge figure whom I didn't know.

Even in those days Hugh Thomas sparked off animosity, merely by entering a room or by his silence. There must have been something chemical about his insolence – the opposite of dumb – yet the certainty of his assumptions and his displays of superior intelligence threw people instantly. I remember my younger brother Peter, a mild and temperate lad, loathing him on sight. Of course, *I* liked Hugh and found him loyal, funny, open and even humble about his ambition. He had winning ways and lived for free at the Old Cavendish Hotel, where his main function was to open the door for the cat. He went to the cinema in Shaftesbury Avenue, courtesy of the usherettes, and was often sick in the loo. On the other hand, he was regularly dined by Harold Nicolson at the Beefsteak Club.

Hugh quickly drew up a list of contributors and their subjects. The former were all friends and the latter suggested themselves. Thus, Henry Fairlie wrote on politics, John Vaizey on education, Victor Sandelson on the City, Thomas Balogh on the Civil Service and Simon Raven on the Army. The stuff came in tickety-boo, except for Henry Fairlie's piece, which I managed to obtain only by driving down to Lewes and waiting outside his house while he wrote it. The book's jacket, printed in dark blue on a pale blue background – 'a one-colour job' the technical might note –

---

* Now Lord Thomas of Swynnerton. Hugh was rather left wing in his youth; indeed he hoped to be adopted for Ealing in the Labour interest. I once reproached him for not including his editorship of *The Establishment* in his *Who's Who* entry. He promised to correct the omission, though whether he did or not I do not know. Probably not.

explained the contents of the book. The people and the subject fitted the climate; needless to say the book took off.

The launch party in Chester Row lasted the whole of a fine summer night, and I remember towing Tom Chetwynd, whose novel *Rushing Nowhere* I had published and with whom I was in love, across the road to the Duke of Wellington. The pub, authentic in those days with sawdust on the floor of the public bar, was run by two gloomy brothers called Pettet or Pettit. One of them was wiping the bar, so I ordered two large brandies. He refused payment and when I asked why replied, 'It *is* two o'clock in the morning.' At breakfast time I found John Raymond,* dressed for departure with his bowler hat on his head, sitting bolt upright on the half-landing loo, clutching his umbrella, fast asleep.

I had still not met Simon Raven. Nevertheless, when Hugh Thomas suggested that, as Simon was patently talented and broke, I should commission a novel (then an unusual gambit), I said: 'Tell him to send a synopsis.' Simon was more a heroic, legendary figure to me at that time: when in the Army, his reply to an urgent cable from home, WIFE AND BABY STARVING SEND MONEY, had been, NO MONEY SUGGEST EAT BABY. I might also have known then, but was certainly to hear it repeated many a time later, that, in the words of one particular reviewer, he had left Charterhouse under a cloud 'no bigger than a boy's hand'. Moreover, he had prematurely left King's College, Cambridge, where he could have been a don, and the Army, where he could have been a regular officer, on account of an addiction to the horses and roulette. None of this put me off. I gave him a regular retainer of ten pounds per week, on condition that he lived more than fifty miles from London: the remittance man's distance. Having met him in his seedy, if genteel, lodgings in Collingham Gardens, Kensington, I decided his amusing friends were of no use to him; he was grateful to be ordered from their arena.

---

* Literary editor of the *New Statesman*, then as chic and influential as the *Spectator* is now. He dominated in a Johnsonian manner a few tables in the Reform Club known as 'buggers' corner'.

As the manuscript came in chapter by chapter, I experienced that sense described by Isaiah Berlin, when he was listening to Namier talk, of 'sailing in first-class waters'. To promote publication of *The Feathers of Death*, London's glitterati assembled in the committee room of the Reform Club, to which I had been introduced by Herbert 'Bertie' van Thal, a tubby chubby publisher whose wife was the inamorata of Nancy Spain. An engaging conspiracy ensued which has never happened to me since (but then both Simon and I were novices and, therefore, presumed innocent) whereby the literary editors planned to review the book. Terence Kilmartin of the *Observer* reviewed it before the Monday of publication, ditto the *Sunday Times*, Anthony Hern of the *Evening Standard* reviewed it on the Tuesday, *The Times* wrote it up on the Wednesday, and so forth round the clock. Thus, *The Feathers of Death* sold out its first print run of three thousand, a modest number in 1959, in three weeks. Simon Raven became, and has remained, the idol of a tiny cult.

A few days after I divorced my first wife, Charlotte, I was in New York on the first of many annual visits, armed with a few introductions from Fleur Cowles. These were all I needed. The playwright Santha Rama Rau took me to a party given by the John Gunthers for the Walter Lippmanns who were retiring, whither had also been bidden Greta Garbo, Eleanor Roosevelt, T. S. ('Tom') Eliot, the Heinzes, Charles Addams the cartoonist, and the president of some east-coast university. I remember I was appalled and dazed by the banality of these famous people. It was snowing and Garbo insisted on telling my fortune on a sofa in her galoshes. She predicted I would not have any children. Well . . .

Fleur Cowles also sent me to the most elegant public relations consultant in New York. This function, in the days before its abbreviation to 'PR' was new to me and rather mysterious. Baxter Beauchamp (for let us call him that) had a Filipino butler who showed me into a chinoiserie-styled drawing-room, where the proprietor lolled on a chaise longue in a heavy silk dressing-gown, reading, under a spotlight, Simon Raven's recently published second novel *Brother Cain*. My host, who was very funny, very successful and very camp, swore that this performance had not been laid on for me. Outside the salons of the Upper East Side, Simon Raven's novels never grabbed America. I sold US rights in *The Feathers of Death* to a rather dull man, Peter Schwed of Simon & Schuster, who had, as we used to say in the trade, 'done nothing with it'. Although Simon Raven, unlike say Anthony Powell, never alas dented the American scene as a novelist, he did enjoy a brief and comic fling as a supernumerary scriptwriter, recruited by 'Cubby' Broccoli, for a Bond film. His television adaptations of Trollope were later televised by PBS in that country.

Anyhow, Baxter and I, as is the custom in New York, became friends for life, or at least for that night. I actually asked him what he *did*.

'Take the Belgian ambassador,' he replied, 'a new account who had the wrong friends'.

'So what did you do about that?'

'Changed 'em,' he replied.

Baxter Beauchamp epitomised the fan of Simon Raven's works: fruity fellows who like their game high. The trouble for his publishers was, and is, that there are not many of them and, *sui generis*, they do not multiply.

When *The Feathers of Death* was first published* homosexuality was still illegal and, therefore, slightly dashing. To the British upper classes its practice was never offensive. Indeed, at the time of the Montagu affair the *obiter dictum* of a member of White's summed up their feelings: 'It has come to a pretty pass when a peer of the realm can't bugger a boy scout.' To Middle America, however, who never even suspected that Joe McCarthy was in love with the golden-haired Mr Shine, homosexuality was disgusting.

The plot of *The Feathers of Death* turned on the revelation at a court-martial of an officer charged with shooting a soldier in action in Kenya that the officer was in love with the soldier. The officer was acquitted only to be stabbed to death by the company sergeant major. The imaginations of the reviewers and of seven

---

*   The novel now languishes, half forgotten, on the list of that imprint of the special interest, the Gay Men's Press.

thousand members of the public had been captured by both the unusual story and the writer's style. We, because we controlled the publishing rights, sold the film rights for three thousand pounds in cash to a plausible Pole called Gene Gutowski, who had already sold them to a consortium of which Richard Attenborough and Bryan Forbes were members.

The film was never made, but years later Bryan, who had been a neighbour when I lived for two beastly cold years in Albany, told me why. At the time Bryan's lot depended for finance on a distribution deal from one of the American majors, Universal, Paramount or United Artists. When the subject of *The Feathers of Death*, a newly acquired property, came up for ratification at a board meeting of the company, the vice-president in charge of sales made a short but damning declaration that, while he never normally commented on company policy in the acquisition of new properties, he would ask to be excused from having to try and sell this one. 'It stuck, if the gentlemen would pardon the expression, in my throat.' Enough said.

Today 'the love that dare not speak its name' has become loquacious, even boastful, demanding and arrogant, but still the film rights to *The Feathers of Death* are locked in a file belonging to a movie company that by now may belong to the Japanese. They should be taken out and dusted. The film rights in Simon's second novel *Brother Cain* were optioned fourteen times without much luck. Nevertheless, another of his entertainments, *Doctors Wear Scarlet,* was actually made into rather an appalling film, starring Peter Cushing.

In case these words are read by someone unfamiliar with the nature of Raven's oeuvre – which has never changed – I would like to quote from the introduction to a reissue of *The Feathers of Death*. This was one of the four first novels I republished, under the un-catchy title *They Made Their Name*, for the tenth anniversary of the by then fairly established, but financially shaky, firm of Anthony Blond Ltd.*

---

* The others were *The Ha-Ha* by Jennifer Dawson, *The Fourth of June* by David Benedictus and *Barbouze* by Alan Williams.

Simon Raven, who claims to be no gentleman himself, is
interested in the affectations which he feels should accompany
the exercise of that *métier*. The personnel in his novels tend to
bid each other to dine rather than ask each other for dinner,
eschew the handy traveller's cheque in favour of letters of
credit arranged with a foreign bank, travel by wagon-lit, rather
than aeroplane, unless employed by a doubtful international
organisation which is anxious to hurry them out of the country. They talk a lot amongst themselves in their letters (which
they prefer to telephone calls) about loyalty, but when it comes
to the crunch they tend to burble on rather than act . . .

And what a world! There's no mistaking it: officers gentle-
manly or snide, cosy company sergeant majors, dons malicious
or chilly, left-wing schoolboys incredibly *mondain* or beautiful,
the fates relentless.

Simon had chosen for his first exile Hunstanton in Norfolk,
where his father dwelt, a comic horror of a parent, who, from his
son's account, merited crucifixion by the pen. His mother had been
an alcoholic and an athlete, and Simon clearly inherited some of her
genes. I never really got to know my increasingly distinguished
author, whose regular output made him the standard-bearer, as
it were, of a rather mixed list. Of them only a handful – Isabel
Colegate, David Benedictus and Alan Williams – did not lose
money. And at the close of the business some thirty years later,
Simon's ledger showed unearned-income advances of twenty-six
thousand pounds – our fault rather than his.

In the sixties, Deal, one of the Cinque Ports, was so forgotten
that you could get caddies, who had been unemployed miners, at
the golf course. Simon lived there in what his neighbour David
Carritt,* the art detective, called a dog kennel. I thought this

---

* David Carritt discovered the Tiepolo ceiling in the Egyptian Embassy in
South Audley Street, formerly the London house of the Bischoffsheims,
friends of Queen Victoria and Edward VII. He was a waspish queen
with a kind heart. Often summoned to authenticate pictures, he told me

description most unkind until I discovered that the crushed little dwelling, so small that Simon had to crawl upstairs, had indeed been such a doghouse. Simon worked with Trollopian industry, as punctual and puffy as a steam engine. The day was compartmented into periods of writing, revision, typing, reading and reviewing, alleviated by many Camel cigarettes, a Campari before luncheon, and copious beer and burgundy, followed by Armagnac and Armagnac and Armagnac, in the evening. His courtesy was only marred by fits of bad temper. Journalists who came to interview him were amazed that he insisted on paying for lunch.

So it came as no surprise that his last words were said to have been: 'Who's paying for all this, I'd like to know?'

Alan Clark

A well-articulated bray, similar to that made by a very upper-class donkey, was a sound that I relished. It often stretched into self-parody because I had known it, more off than on, for over fifty years.

Alan Clark was three years younger than I; his younger brother, Colin, was a contemporary of my younger brother, Peter. We knew each other well enough to share houses. When Colin and Peter were commuting to Manchester, they shared a prinked up cottage in salubrious Knutsford. The parrot they kept was trained to say, 'Good morning, Mr Colin,' to Colin, and to my brother, 'Good morning, Mr Blond.' The Clarks enjoyed that sort of thing. We were, I suppose, rivals, but the odds were tilted heavily in their favour. They were much richer, more upper-crust and funnier than us. Both Alan and Peter were early owners of the Jaguar XK, a car so fast, as Alan pointed out with satisfaction, that the pigeons had not yet learnt to get out of the way. Only Peter was faster: he raced at Le Mans. The last time I saw Alan at his ministry he confessed rather sweetly that he thought Peter a hero for this. At the time he had said nothing.

---

he had tired of telling Texan oilmen that their Modiglianis were fakes and just said, 'My dear, what a lovely picture.'

I first saw Alan in Upper Rowlands 'socking' himself endless 'bangers', a delicious Etonian confection consisting of a hot sausage with oodles of melted butter and French mustard wrapped up in a slice of damp white bread. He was what we called a 'slack bob' as opposed to a 'wet' or 'dry bob'. We all had to wear black pinstripe trousers, yet the stripes on Alan's seemed to be wider apart than those of anybody else. He always looked healthy though he never played games, and he never put on any weight. Even as a boy there was an aura about him of *fainéant* privilege and indifference to public opinion. (How did he manage to get out of playing games? How did he manage, years later, to get out of joining the Army?)

In the fifties Alan sported an old-Etonian tie, worn with a Guards blazer, the fruit of some six months on the reserve of the Household Cavalry Training Regiment. He was often seen lying in it on the marble floor of Jack Barclay's showroom in Berkeley Square, pondering the merits of a Silver Wraith, and watched by an apprehensive salesman in a blue suit.

Alan's father, Kenneth 'K' Clark, owned the freehold of B5 in Albany, which he sub-let to Sir Leigh Ashton, the director of the Victoria and Albert Museum, dubbed 'Surly' Ashton by Queen Mary. This distinguished old fruit, in every sense of the word, had decided to enter into marriage with another of that ilk, Dame Madge Garland. The marriage was a disaster, but it left B5 vacant and I eagerly agreed to take up the tenancy of the main set, blindly signing a full repairing lease, while Alan had the little servant's room above. Alan liked Albany because he said it was the only address in London to which you could direct a cab driver with a single word. 'No,' I said, 'two words.' Alan looked puzzled. 'Please,' I suggested.

I disliked Albany because for two years I never saw the sun, and had a feud with the secretary, Captain Adams, an acidulous little man who liked 'chickens' (work that one out for yourself). The only advantage was that I could walk a few hundred yards to my office in New Bond Street. Certainly Alan's activities at this time were less definable. Like many people with nothing to do, he got up extremely early and went God knows where. I suspect his life was an adult version of:

'Where did you go?'

'Out.'

'What did you do?'

'Nothing.'

Possibly he went to Mr Spring's garage in Bayswater to contemplate and polish his white XK. He might have had lunch at the St James's where he would get a tip for a hot share. He initiated me into the mysteries of buying and selling within the account, of 'tangoing' and 'co-tangoing'.

Alan was a brilliant companion, funny, often cruelly so, but occasionally affectionate in a sly, ashamed sort of way. He played the stage villain and delighted in outrageous behaviour, to *épater* not only the bourgeois but also his friends. He was an expert in schoolboy demolition: the French were 'bum boys', 'cheeky chappies' or 'General de Gaulle'; the African continent was referred to as 'bongo-bongo land'. Nevertheless, Sir Alfred Sherman once confided to me that he thought Alan Clark was the only Conservative politician who was his own man.

Outings with Alan could be memorable. We once spent a weekend at Finchcocks with Michael Briggs (who at the time was courting Isabel Colegate), Digby Neave and Euan Graham. An enormously tall man, Euan Graham was separated by too many unkindly and undying relations from the dukedom of Montrose. He is a most sympathetic and appreciative fellow, meaning that he laughs at my jokes and sometimes gives me lunch.*

In the high-class grocery in Lamberhurst, Kent, a huge trap door was opened and we descended on broad steps to a vast cellar which must have victualled the local gentry with fine wines before the Boer War. I discovered a rack full of half-bottles of champagne which, when dusted off, were Bollinger 1928, at that moment – it being 1953 – the best year of the century. My heart beating, I

---

* He will be remembered by the readers of Alan Clark's *Diaries* as the friend, a clerk in the judicial office of the House of Lords, who passed on rumours that Alan was to be shuffled out of government.

attempted a mild interest in acquiring the lot. The grocer's assistant tried to dissuade me from buying those old bottles by offering brand new ones wrapped in cellophane. Wearily, I insisted and we settled on a price of ten shillings a bottle, on the grounds that many would have been flat. Digby Neave was so nervous that he dropped one on the floor. The golden liquid fizzled dreamily on the flagstones. We spent two days at Finchcocks doing nothing, eating nothing, only talking and drinking champagne – a Russian weekend. I have never felt so well.

Alan, who always had more money than the rest of us, was the first to have a house abroad, in Zermatt. Of course he skied well, and of course I couldn't. Isabel Colegate and I skated unsteadily instead. On my next visit, I took my current temporary/permanent houseguest, a girl of seventeen called Lucia, with blue eyes and long golden hair, whom *I think* Alan seduced. Both were quite cross that I appeared indifferent.

*   *   *

We often talked about inheritance, an area in which Alan had been, despite his protestations of being 'on the treadmill', quite successful. At Oxford, which gets everything wrong, he was thought to be the heir to Clark's shoes. The truth is that the Clark fortune derived from a more serious source, cotton thread, which, in alliance with J. & P. Coats of Paisley, made his grandfather one of the richest – and laziest – men in England. For at least three generations the Clarks had been able to indulge in whatever they listed: steam yachts, shire horses, old Turners, young Henry Moores and, in Alan's case, flashy cars, a wodge of Scotland and finally politics. This last interest was not evident at Oxford, where his name would not be found on a list of those voted 'most likely to succeed'. We, the Class of '48, put our money on Michael Codron, Ken Tynan, Godfrey Smith (president of the union), Marcus Worsley (a solemn youth), Milo Cripps and, later on, Jeremy Thorpe. They were not all winning bets. No one would have backed Alan: he was too blasé, too rude, too lacking in feck and reck.

There is no sillier saying by the way than 'still waters run deep'. Stillness is not a sign of depth. Perhaps not wholly irrelevant was Isaiah Berlin's reply to the observation that Oliver Franks was 'all right when you crack the ice' – 'What is the point if there is only cold water underneath?'

Alan was incapable of being still. He walked about the room, lithe and predatory, like a cat burglar on his own premises. Apropos of which, the sub-lease of B5 which I had taken over from 'Surly' Ashton had run out and I had to go. When I protested to 'K' Clark that his solicitor was demanding that I pay seven years' worth of repainting his set in Albany, despite our understanding that I would only be responsible for two-sevenths, he replied, 'Yes, my dear, isn't he dreadful?' A good upper-class ploy is to shelter behind a professional when wanting to behave very badly; particularly useful in divorce cases when the cupidity of the offended – sometimes just offensive – wife can be attributed to their greedy lawyer. (Americans use their doctors in just the same way.)

The Clarks have always been tricky about money, towards each other and towards their friends. To Naim Attallah in an *Oldie* interview, his younger brother and sister revealed how Alan had conned them out of their inheritance. Alan regarded the full and prompt payment of a debt as a sort of defeat, procrastination or diminution as a victory.

Alan's first published – well publishable – work was a frisky, witty, cruel little book about a stockbroker called *Bargains at Special Prices*. At that time I was working for Allan Wingate and showed Alan's book to Tony Gibbs who turned it down. It went to Hutchinson's New Authors. Later I did publish his *Fall of Crete*, with the same title and the same jacket as one published almost on the same day by, I think, Heinemann. Desmond Briggs suggested to the Publishers Association that a sort of confidential title bank be instituted to prevent this sort of damaging duplication, but nothing came of this sensible wheeze. Then I suggested to Alan that, as the really serious and bloody conflict in the Second World War was between Russia and Germany and that not much had been written about it, he should turn his attention to Operation Barbarossa. Alan telephoned me a few days later to say that Hutchinson had offered him a commission and an advance of seven thousand pounds for this idea and as this was obviously beyond my means . . . I promptly ordered, from a brilliant hack who never slept called Ronald Seth, the same book; and our *Operation Barbarossa* pre-empted Alan's by a year. We were in competition, Alan and I.

We must also have been slightly obsessed with each other because years later we conceived the idea of a study of the putative successors to Hitler, called, a little pretentiously, *The Diadochoi.** Alan's synopsis was telling and on the strength of it we sold the paperback rights for ten thousand pounds; but after months of nothing from Alan it became clear that he was more interested in trying to make history than to write about it. He had become the prospective candidate for the safe Conservative seat of Plymouth (Sutton) and only when we threatened to sue, in time for the election, did he repay the money.

Alan was a considerable military historian and a master of cold indignation. In *The Donkeys,†* he describes Haig's distress when, on a visit to the front, George V was thrown by a carefully chosen, quiet black mare. Tens of thousands of British soldiers were being shot daily by German machine-gun fire; yet all their commander-in-chief could write home to his wife, a lady-in-waiting to the queen, was how the king had been thrown from his horse. Alan relates how Haig, ignorant of this near tragedy, rode out 'pink-cheeked and well breakfasted' to meet his sovereign. Haig's widow and daughter wrote furiously demanding an apology and retraction. Alan replied with an exact catalogue of what the general had had for breakfast: two kippers, three slices of buttered Hovis toast, Cooper's marmalade, possibly a bit of cold pheasant and lots of coffee. He added that the temperature was just above freezing and their distinguished relative was known to be of a

---

*   The name given to the successors of Alexander the Great.
†   The title was drawn from a phrase attributed to Max Hoffman: 'The British soldiers were like lions led by donkeys.'

eupeptic disposition, so that 'pink-cheeked' and 'well breakfasted' was historically accurate.

*　　*　　*

Alan took easily, if late, to the game of politics. His good looks, good luck and good fortune certainly entitled him to some success. He charmed Margaret Thatcher, who gave him a deliberately boring job as Parliamentary Under Secretary of State in the Department of Employment. Then, as the only person to have benefited from the 'Westland Affair', she moved him to the DTI as Minister of Trade, where he remained until 1989, when he was made Minister of State for Defence Procurement. He thought he might make the cabinet as one of the most intelligent spirits of the Conservative government. He never did.

His home, Saltwood Castle, whence Norman thugs once thundered forth to murder Thomas à Becket, remains a treasure trove, and was once filled with the sound of dukes munching champagne. Later it hummed with the intrigues of fellow members and journalists.

With an income from investments of a hundred and forty thousand a year, on which he said he found it difficult 'to make ends meet', he could afford to be quite a refined man of letters. His diaries, he once told me, would not be published until fifty years after his death . . . When they appeared covering his years as junior minister from 1983 to 1991, he became a national figure. With his well-tuned gaffes, he endeared himself to that section of the British public which raises pints to the sinking of the *Belgrano* – an upper-class Alf Garnett.

Both *Diaries* were well hyped and well timed; they made what for a run-of-the-mill author would have been a fortune. They turned discretion into a dirty word, a retreat for cowards, and created a new model in the field, which only those economical with 'the *actualité*', and with their own feelings, will dare oppose.

His very old friends feature slightly and slightingly. Euan Graham, an intimate for more than forty years, who persuaded Alan to pay for the redecoration of the card room at Brooks's – a

curious quixotry – appears fleetingly. Michael Briggs, one of the
wittiest men in England, is billed as a snobbish bore. Yet both
were loyal to, and patient with, Alan for most of his life. Understandably, I do not feature, though he does mention a house I had
in Netherton Grove – opposite the incinerator of St Stephen's
Hospital – which he moved into, briefly, in 1952 with Anthony
de Hoghton.

It was not difficult to be envious of Alan, of his talent, his
energy, his possessions: the castle in Kent, the empty, spectacular
acres in Scotland, the secret garden in Dorset, the chalet in
Zermatt, the grubby set of rooms in Albany (where 'the crumbs
are in, not just on, the carpet'), the collection of motor cars, and
the sexual vitality which allowed him to run three mistresses at the
same time.

In the *Diaries*, Alan mentions in a moment of despair that he has
run out of Redoxon, a fizzy drink from a tablet crammed with
vitamins. I remember, in the late forties, when there was a shortage
of so many nice things, the performance he made of this daily
libation, which was sent to him from Roche in Switzerland. (We
were never offered a taste.)

These days I take my vitamin C in this way and it reminds me of
Alan – fizzy, healthy, expensive, tart and cold.

Sir John Betjeman
'Fuck Collins, bravo Anthony Blond!'
Certainly not the sort of epistle one would expect from the future
Poet Laureate. It did not rhyme or scan, but John Betjeman wrote it
all right, about my proposal to publish a new edition of *Ghastly
Good Taste*. This was a book about architecture, which had been
produced in the thirties and was embellished with an extensive pull-
out of the changing English townscape drawn by Peter
Fleetwood-Hesketh. John Murray must have turned down the idea
and Betjeman's agent must have offered it to Collins, who had
dithered. *Voilá.* I had known and loved the original, which was
among my mother's books in Greenbank House; and, together with
Hirschfeld's *Sexual Anomalies and Perversions* (carefully bound in

brown paper so that I wouldn't notice it), it was my favourite reading from about the age of eight.

Thirty years later *Ghastly Good Taste* was still valid and, indeed, was the precursor to Osbert Lancaster's designations of 'Pont Street Dutch' and 'Bankers' Georgian', which have since passed into the language. We made a larger book and persuaded the artist, my future wife's uncle and future tenant, to make the pull-out even longer. This he eventually did, using, unfortunately, a different pen. The reissue pleased the *aficionados* and the limited edition went well at Hatchards, though it must have been too much of a period piece for the mass of Betjeman's fans who, according to our sales reps, wanted to see his face on the jacket of the book, as they had on television. I have always been a bit of a purist – a fatal refinement in a publisher.

It was easy to get to love John Betjeman. I had first encountered him while at Oxford, where, for the second number of *Harlequin*, the magazine which Oliver Carson and I had started (it did run to a couple of issues), we solicited two poems from him. He kindly sent us two which had obviously been declined by daintier journals, 'Late Flowering Lust' and 'The Corporation Architect'.

John Betjeman was considerate, even on television where I appeared with him on the occasional BBC programme in the sixties. In the middle of that decade, Blond Educational, an imprint designed for the new secondary modern schools, was launched and was instantly successful. Any police constable over the age of forty-five will have been brought up on our *English Through Experience*, which sold by the tens of thousands. In light of this success, which was threatening to make me quite rich, we decided to run a poetry competition for these children, with Roger McGough, Sylvia Plath (who died on us) and Betjeman as judges. A room in Noel Road, Islington, where I was building a disastrously inventive house, was hired, and the entries, which totalled seventeen thousand, were sorted by an over-educated and increasingly desperate young lady from Newnham. About seventeen poems displayed any sort of talent – not really enough for a book, but we managed. The winning poem's first line was, 'I'm all right, mother, but what about you?'

The prize was to be awarded by Betjeman, to the accompaniment of some pretty stagy effects, at Burton Constable. This was the intact Elizabethan seat belonging to the Catholic recusant Chichester-Constable family where Jean-Jacques Rousseau had stayed. A carriage carrying Betjeman and myself would rattle up to the front door while a specially trained eagle would swoop down and carry off a lump of raw meat placed on an empty pedestal. When I asked the keeper what he meant by 'special training', he replied curtly, 'I starve it.' Fortunately, I thought, the winner turned out to be a schoolgirl from Hull, the nearest big town to that great house. When I telephoned the headmistress with the glad tidings and a modest suggestion that the school, or at least her class, attend the ceremony, which would doubtless be on television granted the glamorous nature of the occasion, silence reigned at the other end of the telephone. Our prize-winning poet – and when we saw her it was not difficult to see why – had been sacked.

Betjeman had agreed to present the prize provided that he was back in London in time for dinner. This I guaranteed, but the state of the railway* was such that we had to book our return journey in a small aeroplane. The outward trip was – there being no other word for it – Betjemanesque. The train stopped by some giant cooling towers in the middle of an already flat landscape.

'Bedfordshire,' hissed Betjeman conspiratorially.

'How do you know?' I asked him.

'Just look at the hedges.'

An hour or so later: 'We must be near Ely. Can't you feel the reeds under the sleepers?'

When the train came to a halt for a third time, by a dense wood crawling up the side of a sharp valley, it was as if Betjeman had trained the train to stop, for he said in that specially lowered voice, 'On the other side of that hill is Tranby Croft!' I had read a play[†] about the scandal in that house which ended up in court with the

---

*   Before the war, the LNER had been known as the great natural barrier to East Anglia.
†   Though the scandal was Victorian, the play had been clobbered by the Lord Chamberlain for portraying a royal person on stage.

Prince of Wales as witness, written by an author of mine who had (understandably) changed his name from Krapf to Russell. I also remember us having an argument about the Lycett Greens, who I said were ship-builders. 'No,' said Betjeman, 'boiler-makers.' It was typical of him not to mention that his daughter, the lovely Candida, was engaged to one.

We had arranged to have lunch with the mayor of Hull, which turned out to be lunch on the mayor of Hull, as that worthy explained that John Betjeman was of sufficient account to be an official guest of the corporation. His worship did not show much interest in the fate of the secondary modern school. I, on the other hand, was interested in Hull: I have always been fond of that city because my grandfather Blond landed there from Russia and lived in what was in fact a ghetto on the site of the comprehensive school which had spawned *English Through Experience*.

After enjoying the corporation's lunch – one understands why one's stomach sometimes has that name – we were stunned by the sight of the winning poetess. She made Lolita look like a frump. Her perfect little body was encased in supple leather; she wore a skirt that descended just a millimetre below the crotch and was separated by only a few inches of bare flesh from the top of her leather boots. She moved like Mae West and stood as still as Helen of Troy, unaware of the effect she was having on the shipping. I don't believe she opened her mouth except to smile, show her immaculate teeth and lick her wonderfully rouged lips. 'I don't think,' said Betjeman, 'we have to worry about her.'

Neither did the eagle swoop, nor did the television cameras roll: the event did not go as we had planned.

When the pilot of the little passenger plane I had hired spotted Betjeman, he insisted that the poet sit in the co-pilot's seat so that he could explain the sights below. He was an ex-Battle of Britain chap with jaunty hairstyle and RAF moustache, which had whitened with age. He pointed out every airstrip between Hull and Luton, and Betjeman pointed out every church. Each was convinced that the other was fascinated by his own lore.

'Just down there, Mr Betjeman, on the port side, is the field used by Fifth Fighter Command when they gave Jerry such a licking after the raid on Manchester in . . . '

'Yes, and there, captain, on the left, is the church everybody assumes is Pugin, but actually . . . '

And so it went on till touchdown. We couldn't find a taxi and didn't get back to London until ten o'clock. He had missed his dinner date, which was nothing more, or less, given he was a considerate man in all things, than with his mistress, Elizabeth Cavendish.

When Betjeman died, he was due, as any poet laureate, a memorial service in Westminster Abbey. Tickets were via Mark Bonham-Carter, whose office at Collins I telephoned – perhaps a little late in the day, because I was told there were none left. He shared with Alan Maclean* the upper part of my first mother-in-law's house. We disliked each other: I had annoyed him by bailing Anthony de Hoghton, whose trustee he was. I rang Sir John Betjeman's daughter, Candida Lycett Green, who handed me an envelope at the *Spectator* party almost the next day. 'Be sure to come early,' she said.

When I showed the tickets to the usher, I thought I noticed a look in his eye. I followed him down the aisle, on and on and on, until we reached the front row of the south side of the Abbey; here he showed me to a pew just under the pulpit, full of Betjeman cousins and aunts. I saw Osbert Lancaster in a wheelchair, holding a gigantic ear trumpet, a caterpillar of aged canons (the Collegiate of the Royal Peculiar) in a variety of wizened fur capes, and the Archbishop of Canterbury in his summer mitre, though he only delivered the blessing. The organ groaned and then the Prince of Wales arrived.

The scene demanded a Betjeman, but the one and only was dead. My face was barely three feet from the lovingly shined toecaps of the royal boots when Prince Charles went up into the pulpit to read the lesson. I could have licked them. At the end of the service, the congregation stood until the family had progressed down the aisle to

* The brother, as in Burgess and . . .

where the Princes of the Church had stationed themselves to bid farewell to the family and the congregation. On the long haul up the aisle of the Abbey, aware of the eyes of other friends of Sir John Betjeman and the hundreds who just wished to be present on such a numinous occasion, I attempted to chat up an implacable aunt, but she wasn't having any.

Later that night – I had not noticed the television cameras – someone remarked, 'Anthony, I never knew you were *such* a friend of the Betjeman family.' Indeed, I wasn't.

Graham Greene

One of my greatest coups as a publisher, and indeed my last coup, was precipitated by a hardish-core pornographic film from Brazil. In the early eighties, Laura and I travelled to Anaheim, an unattractive spot just south of Los Angeles, for a conference held by the American Booksellers Association. Having purchased the British rights to a book on farts, I felt free to accept an invitation to dinner from Conrad Goulden, who had made a lot of money from book clubs, in his elegant suite at a hotel in more salubrious Los Angeles.

Accompanied by Laura, I was sate next to Sam Marks, an octogenarian executive at MGM who had discovered Elizabeth Taylor and who, by dint of keeping his head down, had survived the executioner's axe as an archivist.

He invited Laura to lunch at the studio the next day. I, however, had other plans; but when my date failed to show, I invited myself. Before lunch, we were treated to the Brazilian pornography, whose leading actress was up for a screen-test for a major block-buster at MGM. As one embarrassed executive after another slunk out of the viewing theatre, it was clear that some mistake had been made. Sam, who sat next to Laura, repeatedly offered his apologies and asked whether she would care to move on for lunch. My plucky wife stood her ground (and I followed her lead) right through to climax.

Sam was so embarrassed that after lunch he took us to his office where he handed me a yellowed copy of a typescript stamped: 'This script is the property of LOEW'S INCORPORATED. No one is authorized to dispose of the same.' It was entitled *The Tenth Man* by Graham Greene.

Like Scott Fitzgerald and other writers before him, Graham Greene had been a hired gun, hired to write stories which the studio would then turn into movies. He had been put up at the Hotel Bel-Air and paid fifteen hundred dollars a month. And more to the point, all copyright under this deal had been vested not in him but in his employers.

I read the novella that night and ran the figures through my mind: first print hardcover twenty thousand and then, of course, paperback rights. But the icing on this particular *gâteau* was that Greene's French publisher, Laffont, never printed fewer than forty thousand. I telephoned Sam in the morning.

'I thought you might be interested,' he remarked in his usual gentle manner.

I had my partner, Antony White, negotiate a contract with MGM's lawyers: reasonable advance and provision of six per cent of the royalties for Greene to dispose of as he wished. Nevertheless, I thought it prudent and good-mannered to make the proper investigations.

'You are treading in a minefield, my boy,' said Max Reinhardt of The Bodley Head, Graham Greene's normally imperturbable British publisher.

I had again misjudged the reception with which my own good fortune would be received by others. Though the title to publish in America was clear, Greene's assignment of copyright to MGM under the terms of his contract in 1945 might have been vitiated or certainly muddied by a British Act of Parliament in 1956, or so my partner's lawyer implied in a masterly analysis of a clarity beyond the capacity of most American lawyers.

What was I now to do? Fortunately, the matter was wrested from my hands one evening in New York when Robert Mayall, then PR man to Mitsubishi, invited me to join him at his father-in-law's comfortable estate in the hills just above Nice. From there I could stake out my quarry.

I enlisted the help of a friend, Celestria Noel, who agreed to be my travelling companion. We set off for Antibes on a reconnaissance trip, and our first stop was to take a drink off my former father-in-law, John Strachey, a contemporary of Greene's. Although we had his address, Strachey urged me first to telephone Greene's unofficial bodyguard, a former Gibraltar policeman, whom he knew and who protected the master from the likes of me. Fortified by a pastis (or two), I made the call. I was relieved when there was no reply.

We found out that Graham Greene lunched every day at Felix au Port and there Celestria and I repaired, arriving at two o'clock. Needless to say, our hero was not there, but nor were there many others. As I paid the bill — making sure that I left a discernible tip — I engaged the proprietor in conversation about the habits of his most distinguished customer who, he told me, turned up every day just before *midi*, nearly always lunched alone and only consumed one *plat*. We decided to return the next day . . .

That very night I had a nightmare. In his youth Greene, who had been attracted by danger, had played Russian Roulette. In my dream he had said to me, 'Yes, you can publish my book but first let's play this game.' I woke up in a cold sweat just as I was about to press the trigger. In my waking mind, I rewrote the scene: the revolver goes off, killing me of course, and Graham Greene is extolled for causing the death of an exploitative Jewish publisher.

The next day Celestria and I arrived *chez* Felix at about twenty past twelve. It was pretty hot but we insisted on sitting inside at a table next to a man I supposed to be Graham Greene. I didn't recognise him until I noticed those slightly bulbous eyes I had so often read about. He had been talking in French — but with an accent which owed more to Berkhamsted than Biarritz — to the only other occupant of the restaurant, but when he saw us approach he retreated into contemplation of a sort of posh glossy. I already felt some of that fear and doubt which must shake the resolution of a hunter when the game he has been stalking appears framed so nobly in his sights. I don't remember how the next hour passed but Celestria and I rattled away, exchanging anecdotes which grew in exuberance and colour as the cham-pagne bottle emptied. Then, when we were in mid-flow,

Graham Greene left – it seemed to me without paying the bill. Perhaps he had some arrangement with the proprietor? But he came back and ordered an ice cream.

He appeared to take absolutely no notice of my assault on his attention though I was aware, until I stopped noticing anything, that he had not turned the page of his magazine. Then suddenly he was not there. So intoxicated was I by the vivacity of my own verbosity and three-quarters of a bottle of champagne, that I had not registered his departure.

On the fly-leaf of the book I had been carrying I had written in shaky pencil, 'I see no reason why *The Tenth Man* should not be published. Anthony Blond.' It looked as if this bow at a venture would never be deployed, until Monsieur Felix spotted our distress. Thinking us Graham Greene fans hoping for his signature, he picked up the book and cried out, 'But Monsieur has not signed!'

'I did not like to embarrass him,' I replied nauseatingly.

'Never mind,' said Monsieur Felix, 'he will sign it for me; he is not only a customer, he is a friend,' and he hurried out of his restaurant in pursuit of the maestro.

Celestria, who happened to be seated opposite the exit, provided a running commentary. 'He's caught up with him, he's stopped, he's looking at the book, he's got out his spectacles . . . He's got out *another* pair of spectacles, he's reading it, he's got out his pen, he's writing something . . . ' Monsieur Felix then hurried back into the restaurant. 'Monsieur a signé.' He had indeed. Under the clear and legible message, 'I see every reason,' was the equally clear and legible signature 'Graham Greene'.

'Hard luck, Blond,' said Celestria.

'No,' said I, 'first round.'

We went to a flower shop and bought an armful of tiger lilies and discussed the nature of the message for the card. 'Just put "Well done",' said Celestria.

The correspondence that ensued was fulsome on my part, cryptic (via his sister in Crowborough, Sussex) on his. *The Tenth Man* was written, he complained, under 'a slave contract' when he was in a state of economic distress. No, he couldn't be bothered to write a preface saying why the book shouldn't be published – which we would then publish. His tone was always courteous, however, and in one letter he even agreed to read my own novel which I sent him, provided he broke a leg or something and had a long convalescence. His last letter seemed final since he said that he had asked his regular publisher, Max Reinhardt of The Bodley Head, to repay me my expenses in the matter.

Max Reinhardt gave me lunch at Rules. After half an hour of statutory gossip he announced, 'Graham wants to do it.' On the back of the menu – no envelope being handy – we wrote out the deal: '*The Tenth Man* to be published jointly by BH and AB with equal billing, our contract with MGM [over whose validity under the laws of England and Wales there was a smidgen of doubt] to be subsumed by a new contract between BH and AB with GG giving him a larger royalty and the lion's share of foreign rights.'

A few weeks later Graham Greene sent the revised typescript with an introduction and appropriate reminiscence, and Max Reinhardt flew off with it to Simon & Schuster in New York. The deal was acceptable to us because it involved no fuss, and surely a slice of fruitcake is better than the whole of a penny bun.

When MGM heard the news, the studio mandarins couldn't believe it. How could they have parted with a potential bestseller for so little money? Sam Marks, the archivist, who had by now left the organisation, pointed out that (*a*) they didn't know that they owned it; and that (*b*) having paid Graham Greene (on fifteen hundred dollars a month) for ten weeks' work nearly sixty years ago, it wasn't such a slave contract. Anthony Blond, in association with The Bodley Head, published *The Tenth Man* in spring 1985. The print order was forty thousand copies.

Now that's a coup.

CHAPTER FOURTEEN

English Through Experience

Teaching remains the unfulfilled passion of my life, whose most exhilarating moments have been in the classroom. I always really wanted to be a publisher of schoolbooks, but a wise man told me fifty years ago that I needed a million pounds and ten years. Untrue.

Educational publishers are indeed a close and canny lot: they operate a different system from general or trade publishers, with different sales outlets, representatives, costings, editors and even publishing associations.

In the sixties, schoolbooks were ordered by heads of department, who did not pay for them; they were paid for by local education authorities. (Is this still the case? Aren't certain schools so hard up they can't even afford books?) The books were supplied by a handful of schoolbook contractors and consumed by children who had little choice in the matter.

With this structure in place, a publisher would commission a title, usually from a practising teacher, and pay a small advance and an even smaller royalty.* He would then mail schools with details of the proposed book and await requests for inspection copies; the first print-run would be based on the response. It is obviously impossible to call on all schools, so this part of the exercise was crucial. I say first print-run, for if there were no second, third or forth impression, the whole enterprise would be unprofitable – though schoolbooks tend never to be remaindered. Successful textbooks have long lives: the hits are generally revised to keep the copyright warm and are often, as we remember from our own schooldays, eternal. I once asked Enoch Powell to write one for me. He said no – although I don't think he had anything better to

* Only in recent years have such authors used literary agents.

do – but he did acknowledge that he was still receiving royalties from his father's textbooks.

Of course, it was not texts for grammar- or public-school pupils that concerned me. It was that seventy-five per cent of the school population which had failed its eleven-plus and attended secondary modern or comprehensive schools (then becoming all the rage) in which I was interested. This market was, I believed, inadequately provided for. But I needed to know the children and their teachers.

Fielden Hughes, himself a headmaster in Wimbledon and father of my author David, procured for me a temporary teaching post at Intake Secondary Modern School, just by the racecourse in Doncaster. It was far enough away, I was told, to prevent my coming to London for the weekends (then no motorways). 'So people will take you seriously . . . oh, and by the way, Anthony, when you hit a child . . . '

'What!' I screamed.

'I said when, not if,' continued Fielden. 'Do it like this.' And he thumped my back with his half-closed fist. 'See, it makes a lot of noise and doesn't hurt.'

Further to attune myself to the secondary modern ethos,* I stayed in the house of one of the teachers who, with his wife in the same profession, was mostly concerned to fill up a coach with enough Intake children to secure a free summer holiday in Switzerland. They seldom spoke of anything else.

The children in my class were enchanting: eleven- and twelve-year-olds who took to writing poetry at home, some of which made me cry. The staffroom, where I was suspected of being some sort of spy, and anyway dangerous for not being paid, obviously thought I needed some teaching experience. One day I was told I was taking 3B. In the front row were two huge youths, Gormley and Ramsbotham, who decided within a minute of my talking to the class about Greece that I was fair game. Their barracking and insolence climbed to such a pitch that I was beginning to lose my

---

* Though I did allow myself the daily luxury of calling the office from a public telephone box.

temper. At one point an angelic sixteen-year-old yelled out, 'Give the poor sod a chance, can't you.' But they didn't and I lost my cool – though just in time remembered Fielden's tip, and thumped Gormley – or was it Ramsbotham? – as hard as I could on the back. Eventually the bell sounded the end of the longest forty minutes of my life. I had made the mistake of trying to talk to these children instead of setting them a series of boring tasks, like copying out of a book. The noise the children had made was so loud that the teacher next door told me afterwards in the staffroom, where my ordeal had been noticed with smirks and sympathy, that he had nearly come in to rescue me.

'What,' I asked, 'do you do about Gormley and Ramsbotham?'

'Oh, we send them off to blow up footballs in the gym.'

In the revision period the next day the class were asked to write about what they had learned from me. They were silent in this heavily supervised session, which I attended. At one point Gormley silently beckoned me to his desk. 'How do you spell Onassis?' he asked. Apparently, I was told, they had learned quite a lot. And at least Gormley – or was it Ramsbotham? – had forgiven me.

In 1963, we embarked on the publication of a new basic course, which we called *English Through Experience*. The typescript came from another publisher, Heinemann, through an editor friend, and my man Lyon Ben Zimra thought it was a winner. It was. A chord was struck which reverberated throughout the land and, indeed, as far as Natal, where the course became a set book. In the end we were selling a hundred thousand copies per annum of the four books in the course. We, of course, exploited the success so that the tag line *Through Experience* was applied to maths, science, whatever . . .

The attraction for schools – and this applies more than ever in today's educational system – was that the course paid no regard to grammar or spelling, but simply encouraged the children to express themselves. A typical lesson would have been where a teacher set fire to a pile of salt – a blue flash – and then the class had to write down what they *felt*. It was, of course, this side of the publishing business which Holt Rinehart and Winston, a New York-based dependency of CBS, needed to tap into in order to establish a foothold on the educational publishing front in England; for Blond Educational was soon outselling Penguin's schoolbooks. In light of this success, an educational journal, running a feature on our company, described me as 'the odd man in'. And so I was.

CHAPTER FIFTEEN

Cap'n Bob

There was no reason to doubt Victor Glover, who acted as my first London rep and sales manager. He had been taken prisoner at Dunkirk and spent the war in German camps, leaving him patient, slightly ulcerous and gloomy over the state of the trade. He was also a good man and never told a lie, as far as I knew, except routinely in the course of persuading Hatchards, Harrods, Dillons, Bumpus, Boots and the Admiralty — the last four no longer punters — to subscribe our titles.

So when he told me that when working for Robert Maxwell in the fifties his task had been to pick up parcels containing almost the entire issue of every Pergamon Press scientific journal and deposit them down a disused mineshaft in the West Country, I believed him. One binder's parcel was kept for subscribers and voucher copies for advertisers, who could be shown the delivery notes, proving that the print order was as guaranteed by the publishers.

Maxwell was known to Allan Wingate, where Victor and I both worked, as the new owner of the ancient but shaky wholesale bookselling house of Simpkin, Marshall Ltd. When that institution was going bust, I remember Charles Fry, at a cocktail party at my step-aunt Tilly's flat in Berkeley Square,* taking a telephone call from Maxwell who said that if Charles rushed round fifty pounds he would see that Allan Wingate's account was paid in full. Charles did and it was. No one, not even Jimmy Goldsmith, could have made Simpkin, Marshall Ltd work, specialising as it did in the supply to the trade of single copies; and at that time Robert Maxwell was given marks for trying. He had

---

* Allan Wingate published the novels of my step-aunt Tilly's husband, Terence Kennedy.

not yet been excoriated as unfit to run a public company.

In the sixties John Calder, whose publishing office was such a *capharnaüm* that when the telephone rang no one could find it, started an anti-censorship lobby, clumsily named the Defence of Literature and the Arts Society. (I tried to change the name to DELENDA, which I thought would be somewhat snappier.) John was a small, neat, huffy, puffy walrus of a Scot, and had always been a braver man than I: he published *Last Exit to Brooklyn* by Hubert Selby Jr and defended it successfully through the courts. Mr Justice Salmon's judgment in that case, which I heard, was far more significant for British publishing than that in the case of *Lady Chatterley's Lover*. I had optioned Selby's book in New York but was too scared of the law to take it up. Some people, including John Calder and, of course, Maxwell, did not feel totally alive unless litigating.

Nevertheless, the National Book League asked me to a forum on censorship at their headquarters in Albemarle Street, where the others on the platform were Mary Whitehouse, a crusty duck and the sort of woman who would look after your cat in the holidays, and Robert Maxwell, MC (no duck he, more of an upholstered eagle). Jonathan Guinness of the Monday Club and a friend from some time back sat on the floor at the comfortably shod feet of Mary Whitehouse, hissing her advice like an expensive monkey.*

Mary Whitehouse opened with her attack on the permissive society, which had not changed much over the years, and was prompted by the Honourable Jonathan as to how the decadence of the Weimar Republic had stimulated the rise of Hitler. At this point a modern historian from the floor interrupted to animadvert that priests at that moment in history were running around measuring the distance of ladies' skirts from the ground. It was that kind of audience in Albemarle Street.

Then Captain Maxwell, in his deep and enriched British brigadier's voice, argued that we publishers were perfectly capable of

---

* Forgive these animal similes, but the scene would have been well drawn by Daumier, with myself, perhaps, as a pug.

monitoring the cleanliness of the novels we published and should be left to do it, just as the Hays Office had done it with films in Hollywood.

I chuntered forth with the standard arguments, in which I still believe, about absolute freedom at absolutely any cost, citing the Dutch experience where the spread of legal pornography had resulted in a diminishing level of sexual crime. I also remarked that Captain Maxwell had never published any novels and that – the phrase just slipped out accidentally – the only fiction he ever read was his own balance sheets. There was an amazed, half-frightened, half-delighted intake of breath from all present.

When he rose to reply, as if to steady himself, Maxwell appeared to rest his hand on my shoulder and only I knew, and I hope gave no sign, that his headmaster's grip was torturous. He made no acknowledgement that he had heard what I had said; indeed he used at least once the phrase 'as my good friend Tony Blond has pointed out . . . ', referring to something I had not said. And, of course, nobody has ever called me 'Tony'.

C. H. Rolph, the policeman who became an intellectual for the Left, writing in the *New Statesman* about the forum at the National Book League simply said, 'Anthony Blond was wickedly funny.' Though often a figure of fun, many people were frightened of Robert Maxwell when he was alive.

*   *   *

Captain Maxwell, MC, had been, in the war, a pathological killer of the German enemy, single-handedly destroying a bunker with grenades when his men refused to do so, and killing the soldiers when they came out with their hands up. Bullets directed at such a man are transformed into marshmallows as they approach his chest. (I'm so sure nobody pushed him.) Equally, Maxwell, never believing anyone could seriously wish him harm, bore no malice. He terrified with his violence, but vengeance was not part of his psyche.

For more than thirty years, from the late fifties to his death by drowning, a fortnight never passed without Maxwell being in the

Thirty-two; educated at Eton and New College, where he was an Exhibitioner in History. Served for two years in the Royal Artillery after the war and for six months in a factory in Manchester. Became a literary agent specializing in sensational and explosive books but not liking them much. Has published, since May '58, thirty-odd titles of varying hue and is most proud of Simon Raven's *The Feathers of Death* and *The Establishment*, a polemic symposium from the left. Has been described as the fastest *eater* in publishing and as having 'the features of an amateur boxer', but is in fact frightened of blows and a convinced pacifist. Has a Bentley.　*Punch*, 1959

Daddy – Major Neville Blond, Royal
Horse Guards, 1916.

My mother in the 1920s.

Greenbank House, Bowden, 1936. 'My father turned his back on his upbringing in
the Jewish enclaves of Cheetham Hill, Higher Broughton and Didsbury: so there was
nothing Jewish about our upbringing in *Judenrein* Bowden.'

Mummy and Daddy at Thurlestone, Devon, with Peter and me. 'A typical cameo of family life.'

'I was a Jew at Eton. That wasn't the trouble though – the trouble was me.'

Above Daddy marrying his cousin's ex-wife, Elaine Laski, 1944.
Left to right: Uncle Horace, Daphne Sieff, Neville, Elaine, Aunt Rita,
Michael Sieff, Barbara Benjamin (Elaine's best friend).

Left Uncle Baron (the photographer) with King George VI and Queen Elizabeth.
Below Lance-Corporal Kenneally VC, 1943. 'The spitting image, as is often God's joke with bastards, of my father.'

IWM MH15626

'Poor Neville, he has to put on his own plays.' Neville (*left*) with Lord 'K' Clark (*centre*).

Raymond Chandler, emotional but not tired, who came to town and made a pass at my first wife, Charlotte (*right*).

From Chester Row . . .

. . . to 56 Doughty Street (now the offices of the *Spectator*).

Laura Hesketh, aged twenty-one. My second wife.

My permanent houseguest: Andrew McCall.

My wedding to Laura in Sri Lanka, 1981. Laura given away by her father, Roger Hesketh.

With Ajith at New Concordia Wharf, Docklands:
'the size of a tennis court or, as some said, a small Sainsburys'.

public eye and, as Cap'n Bob in a cartoon strip, in *Private Eye*. He became for me an ideal – not a *beau* one – but an ideal none the less. He was the odd tycoon permanently in my mind. I watched his ups and his occasional downs. He was all I least admired as well as all I most admired: huge and randy* and immensely bold. He became the Labour MP for Buckingham by paying students at the private university ten shillings an hour for research; he turned round the catering at the House of Commons by selling off all the good wines; he once quelled a riot at the Oxford United football ground by standing up and raising his hands. (The police told me that, so believe it if you will.) When he bought the *Daily Mirror* newspaper he fired Noel Whitcomb, the highest paid columnist in the world, but, at the same time, offered him a travel agency.†

OK, it now emerges that he stole; yet he did so gigantically and without regret or restraint, because, being a psychopath, he was blind, tone-deaf and indifferent to right and wrong. If there was money around and he needed it, it was his. No other prescription applied. When the *Daily Mirror* complained to the Press Council that other newspapers had reported incorrectly that Robert Maxwell had stolen money sent in by readers for 'charity', the complaint was disallowed on the grounds that, in the circumstances, such a view was understandable.

We in the publishing game were all Maxwell-watchers, and some of us were apprehensive of his predation. For instance, he nearly got Collins and he did buy Macdonald and Sphere, causing the abrupt departure of clever Anthony Cheetham. Maxwell could not abide other, possibly dissenting, talent and saw no need for the delegation of power, since he monopolised all decision-making.

One day when I was in discussion with my editor at Jonathan Cape, about my second book on the publishing game, called *The Book Book*,‡ she said she wanted to start a club, for the likes of us

---

* Victor Glover once found an international address book of his mistresses, which he blushingly returned to the master.
† Noel, whose autobiography I published, never told me that.
‡ Geoffrey Wheatcroft remarked of the book that it was like being taught to fly by Icarus.

who didn't fancy ordinary clubs, to be called the Groucho. I anted up a cheque for four hundred pounds and became a founder member. At an early meeting, summoned before the idea was anything else but that, the mood was gloomy: the plan might have to be aborted. It was mooted that we approach Maxwell for help. The concept that he should become a member was not even considered: it would be like inviting a whale into the bathroom. No. It was his money we wanted, not him. So I offered to write to him, but André Deutsch, who was there, went out of the room and rang him up. He returned beaming. Maxwell would send a cheque.

'How did you do it, André?'

'A few words in Hungarian,' replied André modestly.*

In the dying days of my last publishing company Muller, Blond & White (as we had re-titled ourselves), we actually had a seller called *This Land of England* by the estimable David Starkey. The book was based on a Channel 4 programme and needed a reprint. The trouble was we hadn't paid for the first impression and the printer refused: it being company practice and all that. The printer was part of the British Printing Corporation, which was owned by Maxwell, and so I asked the managing director to have a note placed on Cap'n Bob's desk saying, 'Anthony Blond . . . ' He rang back a day or two later, quite puzzled, to say the reprint could be put in hand.

A discreet interval after Maxwell's death, I wrote to Kevin, who had decently suggested I write my 'dream ticket' for a publishing involvement with him (I don't know why, but I never did), offering to be his father's bio- as opposed to hagiographer. I was working on the lives of the first five Roman emperors, I said, and thought that a book on their papa would come naturally as a successor. I meant it. I haven't as yet received an answer. I suppose his hands are, as it were, tied.

---

* I wondered if they hadn't been 'Alle yiddische Kinder'?

CHAPTER SIXTEEN

If Only

Publishers admit to making mistakes and, even in their cups, compete with their fellows in boasting of the bestsellers they have turned down. As I grow old I tend to brood on failure; so here, to purge my melancholy, are a few of mine, which it might be salutary and possibly original to record, laced of course with the successes, which in a way provoked them.

The Anthony Blond hardback of *The Carpetbaggers* stimulated to our premises a spate of wannabees from literary agents who must have credited us with a sort of Midas touch. In fact, with a real bestseller, all the publisher need do is reprint and reprint and reprint. I was disgusted by Jacqueline Susann's *Valley of the Dolls* and turned it down, along with a lot of money; but I had so liked Harold Robbins. To fête my buying the British rights of *The Carpetbaggers* and to puff my imprint amongst the New York fraternity, I gave a bash in the Drake Room of the eponymous hotel on East 56th Street. Later that evening, Harold saw my face when presented with the bill and pocketed it himself without a word.

My father, who never read a book, had read *The Carpetbaggers* in the uncensored Simon & Schuster edition on the beach at Cannes and, ever the optimist where I was concerned, remarked, 'Why publish something everybody has read?' Yes, everybody, except the seven factory workers who each subbed five shillings to buy a copy. We had orders from railway-station newsagents, an infallible sign of a bestseller for which we were but the conduit. W. H. Smith had initially refused to stock the book; then they agreed to supply customers' orders; then they sent for five hundred. In the end they sold between fifty and a hundred thousand – I forget the exact figure. Desmond Briggs managed to consolidate our orders

by going to Australia and subscribing thirty-five thousand hardback copies. We subsequently published two more of Harold's
books, *Where Love Is Gone* and *The Adventurers*; both sold well but
nothing, nothing like *The Carpetbaggers*.

Harold Robbins was the archetypal bestseller writer. Disappointed at the reception of his early book, *A Stone for Danny
Fisher*, he decided to abandon literature and go for the money.
And it was not for nothing, for he had made his way from a lowly
shipping clerk in the warehouse of Universal Pictures to become
executive director of budget and planning for the entire company.
When he came over for the launch I put him up in a suite at the
Ritz, where Gareth Powell, Welsh lorry driver turned impresario
who emigrated to Australia with his Rolls-Royce – and so himself
a Robbins character – gave him a party. Harold found the Ritz too
poky and moved to the Oliver Messel suite at the Dorchester,
where he had his own chef and installed his lawyer – cheaper, he
explained to me, than a literary agent. Paul Gitlin, a Rottweiler of
a lawyer, interviewed supplicant European publishers offering the
foreign rights of *The Carpetbaggers*. I saw Danish, Swedish, Finnish
publishers, as well as French and German, exit the elevator,
white-faced and trembling, and head for the bar to recover from
his depredations, having been well and truly screwed by a man
who, unlike the conventional agent, had no regard for goodwill.
Only Steimatzky, then, in 1963, the sole translator of English
books in Israel, got away with paying his standard advance of fifty
pounds.

The shit or bust syndrome in Anglo-American publishing,
together with the efficiency of the global market,* has created
more and richer bestselling authors, mostly English or American.
Visiting him in his vast Edwardian villa in Le Cannet, where he
had only his latest mistress for company, I once asked Harold the
secret of his success. Reaching for the traditionally handy envelope,
he wrote on the back:

---

* In the only bookshop in Port au Prince, Haiti, one of the poorest
  countries in the world, I found a carousel of novels by Barbara Cartland.

SEX
MONEY
POWER
VIOLENCE
SEX
MONEY etc.

He might have added 'user-friendly technical information', though the mantra would have lost its punch. Harold's unique skill lay in explaining the tricks of any trade: from designing a bra to bankrupting a film company, he could do it. A favourite tale was how he took over the controls of an aeroplane when the pilot had turned green and nearly fainted. This most energetic and egotistic of Jews was not a modest man, and in this was the antithesis of another of my bestselling writers.

I trusted no man more in New York than Mark Jaffé at Bantam – indeed, his name should have been 'Gentleman Jaffé'; with him I exchanged books often by word of mouth and always for a lot of money. On one visit he said he owed me a favour because I had recently bought at his behest a title that turned out to be a complete let-down. It has to be understood that these transactions concerned books which had not yet been published by either of us; so when he told me to buy the British rights of *The Exorcist* I did ask if I might read it first. Mark replied, 'You don't read it, you buy it!' So I cabled Desmond Briggs and asked him to do just that.

Desmond had to pay six thousand pounds – this was 1974 – and we were told, after the contract had been signed, that we had already turned the title down when the price tag was only three thousand. No matter, as it happened. Returning to England, I was up all night – I think we might have put that in the blurb – reading *The Exorcist*. The next day I telephoned Mark to say it would sell all right but, boy, what a movie it would make. He replied that the film rights had already been sold for more than any publisher had received for a book.

We sold eight thousand copies and the book sort of stuck. William Peter Blatty, the author, later came to supper in the kitchen at Chester Row, which seemed the appropriate venue for the quiet, religious Lebanese Catholic. He didn't appear the kind of author one could promote, so we waited for the film . . . and waited.

Then I read in the *Evening Standard* that in New York ambulances had been summoned to movie theatres where *The Exorcist* was showing, and I realised all would be well. At the press showing of the film in London, normally attended by a scattering of critics, the theatre was full; moreover the PR people told us they had stopped going to their office and taken the telephone off the hook. One in fourteen Americans bought a copy of *The Exorcist*; and though the British and Commonwealth market was not as enthusiastic, our first royalty cheque was some twenty-eight thousand pounds – enough to take the editor, a former RAF pilot, to lunch in a plane to Deauville.

My return offering to Mark Jaffé was unintentionally a con.

Jo Gladstone, ex Marquand, daughter of Pearl Binder and the Lord Chancellor Elwyn-Jones, was working in Boston and introduced me to Adrian Desmond, a poor and fiery young lecturer at Harvard – such an honour, they didn't pay too good – whom I commissioned to write *The Hot-Blooded Dinosaur*, then a revolutionary concept. It worked and Mark did well too.

Desmond's next wheeze, however, was to write a book to answer the following question: 'If we are descended from apes, then at what point did God invest us with a soul?' A good one, I thought, and so did Mark: he bought the book for an advance of eighty-five thousand dollars. Oh, dear.

Alas, *The Ape's Reflexion* – though the jacket, of a small child watching a baby ape retrieve a floating object with a stick from a pool, won a prize – neither posed nor answered that interesting question. Moral: don't assume that authors will fulfil a publisher's one-line synopsis.

*   *   *

Jo Rosenberg was a pretty, champagney sort of young woman from the Hampstead Jewish ascendancy who became Beaverbrook's last mistress. She was amiable, calm and fair-minded, which were necessary qualities for dealing with the very rich in her *métier*; more to the point, she fancied old men.

When I first met her she was walking out with an ancient typographer who had invented Times Roman. To Desmond Briggs at a party she complained that she had not been given the standard payout for Beaverbrook mistresses, which had been fixed by him before the Great War – no allowance being made for inflation – at twenty thousand pounds. He also was wont to give each of his former girlfriends a hundred pounds on his birthday, equally immutable. Naturally, Desmond suggested she write the book.

She did and it turned out to be terrible. But it had enough in the way of scandal and scabrous detail concerning Beaverbrook's hanky-pankies (and spankies) to keep William Hickey and others foaming for months. I particularly remember his delight in the insolence of his own servants and his swapping with Sir Patrick Hennessy, chairman of Ford Britain, a fleet of girls for one of motor cars.

We had hired Derek Monsey, a former film critic of the *Daily Express*, as ghost and packed them both off to his villa in the South of France, where they jointly and severally complained that the other had made passes. The raw material of the publishing business is more colourful than, say, the raw material employed in the manufacture of sheets of cold steel . . . A typescript emerged from this trying tryst, which would have been publishable had it not been for the laws of libel. Our solicitor, Anthony Rubinstein, estimated the tariff at around ten thousand pounds per page, and if we cleaned it up, well, there wouldn't have been a book – impasse. But Derek Monsey saw a way out. The manuscript should be purchased, he announced, by the Beaverbrook Foundation in Fredericton, New Brunswick for their archives.

To alert the trustees to this opportunity, we had to talk about the publication as if it were imminent and drop a few anecdotes around the scene. 'Now, Anthony, you're going to Paris to-morrow, while I'm off to the South of France. And Desmond, you're doing some interviews . . . '

We obeyed. Nothing happened. We went on waiting and nothing went on happening.

Jonathan Aitken, then working as a foreign correspondent for the *Evening Standard*, had included me in his book, *The Young Meteors*, which was kind of him since I was not that young and too much of a slouch to race across the heavens; but we knew each other. He rang up one day and asked me to lunch. I felt a twitch at the end of our line. I declined and asked him to come to me, for I was giving a lunch party, or rather being given one by a restaurant.* Not wishing to appear too eager, I sate him at the other end of the long table and we did not exchange a word. But after lunch he offered me a lift back to my office, only just in the same direction as Fleet Street.

In the cab he opened directly: 'Jo Rosenberg never got her money, did she?'

I shook my head.

'Twenty thousand, isn't it?'

I nodded.

'I'll send our man to see you.'

In anticipation of the visit from their man, we lit a fire in the *piano nobile* of our fairly gracious offices and replenished the decanter of sherry in the corner cupboard.

The Beaverbrook man was the sort of lawyer every powerful organisation needs at least one of – a right bastard. He declined a glass of sherry and pitched in by accusing us of having 'uttered a libel'; this would have been technically true if we had sent the manuscript of the Rosenberg memoirs through the post. But we hadn't, had we? It had been sent round by hand and reposed in a safe in the rooms of our solicitors in Gray's Inn. Moreover, it would be released to his emissary on receipt of a cheque. (There was no reason to tell him that Andrew McCall had read it with glee, and that the material contained therein would be recycled for his second novel, *The Mistress*.)

---

* I had a sideline in writing features on food for insertion into theatre programmes.

Pause.

'How do I know you've not taken a copy?'

'You don't — you just have to believe us when we tell you we have not.'

We sent Jo the money less the cost of Derek Monsey and ten per cent for our pains and did not receive even a postcard in acknowledgement. After the decease of the famous typographer, Jo settled on an equally elderly baron, who peddled a rather grand marque of champagne.

*   *   *

When Rosica Colin, the redoubtable Romanian Jewish lady who represented Jean Genet, suggested I pay five hundred pounds for the repair, by an English surgeon, of the leg of his current boy-friend, a tightrope walker, as an option on his novels,* of course I agreed. The first printer to whom I sent *Our Lady of the Flowers* rang up and said, 'Shall I burn it, or will you?'

Norman St John Stevas, then a (fairly) simple lawyer, advised against publication, adding that otherwise he and Charlotte (my wife at the time) would have to bring me cakes in Wormwood Scrubs. Nevertheless, we collected signatures from the great and the good, including an old Oxford chum, George Steiner, who attested to the literary worth of the former gaolbird. The Office of the Director of Public Prosecutions, rather surprisingly, tipped us off by telephone that all would go well provided there was no illustrated jacket.

We published all the novels in sombre monochrome with dignity and profit, and consequently were offered, by Gallimard, an extended and over-blown essay by Jean-Paul Sartre called 'St Genet'. After the title page, I thought the essay became unintelligible and boring, but then the profundities of philosophy have always made me feel giddy, like staring down into a bottomless well. I therefore declined the honour. It was a mistake. Sartre's name would have

---

* These were considered unpublishable on account of their militant homosexual content.

sat well on our list, contrasting with Louis-Ferdinand Céline, a great French writer of a different political complexion, whose account of collaborators being shuffled from castle to castle by the retreating Nazis we had happily published.

*   *   *

On one New York trip I took with me Andrew McCall, who installed himself for free in a cosy if dusty apartment above Sardi's, the place for glitterati on the Upper East Side. The only condition for this freebee was that he vacate on the Wednesday afternoon when it was needed by the owner for a session with his mistress. Corlies ('Cork') Smith, a bright editor at a bright house, had given me, as a special favour he said, a manuscript to read by a Canadian singer who was going to be, he said, as big as Bob Dylan. The author seemed to me to be preoccupied with masturbation, an activity I thought better practised than preached. Moreover, it was written in a very modern way, so I asked Andrew, fourteen years younger and, supposedly, more in touch, to assess it for me. *Beautiful Losers* by Leonard Cohen didn't sing for him either. I had turned down a world bestseller.

In no particular order of time or merit I also turned down: *In Praise of Older Women* by Stephen Vizinczey; *The Hand Reared Boy* by Brian Aldiss; *Memoirs of a Princess* by Aisha Jaipur, who came to our wedding in Sri Lanka; and, sadly, a first novel by another friend of Laura's, Jamie Buchan, which went on to win the Whitbread Prize. The most fatal rejection of my career, however, because its acceptance might have saved our business, was of *A Man's Best Friend* by Peter Mayle.

By this time, I had staged a management buy-out of Frederick Muller from Harlech Television with Antony White, Muller's managing director. Muller had been a German, not a Jew, who had come to England in the thirties and had built an eclectic list, which included Patience Strong, Dodie Smith and the *Handbook to Freemasonry*. Muller had a successful line in humour, to which I added only *How Green Are My Wellies* and published a conceited little Welsh bear called SuperTed. At an editorial conference, the three women – rights, publicity and editorial – strongly advocated our taking *A Man's Best Friend*, but were overruled by the two men, as proprietors. Oh dear, oh dear, I do apologise.

When just beginning I interviewed a severe young lady, Fay Godwin, who married Tony Godwin, the sixties' wunderkind bookseller.* She interrupted and asked what would be my publishing policy (wasn't I supposed to be interviewing her?). I replied that I didn't have one – as can be gleaned from the roller-coaster that has been my career. I should, of course, have had a publishing policy: for though the person reading a book in the seat opposite may know the title and author, he or she will not know or care about the publisher. Booksellers, however, do. Publishers do not sell books to people who read on trains, but to booksellers who hardly ever read. These characters just order titles on the recognisable repute and success of a publisher in a certain genre: so thrillers from Gollancz, posh memoirs from Weidenfeld, pop fiction from Collins, but what from Blond? Well, perhaps the odd surprise.

* He later became editorial director of Penguin and was fired by Allen Lane for successfully changing the covers.

CHAPTER SEVENTEEN

The Odd Hoax

Some fairly respectable people were involved in the cases of the Mussolini and, later, the Hitler diaries. I was not one of them. I knew, however, that they were hoaxes and this is for why.

In the spring of 1949 I went to stay with a lady 'qui a vu refleuri plusieurs fois l'aubepine', that is to say of a certain age, in her villa in the middle of the Piccola Marina with a marvellous view of the Faraglione in Capri. My relationship with her – I fancy she may have wished it more complete – was that of a pupil in a *nava scuola*, the phrase used by Italians to describe an affair between a young man and an older woman; but ours was of the spirit and none the less intense for that. I was twenty-one and very impressionable. To this day I keep her prejudices about the only possible scent (Knize), the only way to eat an orange, where to sit at the opera and so forth. In those days there was only one hotel in Capri, the Grand Hotel Quisisana, where Oscar Wilde was once spotted and asked to leave, and no blocks of flats and not too many people, though there were plenty of day trippers. I remember sitting in the bar by the *funicular* with Norman Douglas, watching them arrive. The only taxis on the island, other than the horse-drawn cabs, were three blue open Hispano-Suizas, which belonged to Mussolini's daughter Edda Ciano. She retained her house there and was treated with that distance and respect which the Caprese return to the grandest visitors who behave modestly. (Princess Margaret, with her lady-in-waiting to pay in the shops and carry the parcels, did not go down well.) Through my hostess I got to meet, know and like Edda Ciano; I saw her and her family over the years. I went to her flat in Rome, took her son Mowgli to Wimbledon and her daughter to Madame Tussaud's, where I unsuccessfully tried to steer her away from her grandfather's bust in the Chamber of

Horrors, and went to her wedding. Edda, whose view of men was that they should make love, make war and gamble (her words and intended to shock), assured me that her father never wrote a diary.

One of the more splendid officer cadets at the Royal Artillery's school at Deepcut, where our passing-out parade before Field Marshal Lord Alanbrooke was such a shambles that he turned to the adjutant and said, 'Tell them to do it again' (indeed these were the only words he spoke then or at lunch in the mess later), was a dashing, derring-do, thwacking young man called Bruce Woodall, who was the son or the grandson of a dentist called Lord Uvedale. Why we became friends I do not know. My relations with the military were equivocal, his ecstatic. He wanted to succeed (and did), I just hoped for survival. He joined the Royal Horse Artillery, which is about as chic as you get in that regiment; never, as I was wont to say, more than a million strong. He also married the daughter of a Canadian general, to whom I may have introduced him. And so we kept in touch after my hostilities with the National Service had ceased. He joined my club.

One day at the Reform, where I always thought he looked out of place being young, handsome, healthy and confident, he told me that he had done some off-shore deal for the sale of Mussolini's memoirs. I told him that Mussolini never wrote any, to which he replied that, notwithstanding, the *Sunday Times* had bought them for (I think) seventy-five thousand pounds. This was in the fifties when the Canadian Mr, later Lord, Thomson had bought the paper from Kelmsley – which begs the question as to why are Canadians forever buying British newspapers? The man who had agreed to this transaction was an old acquaintance from my Oxford days, Jocelyn Baines. He had been working quietly at the publishers Nelson (also owned by Mr T.), before being translated, inexplicably some of us thought, to the *Sunday Times* with access to a cheque-book. He was a sociable, literary sort of man, more at ease in the comfort of a double-fronted Bloomsbury publishing house than coping with the hurly-burly of open-plan offices in the Gray's Inn Road. I always met him at the lunchtime sessions at Bertorelli's of the Wednesday Club, which had been founded by and for Philip

Toynbee and Ben Nicolson. These two patronised me in the nicest possible way as a fledgling publisher; Jocelyn Baines also joined in, but not so nicely. He had the face of an intelligent camel with superior eyelids and a mocking expression, which completely reversed when I asked him one lunchtime if he had really paid so much money for the diaries of Mussolini. He besought me to keep quiet about it. He was most distraught. Of course I felt sorry for him and began to rehearse his good points. He was fired and some time later killed himself: let's say for amorous rather than business reasons.

*　　*　　*

My first literary hoax had too esoteric a readership. One evening in Corfu, in Spanopoulos, the house on a hill I shared with Andrew McCall and the site of a libel action – *vide* Simon Raven *infra* – I was thinking about the homosexual poet Cavafy. *En route* from Alexandria to London for a cancer operation, Cavafy had stopped off in Corfu and stayed with the doctor who was so kind to Gerald Durrell. The doctor's chest of drawers, still containing a few papers, had somehow made its way into our house. I, therefore, pretended to have found some poems in a drawer, perhaps presented as a thank-you to his host. One, translated from the demotic, read:

> I don't think much of the boys of the town.
> They walk awkwardly and are not, on the whole, well made.
> You could take a pair of eyes from one, a smile from another,
>   the back of a neck here, an elegant arm there, and put
>   together a real Romoio.
> But I am not a sculptor.
> The other day, driving to Palaeokastritsa, I saw three peasant
>   women on their donkeys, and each one looked like an
>   Empress (κάι καθέ μία όμοιάξουν σάν Βασίλισσα).

I now became ambitious and wrote a longer poem about the tragedy of a policeman who falls in love with a schoolgirl. He tries to woo her, only to be mocked in front of her friends, so shoots her and then turns the gun on himself. I read this poem, in the demotic, to our disadvantaged maid, Vasilike, who was not well formed enough (poor thing) to find work in a hotel. She jumped up and down in a tantrum of rage, excitement and indignation, shouting, 'You knew! You knew!'

*   *   *

My second literary hoax, also conceived in Corfu, had a wider readership, and nearly came off. I was thinking about the programme notes of an opera by Richard Strauss I had seen at Glyndebourne in the summer. Just as at an exhibition of works of art I tend to spend more time digesting the catalogue than contemplating what it describes, so much of my pleasure in opera derives from the printed rather than the sung words. Many people are so intensely verbal that they only read the captions and don't look at the paintings, though few will admit it. The opera, I had read, was first performed in 1943. I, therefore, wondered if the Führer was there; what uniform Göring wore; whether Emma was in one of her Paris hats; whether the Bavarian aristocracy gave parties afterwards and whom they asked (and whom they did not ask) . . . What the publishing world needed, I decided, was 'The Diary of a Nazi Lady'. Elisabeth von Stahlenberg was born.

Gillian Freeman, who was the only person to answer the advertisement for clients for the new literary agency of Anthony Blond (London) Ltd back in 1953, would write the book. She was an inventive novelist in her own right: we had sold her first book to Mark Longman across the road in Clifford Street, but she hit the jackpot in Hollywood with the script of the *Leather Boys*, a novel I had inspired in the same sort of way.

Gillian's husband, Edward Thorpe, the ballet critic of the *Evening Standard*, was a Nazi 'buff' and knew a grown-up Hitler baby, who lived with a Jewish dancer in West Kensington; a gloriously inappropriate association for one designed as a prize specimen for the 'Thousand-Year Reich'. The idea of his researching in Germany appealed to all of us. The plot was simple: Elisabeth was an innkeeper's daughter in Bavaria who married, above her station, an aristocrat, who responded to Himmler's appeal on the radio for all well-bred Germans to serve their nation by joining the Gestapo ('we know you have style and we need it'). He became a member of the Gestapo's film unit, and with this job and her charm the couple lived high on the hog in the good years of the very early forties. The Führer, for instance, though he did not attend the first night of the new Strauss opera in Munich (he had had a quarrel with the composer), did go to Elisabeth's party after the show and ate three slices of her Schwarzwaldtorte! Alan Clark, to whom I sent the book, wrote that it was 'indisputably genuine . . . a contemporary document of the highest importance to social historians of that epoch'. The American publishers offered to double the advance if Elisabeth would tour the United States. A nice buzz was beginning to generate – the book started to sell – then pop! – the *Evening Standard* revealed that Elisabeth only existed in the agile mind of Gillian Freeman. The reviews were pulled and the American publisher tried to get out of his contract. Though we never stated that Elisabeth von Stahlenberg was ever real – people just wanted her to be – the book was damned a hoax.

There is a postscript to the story, which shows how precise hoaxers must be. Staying at the Vier Jahreszeiten in Munich, I showed the German PR lady the book, which had, for its cover, a photograph of a smiling Hitler at Berchtesgarten with two Alsatians, Eva Braun and an unknown lady (our Elisabeth). The PR lady at once remarked that 'Stahlenberg' was not a Bavarian name. We hadn't thought of that.

*   *   *

The technique of mid-twentieth-century forgery had been precisely described in a novel we had published by Alan Williams called *The Beria Papers*. At the time I had a self-denying ordinance – rather a silly rule now I come to think of it – not to put my friends in print. In the case of Alan Williams I had been persuaded by David Gillies, a later aspirant to the favours of Mrs Wriothesley, by the way, to read the former's first novel *Long Run South*; and so began the sort of stormy relationship between publisher and author which made the business such fun. Alan had a Holmesian eye for detail and demonstrated how typewriter, type and tape must be of the right age for the artefact to be credible. Clearly neither Hugh Trevor-Roper, who became Lord Dacre ('Facre' would have done well enough), nor Charlie Douglas-Home, with those patrician 'scimitar-like lips', had read *The Beria Papers* when they examined Hitler's 'Diaries'. Both were deceived. When I heard Douglas-Home on the radio talking about the 'quality' of the typescript as proof of its genuineness, I experienced a sharp sense of *déjà vu*, so much so that I sent him a long cable explaining why the document was a forgery. Apart from the prima-facie evidence, common sense would suggest that men like Mussolini and Hitler have more exciting things to do than write diaries, which tend to be the occupation of retired adventurers like the Duc de Saint-Simon and mysterious Admiralty clerks like Pepys. I never did receive an answer from Douglas-Home; he died without talking to me again.

I think he was just cross with me for pointing out that what he wanted to believe in was false. After the *Evening Standard* had blown our *Nazi Lady*,* a woman telephoned our office in tears, begging to be reassured that Elisabeth von Stahlenberg was alive and well.

Does the human condition perhaps require the odd hoax? I can think of one world religion whose hero led a life no better documented than that of our 'Nazi lady'.

---

* She lost her husband and her children at the end of the war, but managed to start a new life in Toronto.

CHAPTER EIGHTEEN

End Game

I asked Uwe Kitzinger, an Oxford contemporary, who ran an upholstered business school outside Oxford called Templeton College, if I could give a lecture on 'How to Fail in Business'. He demurred. Elements in my case would have included grappa, a too finite capacity for taking pains, and signing a joint and several guarantee – each of which contributed to my disaster. Muller, Blond & White, began well with a management buy-out, which we paid off, as was agreed, in three years. Commodious and elegant premises, formerly the offices of the Society for the Protection of Ancient Buildings, in two adjacent early-eighteenth-century houses in Great Ormond Street* were acquired through a loan from Messrs C. Hoare & Co.† We seemed ready to go.

My partner, Antony White, was an art historian who through his Yugoslav connections was able to secure a stream of expensive looking, but cheap to manufacture, second-eleven Phaidon-esque books. Our coup in this area was to be a great work on the restoration of the Sistine Chapel, paid for by Nippon TV, from whom we bought the English rights. The deal was in yen. We sold ten thousand copies to Crown in New York and insured against a decline of the US dollar to the yen of up to fifteen per cent. We did not however reckon with a drop of twenty-five per cent. The hiatus killed us and we were told to go into voluntary liquidation, having scoured London for rescue.

My joint and several guarantee cost me all the money I earned from Piccadilly Radio; and I still owed the Inland Revenue capital

---

*   Resident secretary uncle-in-law, Peter Fleetwood-Hesketh.
†   I believe I alienated this august firm of Whig bankers by dedicating to them, without permission, one of my books.

gains on the shares I had to sell to pay off Messrs C. Hoare & Co. We couldn't even pay the grappa bill from the friendly neighbourhood Italian restaurant.

People were kind: Sonny Mehta and Peter Mayer, the panjandrums of the publishing business, respectively in charge of Random House and Penguin, gave me lunch; George Weidenfeld spoke to me, as did Paul Hamlyn.* I decided that none of my best friends were Jews; but perhaps I am not cut out to be an employee, of Jew or Gentile, my instinct being to rock rather than row the boat.

Then Laura, to whom I wish I had paid more attention during the declining years of Muller, Blond & White, came up with an idea.

'Why don't you ring up Naim?'

'Naim Attallah?'

We had often been to his parties, which were frequent and flashy, though I only knew him from the public sheets where he featured always with the same story. His father, a Palestinian Catholic, worked for Barclays Bank in Haifa; he had been brought up by women who cosseted him and forbade him even to ride a bicycle; he had been sent to Battersea Polytechnic. In 1948, when the State of Israel was established, his father rang to say not to return home. The Home Office, however, only allowed him to be a manual labourer, so he spent four years painting generators for the GEC and became a steeplejack.

Then he secured a job dealing in foreign exchange where his genius emerged: for he could convert dirhams into sterling into yen into US dollars and back quicker than a calculator. At twenty-five he married a Polish Catholic girl of seventeen and decided to become rich. His first move was to borrow twelve thousand pounds and buy a Rolls-Royce.

It worked. Attracted by the potential of the publishing world – Naim liked making friends – he bought Quartet, a classy, sexy and bankrupt imprint that had been founded by William Miller

* Had I not written of him, 'a megalo publisher of immemorabilia'?

with money from racy young City gentlemen of his Oxford acquaintance. William, when editor of *Isis*, had been sent to gaol by Lord Chief Justice Goddard, a vulgar fellow who was reputed to pay Guardsmen to masturbate, for revealing the location of the British nuclear establishment in Kiel.

I rang Naim and asked if he would give me a job. A second's pause and he said, 'Yes, Anthony, come and see me tomorrow' (instant decision being one of his characteristics).

Naim ran his little empire, which eventually included Quartet Books and The Women's Press imprints, *Wire* and *Apollo* magazines, the *Literary Review*, two perfumes and a PR company, as well as his theatrical and film adventures, from offices in Namara House in Poland Street, Soho. On another floor was *The Oldie*, edited by Richard Ingrams, who, when at *Private Eye*, had regularly satirised Naim's harem, given the latter's penchant for hiring smart young ladies with names like Soames/Emma, Fraser/Rebecca, Sackville-West/Sophia, Sainsbury/Sonamara, Grenfell/Katya, Fry/Cosima, Lawson/Nigella, Guinness/Sabrina.* It was typical of Naim's performing charm that this difficult fellow was converted into a devoted employee.

In fact, Naim, a devoted family man, courted but did not think of seducing these young ladies, though he confessed he dreamed that one of them would one day suck his toes. I remember one favourite whose duty it was to sit next to him on aeroplanes and arrange, with a soft brush, the hairs on his head.

I climbed the four flights of stairs to Naim's offices. There I encountered a macho lair, strewn with tiger skins and occupied by young ladies who supplied his occasional needs, like a glass of water or a pullover when the air-conditioning became too intense. I explained I only needed 'walking money' – an expression employed by the late Dominic Elwes.

'How much?' asked Naim.

'Ten thousand?'

'Too much, that would upset the others.'

---

* All, as somebody pointed out, with first names ending in 'a'.

'OK, then five thousand.'

'No,' said Naim, 'six thousand.'

And so it was.

The 'others' consisted of the editorial director, known only as Pickles, whose great passion was his list of European and New World belletrists – famous in their own countries, but whose obscurity elsewhere was but occasionally illuminated by an international prize or a stunning review in *The Times Literary Supplement*. They did not sell.

Pickles had met Naim through working in a music shop near Namara House, where he upgraded his taste in cassettes, coaxing him gently from Tchaikovsky to Bartók. Delicate in stature and address, with big swimming eyes, he passed so much of his life propping up the bar of the Coach and Horses in Romilly Street that I warned him he might get clamped.

Pickles was tricky and touchy, a militant homosexual with an air of having been scarred in some terrible romantic battle. He loved Naim and glowed like a little girl when complimented by him. Naim, on the other hand, when accused by a not totally sober Pickles of homophobia, one evening at the Frankfurt Book Fair, just smiled.

Quartet Books occupied two adjacent rickety houses in Goodge Street, between which, it was always being mooted, a door would one day be breached. To the young ladies who clattered and chattered up and down the two flights of stairs, I was presented by Pickles as 'seasoned timber' and by David Elliott, the sales director, known as 'dump-bin Dave', as 'a living legend'. The young ladies, however, were understandably more interested in stealing each other's boyfriends on un-monitored telephones than in talking to me. The circus mistress of the *salle de manège* was Jubby, daughter of Richard Ingrams, who cracked a condescending whip and outlasted them all. She was to look after me. Jubby was the Saint-Simon at the court of King Naim, registering his movements, moods and reactions.

I once asked the Reform Club, where I was a member of forty years' standing, if a television company could interview Simon

Raven and myself in the library.* The response was curt: no television cameras allowed in the Reform. But why?

Jubby Ingrams had hired the Reform for a photo shoot and subsequently the secretary was horrified to be sent a copy of *Playboy*, to which surely neither he nor the club subscribed. I am sure the magazine featured a naked girl standing on one of Sir Charles Barry's horsehair sofas, next to the bust of the young Queen Victoria, in the marbled atrium.

I was never allowed to attend editorial meetings, though my modest suggestions were nearly always agreed to. We published biographies of Hugh Montefiore, former Bishop of Birmingham, who was bar mitzvahed, as I had to remind him, at my synagogue, and Justin de Blank. It is odd, come to think of it, that these titles, from a Jewish editor, should emerge from a publisher who was Arab. I did have one coup for Naim, only it misfired.

Jennifer Paterson, a comparatively poor Catholic church mouse, lived with her mother and an uncle, who marketed clerical arte-facts, in a modest mansion flat in the shadow of Westminster Cathedral, where another uncle, Monsignor Bartlett, was part of the top brass. He was a witty fellow, presiding over a nest of Jesuits in Golden Square, whose library I enriched with a set of the novels of Jean Genet, which, he told me, went down well with the fathers. Jennifer claimed she prayed nightly for the death of her mother, which, alas, occurred before that lady was able to witness her daughter's move from, as it were, mags – for she used to work for Norman Kark Publications – to riches.

My acquaintance with the future famous *Fat Lady* was far from slender: one summer Andrew and I invited her to stay in our house in Corfu. Indeed Laura and I invited her for other holidays, so I felt entitled, as Jennifer appeared increasingly in the media, to suggest to Naim she be commissioned to write a book. I wrote to him saying that she could be on the verge of becoming a star, but at the moment she was a Catholic spinster of this parish and would come quite cheap. Those, I'm afraid, were my words and the letter was

---

* I cannot think of a more splendid room in London.

accidentally (?) copied to Jennifer. Oh dear. Jennifer rang me up to say she had found a much better publisher in John Murray. She was right.

Naim continued to pay my honorarium, even when I went to live in France. He was also kind enough to publish *Blond's Roman Emperors*, which was their idea of a title. Eventually, he wrote me a most elegant letter of farewell.

PART FOUR

Life of Bi

CHAPTER NINETEEN

Charlotte Strachey

We were an unlikely couple, Charlotte Strachey and I. She was billed to marry her childhood friend, Burgo Partridge. But Charlotte decided she wanted to marry me.

Charlotte's father, known as 'Spotty John', was the only undistinguished member of a family famous for generations. He was the only one who did nothing. He was also something of a bad hat. 'Am I,' he often wondered aloud, 'a rotter or a cad?' He was an unsaleable painter and spent his life amiably wasting the competences of his wives and mistresses. He was a good cook, a companion of honour (if only in the lower case) and fond of, but not addicted to, the bottle. He said of himself that he should have been a wine waiter, because he had 'bad breath, a shaky hand and a tendency to look down the front of ladies' dresses'.

My mother-in-law, Isobel Strachey, was a novelist and, reeling perhaps from the depredations of her husband, an economical hostess, who served what she called 'guiche', when she could get away with it, and small portions of gin and tonic in little jars that had once contained Shippam's Fish Paste. She wanted to give the wedding reception at her house in Oakley Street, Chelsea, but my father, on being shown the *piano nobile*, jumped up and down and declared it unsafe. The venue was changed to 23 Knightsbridge, big enough to absorb an orchestra and the phalanx of be-minked Marks and Spencer ladies who attended – for my brother and I were then very much part of the family – such events. And thank God they did attend, because for months Charlotte and I lived in the little house in Chester Row, which she had found 'after an intensive search of twenty-four hours' (my father *dixit*), off the sale of the Georgian silver it was their custom to give as wedding presents.

At the time of our wedding in 1955, John Strachey was in Exeter gaol for drunken driving. This was to the great delight of my father, who, like a one-man chorus in *The Threepenny Opera*, shuffled happily round the friends and family of the bride loudly and repetitively asking, 'Where's the father? What? In gaol? Good heavens!'

I have a portrait of Charlotte, aged twenty, by Robert Buhler: slightly sulky, a bit pasty-faced, her hair 'mouse', as it was described on her passport, but with lovely eyes. I thought it not only unflattering but also inaccurate, for Buhler could not show her sweet voice, which tinkled like a bell or descended to a glorious fruity drawl. She could also become, if bothered, as pretty as a picture and was briefly a model. She, however, lacked the essential energy and steel core for that profession, her favourite occupations being, during our brief (five years) but not unhappy marriage, eating chocolates and reading novels in bed. My memory of her is blanketed with oblivion, like a duvet, because I know I did her wrong: more through neglect than betrayal, for I was so taken up with my venture in publishing that I ignored her. Charlotte took no interest in this, only observing that she couldn't understand why Anthony 'didn't get his books from Heywood Hill like everyone else'. She tolerated the *va et vient* in the back room at Chester Row and even put up with Miss Frame's long mink coat. And she liked the parties, which she presided over, fearlessly and without favourites, her indifference to the politics of the literary scenario being, I thought, an asset. We were not a husband-and-wife team.

We were though a reasonably happy couple, in a just-off smart life in a just-off Eaton Square house, with just enough money to enjoy the metropolis and abroad. I remember one summer – in the days when sterling was very strong – we took Paul-Henri Spaak's flat in St Jean de Luz, which had a view over both harbours. Even so, Charlotte was bored. 'If I wake up once more to the sight of those pretty little yachts bobbing at anchor in the glittering blue sea, I shall scream.'

Charlotte put up with my way of life, even enjoyed it, but the stillbirth of our son, whom we had decided to call Adam – that she could not endure. She had had a few miscarriages, but in 1960 she appeared to be successfully and fixedly pregnant. There were problems, however. The family doctor, called Eppel (I said of him, 'An apple a day keeps Eppel away'), who had been foisted on her, lost her blood sample. Her water then turned out to be poisonous and the child turned upside down in the womb. When he was born he had a cleft palate and his heart was on the wrong side. He only lasted twenty minutes, or so we were told, but we never saw him. Removed from his mother, he was consigned to the incinerator. I was summoned by the gynaecologist, an expensive fellow nominated by my father, who swayed slightly, smoking his cigar after a good lunch; he ushered me in to see Charlotte, who lay on a bed, her breasts bound to prevent lactation. Tears ran down her face. I felt bisected by rage and compassion. That night I roared round town getting very drunk and hit David Pelham, the smallest man I knew.* He told me later he quite understood. In the back room of Chester Row, which was to have been his nursery, a gift from my stepmother of a splendid pram awaited our dead son.

What is a non-event in a hospital is a trauma for the parents of a stillborn child, who were not, in those days, consulted as to the disposal of their child – *theirs*, not the hospital's. The result of nine months' gestation may have ended in failure, but that failure has the same rights as a success: to be recorded, somewhere, somehow. Thirty years later, I was interviewed by Danny Danziger for the *Independent* on 'The Worst Day of My Life'. He quoted Charlotte as saying that henceforth she regarded my penis 'as an instrument of death'. The piece was used by a clergyman in Wigan in his campaign for registering the stillborn, which goes to show that some good can emerge from tragedy. But it killed our marriage.

In October of that year, and about to leave for the Frankfurt Book Fair, I asked my friend Peter Jenkins,† to look after Charlotte. When I returned to Chester Row neither Charlotte nor her belongings

---

* A film producer who married Jean Pelham, the tallest woman I knew.
† At that time a correspondent for the *Guardian*.

were there. There was no note on the chimney piece, but then Charlotte had never been much of a letter writer. My mother-in-law eventually revealed her whereabouts. She had gone to live with Peter Jenkins, her first and only infidelity. I cried all night and in the morning asked them both to lunch at the Ritz. I proposed they should have an affair, but that the marriage should not end: an old-fashioned solution to such marital aberrations to which I still adhere. They wouldn't play. So I went to my solicitor – 'I divorced yer father and I'll divorce you' – and he sent a man in a brown bowler hat round to Peter Jenkins's relatively humble lodgings off Oakley Street. Charlotte gave him a cup of Nescafé. She being technically the guilty party, I didn't have to give her any money, but I asked my father if I could. He asked whether I felt guilty, to which I said yes. Even so, my stepmother's secretary rang up and said could I please return the pram.

Later Charlotte developed a form of leukaemia called Hodgkin's disease and started to die. She had produced, however, for Peter, a healthy baby girl, to the delight of Isobel, who left her the house in Chelsea.* Twenty years later, Peter Jenkins died suddenly, his death being announced four minutes afterwards on Radio 4, where he regularly performed. I thought this bad taste on the part of the BBC, but then Peter had always relished purveying hot news.

---

* She grew to become Amy Jenkins, famous, nay notorious, for the amount of money she earned from TV and book accounts of her sexy young contemporaries.

CHAPTER TWENTY

Blond Prefers Gentlemen

Nowadays readers resent, and reviewers disparage, autobiographies where the whole truth, or nearly the whole truth, about the person's sexuality does not emerge. So, here we go. 'Who am I,' I was once reported as saying, 'to ban half the world from my bed?'* I am bisexual: drawn to girlish boys and boyish girls, and have fallen in love with and lived with and been married to people of that style.

As a latecomer to the art of love, I had been chaste, except in my thoughts, at Eton, in the Army and at Oxford. I was a virgin until the age of twenty-four, when one summer night I climbed up to a balcony in St Leonard's Terrace, Chelsea, and fell into the bed of a young lady. She perished later in an avalanche, which she was said to have started. From that moment on, for forty years or so, I led a rackety sexual life – otherwise I was quite stable, in that I lived in the same house for twenty-eight years and had the same job – and ricocheted between the sexes, before settling for the deep comfort of a double bed in the Limousin.

I never concealed my homosexuality: the closet out of which I came had glass doors. And when asked by a lip-smacking vigilante at a Labour Party candidate's interview whether there were any skeletons in my cupboard, I could answer that they had often been exposed, fully fleshed, in the public sheets.

In the sixties I joined the Homosexual Law Reform Society, renamed by its lugubrious secretary, Antony Grey, the Albany Trust, so that contributors might write cheques without embarrassment. Such was the climate. I lobbied Parliament, hired a hall in the London School of Economics for a rally and became, with Trevor Huddleston, one of the (many) vice-presidents of the Campaign for

* A remark that did not go down well in Southport.

Homosexual Equality. I also became a vice-president of a further campaign, to allow women the right to an abortion. Both these efforts succeeded, though I often wonder about the resultant job-losses. I suppose these people moved on to animal rights.

The spark that fired indignation over the nineteenth-century law which imprisoned homosexuals but not lesbians was, wonderfully, a book. *Against the Law* by Peter Wildeblood was to homosexuals what *Uncle Tom's Cabin* had been to Negro slaves. It freed them. I had not been involved in the Montagu case of 1953, though I had known Edward for years at school and at Oxford. As a result of two airmen, McNally and Reynolds, whose faces I shall never forget, turning King's Evidence (or was it by then Queen's?), Montagu, Wildeblood and Michael Pitt-Rivers were sent to gaol at Winchester Assizes.

I did have, however, an expensive affair with Kenneth Hume, quite possibly the oddest man I have ever met. When he was a boy, he once told me, he had organised the pages at the Piccadilly Hotel into a union with minimum rates for pederasts. He became a film director and produced the first commercial-television variety shows for Jack Hylton. As his agent and partner, I had to negotiate his fees. He subsequently married Shirley Bassey, the black *chanteuse* from Tiger Bay, and their quarrels and reconciliations occurred mainly on the stage of the London Palladium. Then, as he had always threatened, he committed suicide.

A crucial figure in the parliamentary campaign to reform the law was Alfred Hecht. He had a gallery in the King's Road and was the Tate Gallery's and – when I could afford it – my picture framer. The trade union MPs were threatening to oppose the bill on the grounds that apprentices might be 'interfered with'. Hecht pleaded with his friend Nye Bevan to use his influence, claiming it was very rare for a politician to have the opportunity to do certain and immediate good. Bevan, whose support was not perhaps entirely disinterested, obliged. Herbert Samuel,* ever popular with his peers, made an

* Herbert Samuel's hatred of homosexuals might have been an aspect of his fervent orthodox Judaism. He believed that homosexuality has the capacity to form a habit, like alcohol.

attack on homosexuals, attracting the support of the *Daily Mirror*, which can't have helped; moreover, Viscount Montgomery* pointed out to their lordships that if the bill became law senior police officers might sleep with each other with impunity. This observation was greeted with gales of noble laughter and the bill sailed through. Edward Montagu told me that Montgomery had been duplicitously encouraged to make this point. The victorious homosexual lobby might have reflected that with enemies like these, who needed friends?

Relief from legal prosecution did not please all those of a homosexual persuasion. A certain *frisson* had now been removed. One of my friends, refusing to make a hefty contribution to the campaign, cried, 'What? Are you trying to deprive me of the thrill of hearing the crunch of the policeman's boot on the gravel outside, as I . . . ?' He was being serious: the secrecy and danger of a homosexual's life had had an erotic appeal.

The coded language ('a friend of Mrs King's'), the international guide with unexplained symbols (which the initiated could immediately understand), the private clubs such as the Rockingham in Archer Street and the Boeuf Sous Le Toit, the shameful thoroughfares like Half Moon Street, the north side of Nelson's Column ('the meat-rack') – all were suddenly *licet*. But for some sex without the *frisson* became, sadly, pointless.† The current system whereby male escort agencies advertise in the London telephone directories or on the Internet must be less fun. And the stridency of some homosexuals is as inadmissible as the laws which were used to oppress them.

*　　*　　*

Fiction and anecdote around the homosexual world are certainly attenuated by the lack of repression. There are no more impresarios like Diaghilev who, pointing to the bed, said to Nijinsky,

---

* Montgomery's passion for young boys, one of whom he made walk naked round his dining-room table, was then not known.

† A pity that Auden never wrote a privately circulated lament.

'The part lies there.' Cecil Lewis, author of *Sagittarius Rising*, who was a pilot in the First World War and should have only lasted three weeks, was a neighbour in Corfu. He told me a story about Diaghilev, which did not appear in Richard Buckle's biography, and deserves to be recorded. One Saturday morning in 1922, Cecil was driven down in a large open car to have lunch with Gordon Selfridge in Old Windsor. (This old man did not forget.) With him were the Dolly Sisters, a pair of theatrical beauties of the day, Diaghilev and his latest find, Léonide Massine, with whom he was much pleased. 'He is so dedicated to his art!' exclaimed Diaghilev. 'Last night he got up in the middle of the night to practise at the bar, and goodness, when he came back to bed, were his toes cold.' 'Of course, I couldn't tell that story to Mr Buckle,' said Lewis.

Another loss is camp, high and low, which has alas all but vanished. How one longs for a drawled 'get you!', with a touch of limp wrist, from a known and *outed* homosexual politician. (He wouldn't lose my vote.) From my circle of friends and acquaintances in that *demi-monde*, in and out of which I was able to flit, here are a few that *got* me:

Brian Howard
Brian Howard was my first fully-paid-up queen; he was the only man in the world who frightened Evelyn Waugh. He was the original effeminate homosexual masochist, smiling as a bunch of Christ Church hearties manhandled him into the fountain in Tom Quad. At a Nuremberg rally, where Hitler was in full flood, he yelled at anybody who would listen that they were fools and was quite pleased when politely hustled off to gaol. He joined the RAF as a second-class airman and worked in intelligence at the Air Ministry from 1942, finishing with the same rank in 1944. Every lunchtime he would walk across Green Park to the downstairs bar at the Ritz, where he held court, in his most un-Ritzy uniform, with scandalous tales of king and queen. One day, a be-medalled young air commodore, pointing out that as an other rank Brian was not allowed to be there, demanded his name and number. Brian looked up at him sweetly. 'Mrs Smith,' he said.

I met Brian in Rome in 1949 when he was staying at a *palazzo* that had something to do with the Millington-Drakes. I remember a glass of water in a silver chalice, which could have been made by Bernini, and a dish of fat black olives. I asked if the olives were grown locally. 'CALIFORNIA!' barked the princess with the American accent.

Brian interrogated me and must have been satisfied with the answers – Who was the only critic in London? V. S. Pritchett, et cetera – because he commanded my attendance the next day. And anyway, he said, he liked Sam – his beloved – to sleep with Old Etonians. The outing was a round of bars and ended with Brian trying to sit on the knee of a violinist in a nightclub at two in the morning. I never saw him again.

A few years later, I learned that he had killed himself to the sound of *Liebestod* after the accidental death of Sam from a gas leak in his villa in the South of France. From his biography by Marie-Jacqueline Lancaster,* which I published in 1968, I read that he was then heavily into heroin and had not long to live anyway.

Beverley Nichols

Beverley Nichols, who was the most promising undergraduate of his day and wrote one of the first Penguins, an autobiography called *Twenty-five*, was my second star in that world. With Oliver Carson, another New College 'man' – we were thought to be lovers, especially by Edward Montagu, but we weren't – I had started a glossy magazine, *Harlequin*, printed on real art paper and very silly. Our first editorial began: 'Because we prefer fountains to factories, wine to water, the individual to the state, we are the revolutionaries of today.' And by its side was a bled photograph of a young man feeding pearls to a china pig – it was that sort of thing. Beverley had contributed a piece about himself which started, 'I was a delicious little boy . . . ' and which the printer, a friend of my mother, whose principal revenue came from making cheque books for Barclays Bank in Manchester, at first refused to print. Oliver and I were invited to a party at Merry Hall, where the

* *Brian Howard: Portrait of a Failure*

garden had been planted, so it was said, with flowers bought that morning from a florist; and the flowers in the salon, so it was also said, had been sprayed with eau-de-cologne. We were stationed in different parts of the room and told not to move. Waistcoated and sweating, we obeyed, the cynosure of a few jaundiced neighbouring eyes, knocking back champagne cocktails. It was like being massaged with sweet poison. Greer Garson was there.

Godfrey Winn

A youthful fan and sycophant of Beverley Nichols, the two of them grew to loathe each other.* Godfrey was as mean a host as Beverley was generous: boy, could he eke out the risotto at his parties on the top floor of that big house he owned in Ebury Street. Godfrey had become a national figure as a broadcaster and columnist by means of a little talent which, he often said, he polished very hard so that it earned him a lot of money. Like many homosexuals he was physically brave, having been frostbitten on an Arctic convoy, and he had written a book about it, *PQ 17*, which became a sort of classic. Photographs of sailors and, for he was fearfully loyal, of the children to whom he was godfather abounded on the top floor.

His real skill lay in (his own) public relations, an expression that did not then exist. Every time Godfrey broadcast, the entire crew would be remembered, their names correctly spelled on boxes of chocolates for the boys and flowers for the girls.† When Godfrey picked me up he imagined I was an exotic from Malaya or somewhere. He was disappointed to discover I was just 'Neville Blond's boy'. Nevertheless, this fact did not deter him from telling me the scenario he had planned for my seduction: he would play tennis with me, win, strip me and have me on the baseline. I only hope his tennis-court wasn't a hard one.

---

*   cf. *All About Eve*.

†   I now advise socially ambitious young men to send postcards acknowledging any hospitality, on the strength of which they can travel the world.

Noël Coward

As a boy and as a young man I was never handsome and indeed suffered so from acne (that most humiliating of all afflictions) that I must have been, as I thought I was, positively unattractive. Once I spent a night at Churchill's nightclub listening to a woman tell me how ugly I was until the arrival of the morning newspapers. I suppose I might have passed as a *joli laid*, but I was fearful of carnal relations and convinced I lacked appeal, until one day, when crossing Piccadilly with Michael Codron (Piccadilly gets crossed twice in this section), I confessed as much. Michael turned to me and very kindly said, 'Nonsense, you ooze sex!' How often the impromptu and unremembered (by them) remarks of others change one's life. I now became a flirt.

Alan Pryce-Jones, the very social *quondam* editor of *The Times Literary Supplement*, gave a party in the Mansion in Albany for Maria St Just. Out of the corner of my eye I spotted Noël Coward.* Out of fifty or so guests, I alone did not approach him, but I did hang in there. He fell over, whether by design I know not, and I rushed to pick him up and dust him down. He said, 'I suppose I had better take you to lunch at the Caprice.' That he did. Naturally he ordered a dry martini. 'Just let the gin and the vermouth cross Piccadilly together, barely touching.'

Having netted Coward, I really didn't know what to do with him, though it was clear what he wanted to do with me. Meanly, I never let him. So I just decided to show him off in Chester Row. At that moment in time my permanent houseguest was a voluptuous blue-eyed and golden-haired young girl who had come for the night and had refused to leave.† She stayed long enough to move from aged seventeen to eighteen; yet when I suggested to her that at her age it wasn't suitable for her to be living with someone of mine, she replied, 'You never said that to me when I was seventeen.' She

---

* Ken Tynan on Noël Coward: 'Hollow as a lemon, taut as a monolith, gracious as a Royal bastard.'
† When Andrew McCall moved into Chester Row, my father attempted to advise me on my lifestyle: 'You know why Noël Coward never got anywhere!'

advanced towards him, her large (cold) blue eyes vast with wonder and said, 'Are you Noël Coward?' Coward nodded. That was the end of that. He wrote, for nothing, the foreword to a book we published called *Les Folies du Music Hall*, and never forgot to send a Christmas card from his house, 'overlooking a tax haven'. A honey man.

Eddie Garrison

I met Eddie Garrison in Rome in the fifties when he was living at the Albergo d'Inghilterra, a favourite of the likes of Marguerite Yourcenar.* Eddie was the son of a central-heating tycoon from Detroit, who, finding him in bed with another young man, banished him. Eddie went to Rome, which was then cheap, subsisting on mama's bucks sent secretly in an envelope. He found a lover in a young priest from the Vatican, who spent his leaves with Eddie instead of with his sick mother, as supposed. One night, when he couldn't sleep, the priest noticed a brochure proclaiming that Garrison Inc. could heat anything from a greenhouse to a City Hall.

'You never told me,' he said to his lover in the morning.

'I didn't think you could possibly be interested, my dear. I'm certainly not.'

The priest explained to Eddie that it had been mooted that the Vatican should centrally heat itself; that a commission had been set up; that he knew the chairman; and that he, Eddie, should now write to his father asking for a percentage of any deal he might be able to arrange in Rome. Papa replied briefly, contemptuously, but in the affirmative. There would be no story had not Garrison Inc. secured part of the contract. Eddie moved to a larger room in the Albergo, though I never found out what happened to the priest. Perhaps he became one of those high-flying banking cardinals.

---

* Her *Memoirs of Hadrian* is among the cult books, along with Mary Renault's accounts of 'upper-class buggery' set against the background of ancient Greece.

Philip Laski

Philip Laski was a queen with a family connection: he was our cousin. He even dressed like a black sheep: a walking stick, a fancy waistcoat, a buttonhole, and a velvet collar covered with dandruff. He was full of deceit and extraordinary tales, having married a Bourbon princess in Barcelona Cathedral during the war, and astonishing connections, many of which worked, like ringing up Laurence Olivier from my office. He was a fixer.

The family tried to have him certified just after the war, but he seduced the psychiatrist with petrol coupons for his Rolls-Royce. He could also supply butter. Befriended by a cousin of the King of Morocco, also a homosexual, he toured the museums of that country, borrowing large *objets* to 'photograph', which he then sold, having broken them into manageable bits, to antique dealers in London.

Philip also behaved badly enough with the local lads to be summoned by the chief of police, who told him to drop his trousers. A bottle of beer was then shoved up his arse. He was handed a ticket for the plane home and told, 'The next time, Mr Laski, the bottle will be broken.' He even had the chutzpah to write a letter of complaint to Neil Pearson, who was chairman of the Campaign for Homosexual Equality, who showed it to me. I just shook my head. His distinguished sister, Marghanita – whose real name, said Philip, was Esther – would only see him when she was dying.

Daniel Sykes

Daniel Sykes married, in 1962, Bridget Chetwynd, mother of one of my oldest and most loved friends, Tom, which is how I knew him. Daniel was a fully-paid-up remittance man: paid to stay away.

With his dyed hair, fluty voice and extravagant gestures, he was a fifties' queen in his forties. His style was not unique but is now extinct. He was also a painter and had been the boyfriend *en titre* of John Minton, a famous painter and illustrator, and a sort of star of the auction room. Daniel and Bridget Chetwynd, a cocktail novelist of repute, were both registered heroin addicts of long standing. Even in his lifetime Daniel was a fairy Black Prince of comic catastrophe. Once, when he was in the money, he bought a Rolls-Royce convertible, which he parked with the hood down on the Embankment to show off to a friend in an apartment above. An appreciative crowd gathered, but then somebody jumped into the driver's seat, pressed the starter and drove it away.* The car was never seen again. And of course, it was not insured.

A later motor car of Daniel's was a shaky, open two-seater Triumph, in which Bridget and he set off to visit Rupert Chetwynd, her elder son, who lived in an elegant eighteenth-century clapboard house near Faversham in Kent. The journey took them three days, during which the pair must have suffered withdrawal symptoms. Fifty years ago, when there were only a few hundred registered heroin addicts, the dose was allocated on a weekly basis; and the week began, as everybody knew, at one minute past midnight on Sunday at Boots in Piccadilly.† The deprived pair arrived at Faversham's highest-class dispensing chemist and presented their prescription. They were asked to wait and patiently they did. Finally, the chief chemist announced that there was not enough er . . . er . . . in the whole of East Kent to fill their prescription.

The Sykeses lived in Dolphin Square in a flat with minimalist décor; the carpet consisted of back numbers of the *Observer*. On the walls of the sitting-room were several families of rats, live in their cages. Both Daniel and Bridget were dedicated chain smokers and spent quite a lot of the day courteously lighting each other's cigarettes. When Daniel dropped a lit match on the carpet the conflagration was speedy. The couple had to make their exit into the inimical corridors of what was then Europe's largest block of flats, followed by – because they are not the sort of animals to tolerate being burned alive – their rats.

---

*   An easy thing to do in a thirties' Rolls-Royce, as I know from my 1934 Barker-bodied Sedanca de Ville. But that was when I had money.
†   Addicts were on a Home Office list that entitled each to an adequate and inevitably increasing dose of a high quality.

The Sykeses found another flat – though not in Dolphin Square – and gave my name as a reference to the estate agent, whom I am happy to name and shame as Messrs Willetts of Sloane Square. I was foolish and thoughtless enough to qualify my recommendation with the sort of cautionary note which prompted the agents to decline the Sykeses' candidature. Daniel told me of this without the faintest whiff of rancour. I wrote off a furious letter and received an apology.

About the time that Daniel died, the Home Office abolished the practice of supplying heroin to registered addicts – it is rumoured that in the fullness of time he had progressed from number thirty-three to number one on the list. A few weeks after Daniel died, Bridget, having hoarded some pills, committed suicide. A broken heart coupled with the withdrawal of a precious, and to her vital, drug?

George Hayim

I first met George with Tony Heckstall-Smith, whom he had picked up, not in the Navy, where he had remained glued to the lower-deck during the war, but in the Boeuf Sous Le Toit, a queer bar in London.

The Hayims were originally from Baghdad, which ranked at the turn of the twentieth century, with Provence in the twelfth century and Toledo before the expulsion of the Jews, as one of the golden havens of the diaspora. Of course it collapsed – Jewish history really *does* repeat itself – and George's mother's family moved to Shanghai where they prospered, even unto owning a racecourse. During the war, both his father and mother, Mimi, were caught by the Japanese and interned; but Mimi's French maid (Japan was not at war with France) bullied the camp commandant into letting them both go on the grounds that her mistress had been constipated for three weeks.

Mimi and maid, now back in London, settled into Claridges for the duration. In 1944, Mimi received, via Switzerland, an instruction from her husband – who still happened to be in the internment camp in Shanghai – to toddle along to Cartier, sell her diamonds and invest the proceeds in Japanese war bonds. Many of Mimi's friends said that he had gone mad, to which she replied that although she never liked him, mad he was not. She did as she was told.

Papa Hayim appreciated that however low the fortunes of Japan might sink – their sun was indeed about to disappear below the horizon – that nation would never renege. In the fullness of time the bonds were redeemed at par, and Papa Hayim, who had bought for pennies, now sold for pounds.

Then they all started to die. First the maid was found dead in Mimi's bath in the Excelsior ('Oh why couldn't she die in her own bath?'), followed by Mimi herself and the rest of the family. George was left alone in the world with thousands of tax-paid dollars per month, together with a bunch of trustees he immediately sued as far as the House of Lords. 'I lost,' said George cheerfully.

I like to think that I helped in the outcome. For one year, George, who had made an annual duty-call to see his father, announced that he could no longer face the ordeal. His distaste for the aged parent was such that on sight of him he had to rush to the loo and throw up. I said that this was not a good enough excuse: that Jewish law decreed one must honour one's father and mother, but said nothing about their being honourable. In this case a visit was worth a vomit. George went and his father died, leaving some but not, as had been the threat, all of his money to Israel.

Though not, by contemporary standards, an achiever, in the eighteenth century (when the concept of 'the idle rich' was meaningless) George would have been considered a man of parts: he is both ruthless and effective in pursuit of his own convenience, using every weapon, including the power of prayer. When George's last obsession, a Lebanese, settled in Sydney, he bought a semi-detached house in the undistinguished suburb of Cremorne, of a style one would see in a seaside town like Rhyl. He recognised that if only he could have the other half and 'lose' the party walls, a decent dwelling would emerge. So he prayed daily for the demise of the elderly lady who was his close neighbour.

God, who E. F. Schumacher once assured me has a sense of humour, which, as we are created in His image, will vice versa include the macabre, obliged. For one day, before his very eyes, the old lady was hit by a truck when crossing the road and killed. George immediately rang up his solicitor and instructed him to buy.

*   *   *

'The Souvenir' was a token from Australia, a young man I picked up there and brought back with me to London. This name for him was, I believe, an invention of Jennifer Paterson's, whose cuisine then was only known to, and patronised by, the *Spectator*, Milo Cripps and myself.

My part-time employer, Adrian Bridgewater, had invented a charity for the employment of graduates, which was so successful that it had to be, expensively and profitably, privatised. Moreover, he was pleased enough with my efforts – I have forgotten what they were – to invite me to accompany him on a freebie to Sydney. Thither we flew, first class on Qantas, with Lord and Lady Glenavy, aka Patrick Campbell, both of whom I had published. Their freebie was even freer because at every staging point an official vehicle roared up the tarmac to the aeroplane to shuttle them, grinning triumphantly, to an official lunch, tea or dinner. Adrian and I, on the other hand, received a bronze plate and a *flacon* of orchids every three thousand miles, together with a refill of Moët & Chandon every five hundred miles.

My partner Desmond Briggs, who knew Sydney, had enjoined me – and the word is precise for he was a magistrate – on no account to go 'up the Cross', a dangerous *quartier*, especially to one of my proclivities. Of course, I booked in there to a modest hotel. Adrian gave me a sleeping-pill to counteract the effect of twenty-four hours of travail/travel, but I went out for a bottle of vodka, deeming alcohol the better drug. It was. I felt fine and set off in pursuit of the love only too willing to declare its name 'up the Cross'. I found him on a bench. He smiled. I held out my hand and he took it. We walked back to my hotel.

Though I had signed John Lennon's advertisement in *The Times* advocating the legalisation of cannabis, I had little knowledge of drugs, other than nicotine and alcohol, but I registered that Kevin was pretty stoned on something.

We were happy together for two days and then he went, as they say, 'walkabout'. One morning he was no longer there. Richard Neville, protagonist of the *Trials of Oz* by Tony Palmer, which we also published, asked me on to his chat show. I told him about my adventure and he sympathised, explaining that Australia was essentially homosexual because when staking out the land a man had to hold on to the piece of wood the other man was hammering in. Good enough. I appealed on air for Kevin to return, giving the grander hotel where I had re-located. He returned that night and the carousel, as it were, regurgitated . . .

Kevin now wanted to go to, as he called it, 'UK'. Flights were full. I, therefore, leant on a gay travel agent and a bona fide passenger was pushed off my plane. Kevin travelled with me, tourist, *bien entendu*. Oh dear.

So what next? I already had a male domestic associate who would not have tolerated another. The enterprise was foolhardy and could go seriously wrong; but I presented Kevin to Milo and the angels sang. Milo instantly adopted Kevin, together with his loud music, with such intensity that he wrote an arcane and unpublishable book on Kevin's addiction. Nevertheless, he bought enough shares in Moog Synthesisers, then floating, to make a fortune. Kevin kicked his habit, met a girl, married her, had children, became a friend of my wife, and is now a businessman on the West Coast. He remains the apple of Milo's eye and his heir.

Did I do wrong?

*   *   *

Whilst the most immaculate and oft recited sexual triangle of our times must surely be that of Strachey-Partridge-Carrington, my own version was more disorderly and obviously less illustrious. It was contrived by a lady novelist, and had two endings – one tragic, the other happy.

Desmond Briggs had bought a novel by Cressida Lindsay, who lived in Notting Hill Gate (then not so salubrious) and who was the granddaughter of Norman Lindsay, Australia's first famous bohemian. She was equally bohemian in outlook and had three children by three different men. When she met me she decided I was to serve as papa no. 4. She stalked me with delicacy. Her current lover, papa no. 3, was a gypsy and a poet called Mark Hyatt. He was beautiful. In the letter she sent me* she included a photograph of Mark. A sensuous poetic face, tender lips, eyes you could swim in and a faultless nose. He is wearing a straw hat with an ostrich feather round the brim, a white satin shirt with lace-trimmed collar and an open velvet waistcoat. The fancy gear was a perquisite from his profession, that of being 'on the knocker'. All he needed was a cart and a nice smile. Mark Hyatt had both. Of course, as arranged, I fell for him. He couldn't write, but with a dictionary and Cressida's typewriter, poems emerged; they were very precious, and are mostly lost or in some Penguin anthology. Our affair lasted as long as we wanted it to. Cressida waited.

Mark led a rackety life. He rang me up once from the prison in Dover. On the seat of a railway carriage in France he had found fifty thousand old francs, which customs had found on him. The customs officers at Dover were notoriously hostile to writers. He was instantly put in the slammer. He said it was because he wasn't wearing a tie. I told Jean Genet, who had also had a hard time with the British customs, this story and said that he must have a tie. 'Même si je la porte à la main?' he enquired in his squeaky voice.

I asked Mark why he had told the customs of what was not a crime in France but was in England. 'What?' he said. 'Me with five hundred pounds' worth of LSD stuffed up my arse?' We, or rather Anthony Rubinstein, got him out. Cressida got her man – me. The fruit of our affair was our son, Aaron. That day Andrew McCall moved into my house in Chester Row. Writing this now, I feel a bit of a shit, but it didn't seem wrong at the time.

Cressida wanted to live in the country, little Aaron having

---

* 'You have my consent to include my participation in your affair with Mark and also my permission to mention the fact that I manoeuvred the situation in such a way that by coming to know Mark, you might eventually notice me!'

been nearly immolated by a lorry in Notting Hill Gate; so I bought her an old rectory, called the Old Rectory, in Norfolk. Mark ended up with a tall young man called Atom, who lived in Burnley. They appeared to be devoted to each other. But one day Atom announced that he was going to leave Mark and live with a girl. Mark bought a jar of aspirins, found a cave – yes, a *cave* in Burnley – and went on eating them until he died.

I was staying at the Old Rectory when Atom came to tell us. He cradled Dylan, Mark's son by Cressida, in his arms and they both cried. Then we went for a picnic by a lake. Atom ran round and round the lake till he dropped down from exhaustion – a marathon penitent.

The homosexual world, which I have been in but never of, is full of natural affection but is not a natural state. The belief that man is made for woman still dominates most of the world. Mark Hyatt was too beautiful, too passionate to live in it for long. His death was a classic of homosexual life.

CHAPTER TWENTY-ONE

Andrew McCall

When we first met I had a house on Ithaca, a charmless, cursed little rock which took three days to get to – from anywhere – and was not much fun when you arrived. Ithaca was the least promising of the Ionian islands which had been mandated to the British – having belonged to Venice and then briefly Napoleon – at the Treaty of Paris and given to the new Kingdom of Greece forty-nine years later.

The absence of anything agreeable on Ithaca, except the sun in the morning and the moon at night, turned most people off; except of course George Devine, the first director of the Royal Court Theatre under my father, to whom I lent my concrete box. He approved of the simplicity and lack of food, and told me it was the best holiday of his life.

It didn't suite Andrew at all who was rebuked for doing the Charleston in bare feet by our neighbour, an ex-jam manufacturer from Newcastle, Australia. This tiresome Greek had, like anybody who could stand up in the island, emigrated and returned to gloat over those who had not . . . 'The mode has not yet reached Stavros,' he said. Stavros was a one-donkey village, with a view Odysseus might have admired, but otherwise of no interest whatsoever, except that I, the only foreigner, had a house there.

Andrew had sniffed out the fleshpots of Corfu. (Certainly forty years ago there were few more agreeable places in which to recreate and create.) He was a beautiful, pleasure-loving young man with no ambition other than to continue as he was and smoke twenty cigarettes a day from a round tin, which appeared to be his only luggage. Nevertheless he was determined about one thing: to find the best place on the island, and if this involved having to learn demotic Greek in order to bully and cajole the Corfiots, then that he would do.

The Ropa Valley is – or was – a flat marshy plain lived in by mosquitoes and wild horses, and bounded to the west by rather high mountains and to the east by three lower hills. On the middle of these hills was a Venetian farmhouse, with its own separate chapel and a hundred and seventeen enormous olive trees, which had grown tall because for a hundred years or so nobody had bothered to prune them. Indeed the whole property – including huge olive press, piggeries and cowsheds – had been uninhabited since 1944, when the proprietor and his young pregnant mistress had been murdered. The estate agent who was showing him round the island maintained, when Andrew spotted the likely site, that no house was there and anyway no road. 'Then,' said Andrew, 'we will walk.'

Centuries of occupation have made lying (or, more kindly, reluctance to help the authorities with their enquiries) first, not second, nature to the Greeks. And it was through a child, miming a killing with a decrepit rifle, that we discovered the true story of Spanopoulos – the place of the (rare) bird, our house. The last owner was a widower and a certain age; he had taken unto himself a girl, possibly a servant from the now abandoned nunnery in the little valley below, whom had got with child. His three grown-up daughters, who were all married, feared that if a child were born, an inheritance would vanish – Corfu had belonged long enough to the French for the Code Napoléon to apply – so hit men were hired to deal with the matter, under the guise of Maquis avenging collaborators.

The house took time to restore and Andrew became, with his intransigence and addiction to straight lines, like the Duchess of Marlborough. The olive press was a banqueting hall, the cowsheds a saloon, the piggeries appointed for the sort of guests who would never go to bed; apropos of which, if guests didn't suit, since charter flights were then only fortnightly, one was stuck.

One such was Jennifer Paterson,* who had kindly offered, at a time when the house was still not yet finished, to take over the

* *Private Eye*, that organ of righteousness, told of the following alleged encounter between Andrew McCall and Jennifer Paterson. Jennifer is

cooking. Cars had to be left out of sight – an essential restriction I believe – so that the last steps had to be made on foot, and in the process Jennifer fell and severely sprained her ankle. Instead of her feeding us, we had to feed her.

In return for our attentions, she promised, with the assistance of some American Express traveller's cheques, to take us all out to a memorable meal in the town. When strong enough, Jennifer accompanied us to the beach for a paddle and, with her handbag over her shoulder, for she did not trust the natives, she entered the Ionian Sea. She again slipped and fell.

Now American Express has thought of everything. Suppose a passenger aircraft were to crash into the Pacific, near, say, Guam – a place indeed only visited by aircraft – the company could not risk the possibility of predatory local fishermen snuffling through the sodden wreckage for the wallets of rich tourists with traveller's cheques. An element was therefore introduced which, on contact with the water, caused the appearance of the letters V O I D on the cheques. And so bang went Miss Paterson's beano.

Andrew and I became friends of our neighbours, Christopher and Elizabeth Glenconner, with whom we arranged picnics on parts of the island untouched by development.* This frequency of intercourse attracted the pen of the writer Simon Raven, whose ink was increasingly mixed with vitriol and lubricity. His last memoir, *Is There Anybody There? Said the Traveller*, pullulated with scenes of such libellous nastiness that Andrew and I and Guy Nevill, 'heir to a fine marquisate', sued. The book was suppressed and we all received settlements out of court, though the 'heir' rather more than us, which Simon, with whom I remained on

---

bien enrobée, as the French say so prettily, and only dressed fashionably when the sack was the rage.

> ANDREW: Really, Jennifer, you should take yourself in hand, your bum is so wobbly.
> JENNIFER: While yours of course, dear, is so taut . . . yes, and who taught it?

* The accessible coast was already beginning to fill up with the sort of tourist who loves Benidorm.

lunching terms throughout, regarded as only right and proper. My indignation, however, was directed towards the publisher – Frederick Muller, then an imprint of Century Hutchinson – who had not bothered to have the book read for libel. By this time Andrew had sold Spanopoulos rather well. Yet I learned later that the olive groves had been cut down 'by mistake'.

PART FIVE

Multimedia

CHAPTER TWENTY-TWO

Piccadilly Radio

Neil Pearson was married to Ruth, the first eccentric I ever met. I liked her because she treated me like a grown-up at the age of eight. Her mother lived next to a graveyard whose flowers she was said to plunder when she had a dinner party, which was rather wild behaviour for North Cheshire in the thirties. Ruth herself was impatient with convention and after a tiff would roar through the genteel shops of Knutsford demanding, 'Has anyone seen my lover?'

She didn't like to be bored. At one of her dinner parties, when Sir Bernard Lovell was at the table, she decided to go to bed, made for the door and, spinning on her heel with all the dignity of a tipsy lady, said, 'And by the way, Bernard, fuck your telescope!' Neil just smiled.

Neil Pearson was a senior partner in an ancient Manchester firm of solicitors and his speciality was international arbitration. He would discover, for instance, that an Italian contractor and the Lebanese Minister of Public Works, whom the former wished to sue, both liked Bach, and settle the dispute that way. A just, dry, tolerant man, respected and devoid of avarice and envy, he was chairman of the Campaign for Homosexual Equality, an office that might have embarrassed anyone else.

In the early seventies Edward Heath had given the nod to the concept of independent radio, disregarding the conspiracy between the BBC and the Post Office, who maintained there was no further room on the air. London began to buzz with consortia planning to present themselves for the first swathe of franchises: two in London and one each in Birmingham, Manchester, Liverpool and Glasgow.

I have always preferred radio to television as a medium, believing, in a phrase I have yet to place, that 'radio has more to offer than meets the eye'; moreover, I enjoyed the mildly anarchic concept of every district having its own radio station. And why not? With an aerial the length of a clothes-line, a transmitter as powerful as a small electric stove, a microphone and a bunch of old 78s, one could create a radio station; indeed this equipment, plus a dog, a bottle of rum and a pack of cigarettes, was all that one station from which I broadcast in Trinidad possessed. Perhaps Lord Reith had perverted, with his imposition of national radio (so valuable for propaganda in a war) and with his commissionaires and Brylcreemed gents reading the news in their plummy voices, what was naturally a *local* medium. I dreamed of a man leaning out of a window with a microphone in his hand describing a smash-and-grab raid in the street below.*

My first move, therefore, was to approach a dentist who headed up a group he called Capital Radio, which would apply for the number-one spot on the dial – the music station for London. I booked the business room at the Reform Club and made my pitch. The dentist can't have been impressed for he sent me a letter saying that as a publisher I was ineligible to apply for a franchise under the act. *Music* publishers were indeed so, but I thought that if he had confused me with Tin Pan Alley – much more lucrative and quite as respectable – he must be a *Dummkopf* and wouldn't get any-where. How wrong I was.

In the end Capital Radio, stiffened by John Whitney, who became the instant doyen of this new profession, won the franchise and the dentist retired to a Swiss Alp to count his money. I complained to John Thompson, in charge of radio at the IBA and an old friend who, when editor of *Time and Tide*,† had given me my first proper assignment as a journalist. (I went to do a profile on Southend and was poisoned by an oyster I ate on an August Bank Holiday; the article was interesting enough to provoke the town

---

* This became a reality, especially in places such as Liverpool where smash-and-grab has become a way of life.
† At the time owned by a rich clergyman, Reverend Tim, later Lord, Beaumont.

clerk to sue.) John said that everybody was after London and why didn't I go for Manchester, which is where I came from, wasn't it? The only serious candidate was the *Manchester Evening News*.

'Only?' I said.

At least a chairman sprang to mind in the form of Neil Pearson. He agreed, not with alacrity, because alacrity was not one of his characteristics, but agreed nevertheless, though he was on the Regional Advisory Council of the BBC. From then on, the austere eighteenth-century farmhouse of the Pearsons, outside Knutsford and a few minutes from the aerodrome I had known as Ringway,* became the HQ of the consortium. With its old red-tiled floor, décor and mod cons frozen in the thirties, it was the setting for a plot. Appropriately there was no television. The only warm room was the kitchen, with its vast Aga and patient bottles of claret braced for an attack.

Ruth had a daughter called simply 'H': the result of a roll in the hay with a person or persons unknown. She was spare, half-sharp, and, like all mentally disadvantaged people I have met, self-obsessed: her continual daily concern was her bowel movements, or the lack of these, which she would describe to her mother at length every morning. Ruth, short-fused with everyone else, listened with saintly patience. H's husband was a railway clerk who wore a tightly buttoned blue suit and pullover, in all weathers, and a NUR badge stuck in his lapel. He had read *Bradshaw* with the concentration of a Jehovah's Witness on the Bible. And I had to pretend to want to go to Porthcawl from Macclesfield on a Sunday. He didn't seem to notice I had a car.

We also needed a bank. I had met difficulties – strange in retrospect – in raising money for this enterprise. Rich young Lord Hesketh had entertained me to lunch† with his *équipe* at the Westbury Hotel but seemed to be only interested in a station if it

---

* I had my first flight for five bob at Ringway before the Second World War.

† He asked that the bones be removed from his chicken curry, a detail of gastronomic fastidiousness which took some audacity.

were called Radio Hesketh. I had a more successful lunch at the
Ritz where I took Norman Quick, whose father had imported the
first Ford car into England and had the concession for the north-
west. He wrote me a cheque for five hundred pounds – walking
money for me to muster the consortium – but we needed proper
money to show the application. Norman's money gave me the
necessary funds to hire Michael Peacock.

When I met him, through my friend Michael Briggs, Michael
Peacock was the cleverest player and thinker in the communica-
tions game. He was also unemployed, though he had produced
Panorama, controlled BBC2 and so forth, and was therefore
prepared, for an embarrassingly small fee, to contrive a document
on the potential of a commercial radio station in the north-west.
The document was masterly. It convinced the newspapers to join
our consortium and even impressed Granada. Michael later
joined the board and became our guru. Wise in counsel, eloquent
and persuasive, at ease with both government and big business,
sure – perhaps he had been too sure – of himself, he quickly
became enough of a friend for me to invite his son to join mine
for a week on a Thames barge. It rained solidly in the estuary for
a week, and the children (as I called them) never once ventured
on deck, but spent the time smoking pot and playing poker.
Michael has since become successful again and has made a fortune
out of management-training videos with the comic actor John
Cleese.

Like many Jews with literary pretensions, I just couldn't have
remained in the north and had had to leave for London. One
wouldn't have got very far with a literary agency in Deansgate. I
may have left my roots, but brother Peter, though he lived in
Belgravia, still had a factory in Wigan and knew the score in
Manchester. He said I should go and see John Foster. Sir John
Foster, MP for Northwich, was, among many other things, the
chairman of the Northern Commercial Trust, which belonged to
the Lever brothers, Harold and Leslie, also both MPs but in the
Labour interest. Although, or perhaps because, he was a foundling,
Sir John had been one of the youngest ever fellows of All Souls and

had rocketed to fame as a lawyer. He was a legend for probity, refusing, for instance, to declare the Scientologists* illegal, as suggested by the Home Office. Comfortingly, though dauntingly, incorruptible, he was very social, a ladies' man, was suspicious of the police, and had a very soft spot for Jews.

Sir John was affable and reminiscent, and did not seem to be pressed for time: a characteristic, I have noticed, of many great men. Although a Conservative politician, I sensed his heart was on the left. He was pleased that I was on the committee of the National Council for Civil Liberties (as it was then sensibly called), and told me how, as a young lawyer, he had accompanied a chief inspector on a raid of the Communist Party's HQ, at the time of the Cable Street conspiracy, in search of incriminating documents. He had asked the chief inspector if he was sure he would find any. 'Quite sure,' he replied, tapping his overcoat, 'I have them here.' Sir John told me to see Sidney Friedland, of the Northern Commercial Trust, the next time I was in Manchester; he was, he added, 'very *frum*'.

Not some but most of Sir John's best friends appeared to be Jews; one of them was Sidney Bernstein, chairman of Granada Television (the 'Voice of the North'), with whom he said he would also have a word. Then he led me downstairs and escorted me to my car. Just before calling on Sir John I had swapped my black Lincoln Continental convertible, the sort of car favoured by comedians and pop stars, for that dark green Rover saloon issued to directors of the Bank of England. I added a chrome rod designed to display the sort of flag to which two-star generals are entitled and covered it with a leather sheath. For good measure I left a copy of *Moriarty's Police Law* in the back window, plus a tightly rolled

---

* This extraordinary sect had bought Saint Hill, which my stepmother rented during the Second World War. The locals were uneasy about them, but the shopkeepers liked their business. When L. Ron Hubbard's great yacht turned up in Corfu one winter, I told the man in charge of tourism, who also ran the casino, that they were not 'a good idea', to which he answered, 'Maybe, but at this time of year no one else is spending a thousand pounds a week on vegetables.'

umbrella on the back seat: thus ensuring *carte blanche* for any official car park. I noticed Sir John's approval.

Though a lumbering, stooped, beetle-browed figure, Sir John was quick on his feet. Sidney Bernstein not only agreed to put in money but also suggested Granada fund (and therefore takeover) the application. H'm. I checked with John Thompson whether the IBA would approve the involvement of Granada in a Manchester radio station. The answer was OK, but not to any great extent. Ha.

I had had a dust-up with Lord Bernstein before. He was also a publisher, owning the paperback house Panther, where William Miller was the editor.* He coveted our Blond Educational list, which was as successful as the general imprint, though not as much fun; moreover, he wanted it without me. (Tom Maschler had apparently told him I was a playboy.) We broke off talks and sold the business lock, stock and barrel to CBS for a decent sum. I sent a case of Krug to Sidney as a *douceur*; needless to say its receipt went unacknowledged.

Sidney Friedland sat on the edge of my bed in my modest room at the Midland Hotel in Manchester. He listened carefully to my tale, which included the Lord Bernstein saga, and then uttered in his uncompromising Cheadle accent one of the sweetest sentences I had ever heard: 'We'll lend yer the money,† Anthony. That'll tweak Sidney's nose for him.'

At the first full meeting of the consortium, Lord Bernstein sat at one end of the board-table (his) and John Gould, founder of the Writers' Guild, sat me firmly down at the other. (Neil Pearson, who was often away arbitrating, took an Olympic view of these proceedings and was happy to let me conduct the day-to-day affairs, as he called them). John Gould, of blessed memory, for he died soon after of cancer of the throat, was a natural Hampden and

---

* Lord Bernstein was left-wing, patriarchal but chummy, hence the following exchange at a board meeting of Panther Books:
    BERNSTEIN: William, will you please call me Sidney.
    WILLIAM: No, Lord Bernstein, I will not call you Sidney.
† One hundred and sixty thousand pounds.

disapproved of tyrants. Sidney addressed us as if we were junior executives of a company he had just taken over and described his plan to acquire the franchise. Signalled by John, who could hardly speak, but had noticed my irritation, I rose to say that grateful as we were to Lord Bernstein for his hospitality, if it were apparent that Granada were controlling our application, or had more than a modest shareholding (the eight-per-cent figure suggested by John Thompson), our enterprise would be doomed. The IBA, we knew, would not tolerate a radio station in Manchester dominated by Granada Television. This was a line of argument to which Bernstein was unused and, since he was equally unaccustomed to conceal his displeasure, it provoked a slanging match. (Jews have not the Anglo-Saxon distaste for public scenes: indeed they enjoy them.) I had known Lord Bernstein, as Simon Marks once said of Mike Todd, 'for a thousand years': a patriarchal bully, big-hearted, loyal if you loved him, and not wholly scrupulous. Of course, I admired him and wanted him desperately to admire me, and indeed used his appearance as the model for the hero, Sir Ezra Sterling, in my novel *Family Business*.

I was also determined that our little barque should not flounder on the rocks of his ego. On this point *Private Eye* printed a neat story, presumably from a disaffected employee. Driving through the dense rain on the M6, Sidney's Rolls-Royce stopped for petrol. He lowered the electric window and demanded to see the manager in order to complain about the graphics. 'Ah, piss off,' came the response from the attendant, 'this is a Forte!'

A few of us were selected as a working party for the next meeting, sited neutrally in the Midland Hotel. Sidney did not attend but fielded his brother Cecil Bernstein. All the members' names were neatly typed on cards, except mine. I wrote one out for myself and sat down quietly, but afterwards employed the 'screech factor' with Neil. Cecil was replaced by an amiable ex-brigadier, Sir Paul Bryan MP, also a director of Granada, who had run Sandhurst and was like most officers of field rank, mild and wise. When we were having trouble restraining Michael Winstanley, the popular face of Granada and a Liberal politician, whom I had recruited with the object of covering the field, Paul advised us to 'overwhelm him with papers . . . '

Any application to the IBA for a franchise had to be financially sound, show technical and administrative competence in the constitution of the board of directors, and on air reflect the interests of the community: we saw the emergence of a new buzz word, 'accountability'. In the next months I busied myself concocting a convincing document, which Granada again tried to takeover, putting up a numbskull whom they eventually fired. I trolled the minorities of Manchester: the Gays of both sexes (less sure of themselves than they are now), the Pakistanis, the Gujaratis and even the Chinese, united only in their dislike of each other and their wish to be broadcast to in English.* Weekends were now spent at Neil's farmhouse, where he modestly let me rehearse him for the crucial interview with the IBA.

I played the aggressive and disbelieving members of their board and he our chairman. Sometimes I overacted and Neil, the gentlest of men, was upset. We had passed the first hurdle, which eliminated the eccentrics, and were into the finals with the *Manchester Evening News*, the odds-on favourite, whom I had encircled with the *Rochdale Observer*, the *Bolton Evening News* and the *Altrincham* and *Warrington Guardians*. We also had someone from the Co-op and two women, Dame Kathleen Ollerenshaw, a deaf mathematician who would become leader of the Conservative opposition in Manchester and lord mayor, and Mary Mason, who was an old girlfriend of Neil's and was now wife to the irritable and belligerent high master of Manchester Grammar School.

Then occurred a turn-up for the books in the form of Philip Birch, who had run the pirate station Radio London and had failed in Associated Newspapers' bid for the London news station. He announced he was prepared to be our managing director. He had a high but correct opinion of his value to us as an experienced Englishman in this new medium. (London was awash with former

---

* David Harlech once told me the Welsh despised programmes in their own language. I wasn't convinced. Maybe they just despised programmes.

executives in commercial radio from Canada, Lourenço Marques, Luxembourg, et cetera.) Norman Quick, Paul Bryan and I, having interviewed him, shared this view of him. Nevertheless, Norman, who admired American business methods, said we should first take a look at Mrs Birch, to which Paul and I said 'no', which was fortunate as she turned out to be a bit potty and was soon replaced by another Mrs Birch. In addition to his salary and share of the profits in the draft agreement for his employment, Philip told me that what he really wanted was a pink private aeroplane. I said that I knew enough of my native Manchester to be sure that such an object, of whatever colour, was not on, and that I would do him a favour and not mention his request.

Encouraged by a glass or two of champagne – the prescription of the late David Webster to be taken before any interview – served in Norman Quick's room in the nearby Hyde Park Hotel, we filed into the IBA's little theatre in their offices opposite Harrods. The chairman, Lord Blackstone, thanked us for coming all this way – in my case all the way from Sloane Square – and proceeded immediately to his first question. Would we please turn to page 85 of our application, section three, second paragraph: 'only *two* outside broadcasting vehicles'? My insides froze. I noticed John Thompson staring firmly at the ceiling. The question was a torpedo designed to sink us in one. They had gone straight for the small print. The interview was a formality: we were not being considered. But Neil did not blink. He gave the ghastly Blackstone an enchanting and understanding smile, thanked him for his welcome and for the opportunity to present to the chairman as well as to the other members of the IBA. He now introduced his team: 'Philip Birch, who has agreed to be managing director, with whose proven ability in this new field, of . . . er . . . independent radio the IBA must be familiar; Norman Quick, a foremost businessman and philanthropist in Manchester, the largest distributor of Ford motor cars in the United Kingdom and the managing director of the *Rochdale Observer*; our . . . er . . . banker, Sidney Freidland; Sir Paul Bryan, a parliamentarian who has been prominent in promoting the concept of independent radio; and finally [the joker in the pack, because every pack must have one] Anthony Blond, who, though he now lives in London, still, I know, has his heart in Manchester . . . ' (tolerant, deprecating of me, smiling – a perfect touch). At this point I imagined that Baroness Sharp gave me a complicit and not unfriendly glance.

Baroness Sharp was the only *mensch* at the IBA. We had met before. Parallel to my function in the Piccadilly consortium I had joined a group trying for the franchise in Birmingham – formerly one of the most corrupt cities in Europe, where it was a matter of local pride that local officials should end their terms of office with money in their pockets. Again, the front runner was the dominant newspaper in that city, the *Birmingham Post*, which gave every old-age pensioner a pudding for Christmas. We couldn't win: they had insinuated a spy on to our board and arranged for our bank support to be withdrawn. We also suffered from the participation of the Mecca chieftain and promoter of *Miss World*, Eric Morley, who told the IBA that he could easily commute from his London HQ to the radio station in Birmingham in his helicopter, and would personally pay for a pad. At the equivalent interview the baroness asked me, 'Mr Blond, I notice that you are also part of a consortium applying for Manchester. Which one did you want?' A cruel and clever question. Answer: 'Both.' (My only success in that grim city was to have parked my dark green Rover in the City Council's car park, with impunity.)

Neil rolled gently on, with an eloquence and persuasiveness I had never seen or guessed at. His speech was harmony itself and not a beat too long. When he had finished, leaving just enough time for a warm silence to suffuse the theatre, he turned to Blackstone and said briskly, as if there had been no interval between question and answer, 'With reference to page 85, section three, second paragraph . . . "only two outside broadcasting vehicles" . . . I should like to ask our technical director . . . ' But the IBA was no longer interested. We were not home and dry, but we were not floundering in the sea.

When we left, I was later told, a clerk was sent to get a copy of *Who's Who*; previously they had not bothered to check any of us out. John Thompson admitted that he had been encouraging me in the pursuit of the franchise because, as a good steward, he needed more than one horse in the race. Finally it emerged not only that we had won, but that the favourite had lost. Their chairman, Lord Hewlett, a self-made chemical tycoon, asked by the statutory left-wing member of the IBA how he handled a strike at his factory, had replied arrogantly that he had never had one and never would. That remark, apparently, lost him the franchise. Subsequently he was accused of having his fingers in the till and committed suicide by stabbing himself in the throat with a pair of scissors. Coincidentally, I heard this news on our radio station in the office of our managing director a few months later.

*   *   *

When John Thompson rang Neil to say our group had won the franchise, and Neil then first rang Philip, I should have realised my number was up. Thank you and goodbye was the message. I had entertained, of course, all sorts of ideas as to how the station should perform; perhaps slightly according to the noble sentiments of the application which I had so painstakingly composed. Philip was succinct. 'Piss off back to London,' he said, 'and get rich.'

When I was the lone standard-bearer, recruiting almost all the directors (far too many and, as it turned out, irrelevantly), Sir John Foster had suggested to Sidney that 'if this comes off something should be done for Blond'. (Oh dear, echoes of my father.) Sidney had – verbally – agreed. When it happened Sidney said that any recompense to me would have to be passed by his board of directors. Nonsense, John had replied. And so it was arranged that I be lent eighteen thousand pounds, interest free for three years, and that I acquire eight per cent of the equity, the same fraction as Granada. Had I been able – or, more to the point, mean and cautious enough – to hold on to this dollop, it would have been worth four million pounds ten years later when Owen Oyston bought the company.

Once upon a time *Picture Post* agreed to let me write an article, on what theme I can no longer recall, but I do remember the rage of the man in the features department in charge of me when I submitted my expenses. 'What do you mean by this?' he roared, pointing to an item of a penny-halfpenny for a bus fare. I replied that that had been the cost of a journey from Trafalgar Square to Fleet Street. He said, 'You took a taxi, journalists take taxis. Don't you forget that, son!' He then crossed out the offending item and inserted 'taxi, 3/6*d*.'. I was shocked, for though guilty of most of the seven deadly sins, avarice is not one of them.

Possibly because I have spent more of my time paying expenses than claiming them, the art of creative accountancy has never much mattered to me. The application costs of the eighty-six consortia, of which five were successful, were published and ours was the least. Neil arranged for me to be rewarded for my economy. Philip Birch and the new director of programmes, Colin Walters, both very tall men, were sending signals that it was bye-bye for little me and from that moment on, apart from changing the starting date of the station from 1 April to 2 April* and inaugurating the AIRC (Association of Independent Radio Companies) with a long memo nobody read, I had no dealings and no influence with the station. Were the promises of the application document to have been implemented, Piccadilly Radio would certainly have gone bust. So surely I was better out of it.

I retained ambitions radio-wise and commissioned from Simon Raven a pilot for a serial on the Crusades. Tom Jones, a pretty man (but so what on radio?) was to play the Crusader, Miriam Karlin a camp follower and Christopher Lee the cunning Sultan. It was lovely but nobody was interested. Only the BBC can afford radio plays. I lingered on shamelessly on the board of Piccadilly Radio through three other chairmen and two takeovers, rarely attending but taking my modest fee.

*   *   *

---

* I happened to be at the station on that April Fool's Day when the discovery of *The Tenth Man* – the property of MGM and subsequently published by me – made the front page of most newspapers internationally. Piccadilly Radio thought it was a joke but BBC Bush House rang up and, for fifteen minutes, I was famous.

I had met Owen Oyston through Ian Coulter, a sharp Scot, whose wife became the first lady chairman of the Reform Club. Owen, brought up in a Catholic orphanage in Newcastle, was definitely a card. He was the first estate agent to put properties on a computer and later sold his business to the Prudential just before the crash for millions. Owen appeared to want to buy our offices in Great Ormond Street and indicated that he thought Laura should be included in the deal. She thought otherwise but to show willing – times were bad – I prevailed upon my benevolent brother-in-law to invite him to shoot at Meols Hall. He showed up in his white convertible Rolls-Royce and his son shot a hare. This, in Waterloo Cup country, had the same effect as when Ribbentrop killed the keeper's pet Chinese pheasant at a shoot in Windsor before the war.

Owen began collecting radio stations. He created Red Rose in Preston and had another in Oswestry; but above all he coveted Piccadilly Radio and made heavy overtures, which our (third) chairman, an accountant, reported and resisted. We were planning a merger with Birmingham at the time, and Owen's bid was considered inopportune, though the IBA had ceased to care how independent stations behaved, provided only that they survived. Indifferent to our careful negotiations and supported by an invest-ment bank, his hostile bid rose and rose and rose every time we said no. It might have seemed that we were playing a clever game, but our board meetings grew more frequent and more hysterical. I longed for Neil. I was still a substantial enough shareholder for Owen to offer me fifteen thousand a year for life to change sides; but I reckoned there was a special spot in the Inferno for those who agreed to that sort of proposition. Owen then drove to see Desmond Briggs in Castle Combe late one night. His chauffeur was ushered into what, in a larger establishment, would have been the servants' hall and offered a cup of coffee. He said no thank you and could he return to the car, as he had to make some telephone calls. Owen also lobbied Andrew McCall, who also had shares. Both were impressed enough to stay in the company and not, as *I* did, cash them in, for the board collapsed and accepted his offer.

Ridiculous. At the first board meeting attended by Owen he proposed that the fees of the non-executive directors be halved. When the motion was unanimously passed, Owen buried his face in his hands and almost sobbed, 'Oh, now I feel *so* mean!'

It was difficult to dislike the man but some people managed to. I was summoned by the takeover panel of the London Stock Exchange to answer the rumour that he had tried to bribe me. I told the two Wykehamists – clones of the couple at MI6 who had asked me to spy on a Russian many moons ago – that I wouldn't say he had, and I wouldn't say he hadn't; but that if they pushed me formally I would deny it. I tried to explain to these polite young gentlemen that, though an utter bounder, Owen was not in the prayer-book sense 'a bad man'. He had attracted hostile attention (particularly from one financial journalist on the *Sunday Times*) as much for his exuberance and lechery as for appearing to operate on the windy side of the law. He was also woefully naïve, having asked his PR man to take him to tea at the Ritz to meet society ladies of loose morals. I think that must have let me off the hook, for the inquisitors laughed. I also like to think that Neil would have been proud of me. Owen Oyston was subsequently imprisoned for rape. Along with certain sections of the media, I was convinced he had been framed.

Neil died, but not before he had seen Piccadilly Radio become the most successful station outside London, turning over its capital ten times a year. He once introduced me to each of the sixty or so employees with the words, 'This is the man without whom you would not be here.' Some of the senior figures looked alarmed. We made some provision for his widow, Ruth, but she also died. I like to think of H making endless cups of tea in the kitchen of that eighteenth-century farmhouse.

CHAPTER TWENTY-THREE

The Eye *and* I

In October 1961, in the same month as The Establishment club opened, the first issue of *Private Eye*, printed on yellow paper, appeared. The inventors were Andrew Osmond, Christopher Booker and Willie Rushton. After some trials and tribulations they ran out of gas and enthusiasm and sold, for fifteen hundred pounds, seventy-five per cent of their shares in Pressdam Ltd, a company Osmond had bought for twenty-six pounds 'from a bloke in Fleet Street'. Nick Luard took me to lunch and persuaded me to help the *Eye* and, in return for guaranteeing their account well into four figures, I received nine point two per cent of the shares. In 1989, I sold my stake in the *Eye*, after a meeting with Peter Cook and his lady at the Hôtel de Crillon.

I was only peripherally involved in *Private Eye* and not at all editorially. I only volunteered my services when there was trouble, as in the case of Lord Russell of Liverpool. The *Eye* had libelled this fearful fellow and the damages were quite punitive – five thousand pounds – and designed to sink us. So one day Andrew McCall said to me, 'If, as you say, the readers are so fond of the magazine, why don't you appeal to them for money?' So, for twenty-five pounds I bought a full-page advertisement, in which we appealed to the readers for support – the original Goldenballs fund. It was successful. Moreover, I remember going to see Malcolm Muggeridge, former editor of *Punch*. He said he would try the Agnews. He attempted to appeal to their sense of heritage and quoted what had been said about *Punch* by *The Times* in the nineteenth century.* The Agnews were not moved.

---

* This was identical to the hostile comment in relation to the *Eye*.

The next time I became concerned with the magazine was over the Ingrams–Goldsmith feud. The *Eye* had been continually offensive to Jimmy, whose style offended the puritan and allegedly anti-Semitic minor-public-school ethic of Ingrams and his chums ('When a man marries his mistress, he creates a job vacancy' was a typical Goldsmithism). But when the *Eye* claimed, without foundation, that Goldsmith had masterminded the escape of Lord Lucan, it was in effect accusing him of being an accessory to murder.

Criminal libel was an obscure and dreadful corner of English law, which rich and terrible men like Captain Maxwell had made their own. Jimmy frolicked happily in these dangerous waters like a man-eating shark which has tasted blood and enjoyed the taste. He immediately invoked criminal libel.

Out of concern for both parties – and a natural pleasure in interfering – I thought I should attempt to mediate. My oppor-tunity came when Jimmy was knighted: I sent him a telegram saying, 'Congratulations. Why not drop the suit against the *Eye*? Noblesse now oblige.' He rang up and summoned me to tea. He was then living in South Kensington. I recall a discreet Daimler outside the door. We did indeed go through the motions of having tea – a Georgian teapot, hot-water vessel and elegant china. After a while he allowed me to have a glass of whisky and soda.

The interview reminded me of a description by Alfred Victor, Comte de Vigny, in *Servitude et grandeur militaires*, where he recounted the experience of a young page at the court in Fontainebleau, who witnesses by chance, having been trapped behind some curtains, an interview between Pope Pius VII and Napoleon. Apart from that emperor's tiny testicles, witnessed and observed by Dr Henry who performed the autopsy, Jimmy and he had many resemblances. In de Vigny's story, the Pope enters the audience chambers and sits in a Roman chair, while Napoleon paces up and down, protesting to the Holy Father his faithfulness as a son of the Church. This is a preamble to attaining a complete surrender from the Pope, to which the Holy Father simply says a single word, 'Commediante!' Incensed at this refusal, Napoleon falls into a tremendous rage and, likening the Holy Father to a parish priest, claims himself to hold the Holy Father in his hands like a puppet. In response, the Pope smiles bitterly and says, 'Tragediante!' At which point, Napoleon picks up a Sèvres vase from the marble chimney piece and smashes it to the floor. Ours was not *that* dissimilar.

Although the interview has been recounted by Patrick Marnham and by Richard Ingrams in his book *Goldenballs,* there is one important point they both have missed. Jimmy was indignant – and with some justification, I thought – that the *Eye* was attacking him and his family by using doubtful evidence. He was determined to pursue them to prison or to the grave. He was prepared to see weeping widows lick his boots, pleading for the release of their husbands. I pointed out to him that in Richard Ingrams he had a dangerous adversary, a martyr even, somebody who would enjoy the flames tickling the soles of his feet. I also added quite casually that he was an amusing fellow and why didn't we all have lunch together the next day. Jimmy instantly said, 'Why not?'

I telephoned Ingrams at the *Eye.* He sighed and said, 'Oh dear, oh dear. You don't know what's been happening. Of course I can't have lunch with him. Come and see me.' This episode was not recorded by Ingrams, but it shows Jimmy's ability to do a U-turn. I reported to the Coach and Horses for a briefing by Ingrams who told me that Jimmy was terrifying everybody opposed to him. Jimmy had indeed behaved with a ruthlessness and savagery which illuminated his behaviour, coupled with characteristic attention to detail (which made for splendid parties). In this case, I discovered that Jimmy had paid almost every private eye in the Yellow Pages as a spoiler for others. I was also warned by Arnold Goodman not to dive into this nest of crocodiles. When Jimmy was in a rage the Inns of Court cringed. His agents had blackmailed unto death a distinguished Jewish solicitor, Leslie Paisner, and had extracted a confession from a PR man, John Addy, who told me, 'I was terrified and tight.' But with Ingrams I was never sure if he was frightened of going to jail.

Nevertheless, I turned up at a hearing and saw Jimmy and his lawyer, Eric Levine, in court. When I went towards Jimmy, Levine said, 'Don't talk to Anthony Blond,' Jimmy replied, 'Nonsense.' At the back of the court the following exchange took place:

ANTHONY: Jimmy, last night I had a dream and your father said to me, 'Tell my boy to stop the case.'

JIMMY: (*without blinking an eyelid*) Anthony, last night *I* had a dream and my father said to me, 'You carry on, Jimmy.'

With Jimmy Goldsmith you couldn't win.

CHAPTER TWENTY-FOUR

Making Movies

When I was young I nourished three private ambitions: to write a novel, to grow my own wine and to direct a film.

Family Business was published in 1976 in London and New York, and later, for some unknown reason, in Holland. Lord Snow reviewed it and liked the hero; Lord Willis wanted to make a television series out of it; but Master Grade thought the hero a caricature of his father, Lord (low grade) Lew.

Although the orchard I bought years later in Blond had once been a vineyard – and very nasty much of it must have been – I decided to leave viticulture to longer purses, like those of rich Californians who need tax breaks. Little wine is produced in the Limousin and none at all in Bellac.

I did however make four films – though at irregular intervals – with my oldest friend, Christopher Mason, over the fifty years of our acquaintance. The first was made in Ithaca, where I had bought for a thousand pounds, while on a cruise with my father, a boring concrete house with a spectacular view. At least it stopped us thinking about food, of which there was very little in the isolated north of that then inaccessible rocky island. I don't remember much about the film except that Christopher was extremely cross when I lost it.

The second, in 1963, was more ambitious and was booed at the Tours Festival for films of *court métrage*. *Christmas Rose* was the story of a hospital matron, past childbearing age, who falls in love with a young guitar-playing car-park attendant; she sleeps with him, conceives and . . . gives birth on Christmas Day (somewhat hackneyed, I know).

When I first saw, at Heathrow Airport, the actress Christopher had engaged for the female role, it was clear a major rewrite was necessary. Otherwise the film would have to be shot in the dark, for this elderly retired opera singer could not ever pass as a matron; and no camera angle, however ingenious, could disguise her embonpoint as *grossesse*. Christopher and I quarrelled constantly and the crew – what crew there was – seethed with discontent. During one take in the Mall, in thick snow, our script girl, who (I thought) was my current affair, announced, 'I've had enough of this. I'm going to get a taxi and marry David Gillies.'

I don't know how she found a taxi, but she certainly married him, though it didn't last.

The next film opportunity did not arise until 1968 when I was building a house on a double bombsite overlooking Regent's Canal at the Angel, Islington. The family business had been sold and my share was a swathe of shares in Emu Wool, enough to lash out on what John Betjeman called 'a little quiet developing'. It was going to be quite a house, with a sixty-foot pavilion bang on the canal, a lawn on the roof, a fountain and a scattering of sculptures by David Gwynne, a friend of Alistair McAlpine. Needless to say the local busybodies took against my plans to cover two of the gardens, which had been painted by Sickert.

McAlpine had had an exotic career as fund-raiser for the Conservative Party, collector of aboriginal art, salesroom correspondent for the *Spectator* and columnist for the *European*, but was then in charge of 'small works' in the family's construction business and clearly fretting. He agreed to finance a film about the building of the house. I then persuaded Spike Milligan to play the part of a man fishing in the canal, while the works were going on the background.

Christopher, who directed, had trouble with Spike, who often did not roll up if he didn't feel in the mood. Nevertheless, the film had one great moment, which only an artist of his quality could have pulled off. We needed to *lose*, as they say in the film business, a tree that was in the way of the building: we therefore had it fall accidentally. Close-up of Spike placidly fishing – cut to bulldozer nudging tree – tree starts to crackle and to fall (but not at the intended angle) – tree crashes within inches of fisherman. Close-up of Spike – he does not blink. *Fish and Milligan* played at a cinema in Piccadilly Circus; the distribution company went bust and we were never paid. Nor was McAlpine: my Emu shares had gone into a tailspin and I had to abandon the exotic part of the development, leaving only a small boring block of flats above my bit. I could not even afford to finish the largest room, which was meant to stretch down to the canal, so I put the property up for sale at forty thousand pounds. I was forced to sell at a loss to an abdominal – I nearly said abominable – surgeon (probably was).

I mentioned to Max Rayne that I was the only person to have lost money on a property development in London.

'Was it,' he asked, 'in any way interesting?'

I said I thought it was.

'Ah well,' he said with a sigh.

When I sold my publishing business to CBS, their prize boffin, Robert Mark, had come up with an idea to rival the tape cassette, which was being touted by Sony and Philips, but which was not yet in production. Mr Mark's invention used wire instead of tape, and CBS were sure it would be a world-beater. Somehow I convinced my new masters that they needed a demonstration film to show off the versatility of their invention and its superiority to tape. I hired the producer who had made *Performance*, a sexy but prestigious movie with Mick Jagger and James Fox, to give the project credibility. Christopher Mason, that promising young man, would direct.

There was a star-studded cast. Yehudi Menuhin, whom Christopher knew, performed free, and with burning sincerity in praise of the product whose name I no longer recall. The Royal Ballet School danced for us. Moreover, I procured the organist of Notre-Dame, Pierre Cochereau, who insisted on money in advance *in situ*, so I dubbed him 'cash-in-the-loft' Cochereau. He showed me the mirror by the narrow window (his view of the world) which had reflected his finest hour when he had played the organ at the memorial service for President Kennedy, when thousands of Parisians, unable to enter the cathedral, had packed the Ile de la Cité. His favourite pastime was to drive into the forests of Les Landes in a truck containing an organ and a generator, and play to the trees: an entertainment Huysmans, who describes how the forests inspired the Gothic, would have appreciated.

The film was sent to 'Black Rock', as the headquarters of CBS in New York were called by disrespectful employees – a magnificent structure, the creation of Dr Stanton, on West 51st Street – and never heard of again. A similar fate awaited Dr S. himself, for the invention of Mr Mark, which he had sponsored, was a total and costly failure. I was *limogé*, as the French say, meaning transferred to a post with similar pay, but without responsibility of any kind. I refused to go, but CBS accepted with relief an offer from my partner and myself to buy back the general part of the publishing list.

*   *   *

Christopher and I had met more than fifty years ago at Eton, where he was painting as well, everybody said, as Augustus John. Nevertheless, we did not become friends until I began to visit Paris, by which time Christopher had got to know France much better than I.

Although my adventures into film, always disastrous, involved Christopher, the reverse was not true. Christopher, with his painter's eye, was a remarkable cameraman and following the technique of his hero, Truffaut, made a film about the Festival of Britain and England in the thirties; the latter included a sequence of a bishop bowling through a development of new houses on an arterial road in his Rolls-Royce, and complaining in a plummy voice that it was 'a spiritual desert'.

His talent was indeed remarked upon by a television company which commissioned a series of topographical films on England. Christopher was however a perfectionist, seething with integrity, and could not tolerate the compromises required of an artist in any commercial undertaking – so he abandoned the profession. I also suspect he recoiled before his own success, which would explain his switching from his admired facility as a portrait painter to a form of abstractionism which earned reviews like 'at least the artist has the courage of his own bad taste'. Christopher, of course, relished these comments. Joanna Carrington, also a painter and a free spirit, and niece of the now (but not then) internationally known Carrington, so loved this quality that she married him.

PART SIX

A Lancashire Lass

CHAPTER TWENTY-FIVE

A Lancashire Lass

She was a waif, small, drenched by the rain, looking as if she had walked out of *Les Misérables*, which was playing not far from Leo Cooper's office off Shaftesbury Avenue. She was soliciting sponsorship for a walk to raise money for distressed booksellers. I was touched and sponsored her for miles and miles and miles. She agreed to let me take her for a drink in the pub where Leo held court with the eximious Tom Hartman and miscellaneous military historians, who worked on arcane regimental histories and non-blockbusters like *Our Enemies the French*, which it was her job to publicise. When Leo saw me escorting her he shouted, 'Watch out, Laura. He'll have your knickers off!' (That had to wait for the fullness of time: I was then living with Andrew.)

Three years later Blond & Briggs, now reduced from thirty-odd employees to two, Desmond and me, needed publicity for a book by a randy granny. William Miller suggested we hire Laura Hesketh, who had gone freelance. She turned up at our offices, a room in Desmond's grand but cosy house in Bayswater, which he shared with a Lloyd's underwriter.* A notice on the front door for a time read: TWO BACHELORS LIVE HERE, SO NO FURS OR JEWELLERY. TRY NEXT DOOR. Laura did not recognise me but agreed to come out to lunch. At our second lunch, which followed swiftly, Laura revealed that her favourite book was *Confessions of Zeno* by Italo Svevo. So was mine. Love at second sight.

The randy granny was a great success and was serialised by the *News of the World*, so posters all over the kingdom. Laura was an inventive publicist and once persuaded whomever one has to persuade for these events to let the Royal Engineers build a bridge

---

* I never did find out whether he lost him any money.

across Fleet Street one Sunday morning, to publicise a book on the Sappers. Her current amour was Hugh Bredin, a polymath copy-writer who read for Penguin. Of course Hugh and I disliked each other, and of course we are now buddies (a standard evolution with men, but rare with women).

In Laura's overheated flat in the Fulham Road the three of us watched the television programme where Jimmy Goldsmith, stage-managed by his friend Peter West, walked off set. Surely a first? Hugh was shocked; I was thrilled. The flat was hot because the shop below sold artificial log fires; the heat melted the vinyl records and parched the air. Laura sued and won. Laura always wins and is as clever with money as I am stupid. When I met her she was lending money to a man who sold skateboards and was happily paying her twenty-five per cent. I stopped that but did introduce her to Elaine Dundy, Ken Tynan's wife and author of *The Dud Avocado*, who bought her flat, redundant when she moved into Chester Row.

At some point I had to meet the Heskeths. And it would have been difficult to conjure up a more unsuitable candidate for the hand of the elder daughter of Colonel and Lady Mary Hesketh, née Lumley, daughter of the Earl of Scarbrough,* than myself. I was twenty-five years older, sexually ambivalent,† Jewish and, later, insolvent as a publisher.

Moreover, Nanny who lived in a cottage in their village, and was still vocal in the family, had discovered that I had published *The Carpetbaggers*, which she had taken out from the library and read with equal measures of relish and distaste. 'Oh, what a blow!' Lady Mary had cried when she heard of our liaison. For had not Laura been destined for a Stanley or a Naylor-Leyland, or someone else in what Elaine Dundy calls 'the battalion'? In time the Heskeths not only rallied, but both Laura's brother and her mother gave me – without being asked – substantial sums to help in the

---

* The last Lord Chamberlain to censor plays, the last Governor of Bombay, Grand Master, et cetera, et cetera.

† 'Blond prefers gentlemen' had been used more than once by *Private Eye*.

crises caused by my having to pay the debts of the publishing company and the capital gains tax subsequent to selling shares in Piccadilly Radio to pay those debts. Moral: never sign a joint and several guarantee.

Just after we met, however, I was riding high. Graham Watson, director of Curtis Brown, had sold my novel, *Family Business*, to André Deutsch for ten thousand pounds, a decent sum in 1976. I now decided to fly to Tokyo and stay with Peter Thompson, brother of Sheila, who had worked for me and then the Lord Chancellor. Peter was head of the Edinburgh-based Ben Line and would arrange for me to return in a cargo ship and meet Laura halfway, which meant Sri Lanka, a country I had always wanted to see since my friendship with Guy Amirthanayagam (of whom more anon).

Peter chaired the tanker consortium in Tokyo, lived in a large house (which had been the Korean Embassy), with a garden (so rare in that overcrowded metropolis), and his hospitality and style matched his position. He was also efficient and successful in all manner of ways and a fast runner.

Every morning a typed sheet was slid under my bedroom door, detailing in goof-proof fashion the arrangements for the day. Although a car and chauffeur were put at my disposal, the congestion and pollution in Tokyo were so dreadful that it was wiser to travel by metro (though not at rush hour).

Japan was beginning to intrigue me. It was the only country I had come across where workers arrived half an hour early for a go-slow strike; where an adulterous husband, nominally out of town for a company weekend, could buy at the metro a souvenir of the resort he never went to and have his golf clubs muddied by an understanding hotel maid; and where a Minister of Agriculture, retained in a cabinet reshuffle, was described in a newspaper as 'popular on account of his fondness for sake and young men'.

Through the British Council in Tokyo I recruited their previous representative and started, with the approval both of the Japanese publishing establishment and my partner Desmond Briggs, the English Agency, Japan, with William Miller. My thinking did not work, but William's did. Over the years, thanks to William, we recovered our (actually Laura's) investment, with a bonus.

Peter arranged my appointment as assistant librarian on the SS *Ben Cruachan* from Nagoya to Colombo, a long voyage on which to write my disastrous second novel.* For two large air-conditioned cabins and three Edinburgh-prepared defrosted meals – mean, except for the once-a-week haggis with whisky – I paid five dollars a day. So, in the company of a cargo of CKD (completely knocked down) Toyotas, I chugged across the China Seas towards my true love, calling at arseholes of the Empire like Port Swettenham, where I bought the fresh vegetables the owners denied us. Nevertheless, I did make friends with the wireless officer, whose ambition it was to construct a concrete boat, fill it with unusual goods and drop them off in ill-considered places – like Port Swettenham – around the world. We discussed the plan in some detail, time hanging heavily on our hands, and I promised to write to an Oxford friend, Sir Jeremy Morse, offering Lloyds Bank, which often advertised its interest in adventurous projects, the opportunity of investing in the scheme. Sir Jeremy did not immediately jump at the idea; indeed my letter went unacknowledged. After some weeks I asked my secretary – even in those days I had one – to telephone to his. The reply was curt: that no proposition of any kind emanating from Anthony Blond could be of interest to Sir Jeremy.

Laura meanwhile had been kicking her pretty heels in a suite at the Galle Face Hotel, so spacious that after three days she discovered another bathroom. She had gained this eminence, or rather spread, because of a rat she had detected in a previous, smaller apartment, and the behaviour of her predecessor, Ursula Andress, who had made herself unpopular by writing rude remarks in lipstick on the mirrors. My boat lay outside the harbour, waiting for a berth, and waited and waited. Laura

---

* *Son of the Lord.* This is a terrible novel I had written hastily, flush with the success of *Family Business.* It was rejected by a New York agent and continues to gather dust with my editor.

arrived at the customs and announced that she would kick and scream until her man was let off the vessel. The officials complied, as I have since learned to do.

*   *   *

When Disraeli married his Mary Anne he listed their characteristics, e.g., 'She vain, He conceited' (this could apply to Laura and myself). After twenty years of cohabitation, as the French say, I sat down in the evening sun in our garden and came up with:

LAURA	ANTHONY
aristocratic (1,000 years of Heskeths and Lumleys)	*haut bourgeois**
unsnobbish	snobbish
quiet, except for tantrums	noisy, intemperate
goer and doer	lazy, procrastinates, but 'good on last lap' (said my mother)
always prepared to look on the dark side	optimist, but broods on failures
careful with money but occasionally generous on a calculated whim	extravagant, incompetent
always elegant and pretty	often shambly and rough
cautious	gullible
at ease with machinery	no empathy
susceptible to maladies	amazingly healthy, considering
arythmic, hates hard seats	loves dancing, opera, concerts
digests books slowly	smells them

*   I once asked Professor Leo Löwenthal, founder of the Frankfurt School of Social Science, what class I was and this was his answer.

plans her diary	likes unexpected guests
an exemplary cook	not allowed in the kitchen
irritating	irritable
has never thrown a dress away	wears odd socks
conservative by tradition	socialist and pacifist
enterprising and thorough	many ideas but high failure rate
always right about the route	always wrong
will order lunch in her room	will go anywhere for lunch
morals above suspicion	suspect and rackety
balanced and moderate	intolerable in victory and grovelling in defeat
mildly Protestant (ex-recusant in the eighteenth century)	prayerful, lays *tefillin*:* a 'church-crawling Jew'
grateful and punctilious	bites the hand which feeds him
naturally discreet	follows Churchill: 'always be indiscreet'
chatterbox	surly but likes to dominate
can't remember jokes	remembers them well
always changes her mind, especially in restaurants	decisive and often wrong
trustworthy	fairly trustworthy
fairly loyal	loyal

* Phylactery laid by Jews on the arm and forehead every morning.

CHAPTER TWENTY-SIX

The Heskeths

Peter (Charles Fleetwood) was my first Hesketh. He had devised the extravagant pull-out for *Ghastly Good Taste* by John Betjeman in 1933 and extended it for our edition in 1970. I attended him in his lodgings: in the ground floor and basement of a pair of early-eighteenth-century houses in Great Ormond Street, the offices of the Society for the Preservation of Ancient Buildings, of which he was the *quondam* secretary. He looked the part, being well preserved and encased in a tight-fitting suit with matching tie and handkerchief from Sulka. He was also always well shod. I bought the houses and inherited a pair of his shoes, complete with three-piece trees in a box neatly labelled 'thin, brown shoes'; but that was later.

He was a flattering listener and punctuated one's quite ordinary remarks by leaning forward with a fixed stare and a great exhalation of, 'My dear, I say!' He walked delicately and was reputed to dye his neatly plastered hair. That he did not was the burden of a letter to the *Spectator* from Gavin Stamp, a sign of the respect for him in certain sections of the aesthetic community. Like all other mannered people of his generation, Brian Howard and Harold Acton among them, he was physically intrepid. During the Second World War, he was parachuted into France with the 2nd SAS, complete with his ivory-backed hairbrushes and a load of French francs – enough at least for one of his equally well-bred colleagues, one Courtney-Gosling, to buy a farmhouse with and to abandon the war and live the rest of his life, with the unspoken complicity of his superiors, happily near Angers. Peter eventually met up with his brother Roger, who had been given the assignment of travelling the Rhine to find hock for SHAEF, in the bar of the Crillon in Paris.

The second Hesketh was Laura of course. The third I met was the second, or was he the third, Lord, who had inherited Easton Neston and a fortune at the age of ten.

The fourth Hesketh was, of course, Laura's father, Roger. If he ever thought that I was not the ideal son-in-law, he never said so. He did once write me a less than enthusiastic letter, but rang up asking me to lunch almost before I had had time to open it. He was an unexpected figure to be in my life – so different from my first father-in-law, John Strachey, a rakish, boozy, broke bohemian – for Roger was an upper and lower case Conservative, occupied with duty and patrimony, courteous, kind and cunning, indeed a master of deception.*

When his brother Peter lay dying in Sister Agnes, and he was determined, as in all matters in his life, not to be hurried, he said to me that he had just reached the conclusion that his father had been a wicked man. Such a judgement, at the age of eighty, is not that remarkable: for it is common for those at the end of their lives to reflect on the beginning, and often in an unforgiving way. For Peter was saying, what his brother Roger only felt, that his father had betrayed them.

The Heskeths had been at North Meols in south-west Lancashire for a thousand years. The name is Saxon and means 'sand-dune' or perhaps 'racecourse'. A Norman knight, Roger de Coudray, had married a Hesketh and the family, through judicious alliances, had prospered; to such an extent that a great-uncle, Sir Peter, was the patron of ninety livings and owned great chunks of Southport, Preston and Blackpool. He commissioned Decimus Burton† to build Fleetwood (named after himself) in 1836. It was designed as a port for traffic by sea to Scotland, since it was well known that the land route via Shapfell was impassable

---

* He started what became the third largest tree nursery in the country, selling partially grown trees for motorways. He earned a lot of money and supplied his charitable obligations from letting the park at Meols for caravan outings and from the Game Fair. In these enterprises, he made money, provided employment and gratified himself.

† The architect of the Palm House and Temperate House at Kew.

by railway. Victorian engineers cut through the impassable and Sir Peter Fleetwood-Hesketh-Fleetwood went completely – this being before the Companies Act – bust.

His family was left with some engravings of Queen Victoria at the opening of the port and a pair of her gloves; his great house, Rossall, was turned into a public school. Nevertheless, the family survived – they usually do – so that much of Southport and some thousands of acres of prime potato-growing land was still in the family when the father of Roger and Peter, Charles Fleetwood-Hesketh-Fleetwood, inherited.

He had in fact been born a Bibby and married the daughter of another ship-owner, Brocklebank of the Cunard Line, but his mother had been a Hesketh and he had changed his name, rather elaborately. When their father divorced their mother and put up all he could of the estate for sale in the twenties, the two elder boys turned against him. The sale had been caused by Roger refusing to persuade his mother to divorce his father, which his mother was reluctant to do as she thought it would prevent her daughters, Joan and Elizabeth, being presented. Although Roger loved the estate, his loyalty to his mother was greater still.

Roger, then at Christ Church, was summoned by his Oxford bank manager and told that his allowance had been cut off; Peter, the aesthete, was sent to a sheep farm in New Zealand. Their mother was in every sense a great lady. She was as wide as they were narrow and was known as Mrs 'Square'-Hesketh. She was drowned during the Second World War when her ship the *Star of Benares* was torpedoed in the Atlantic; she had insisted on giving up her place in the lifeboat, which, she said, would be better used by three people of normal size.

Their mother's sister had married George Westinghouse III, son of the compressed-air-brake inventor, a millionaire with his own train, which included, Roger was fond of remembering, a compartment for hens. Roger wrote of his predicament to his Westinghouse uncle, who cheerfully supported the two elder boys. The younger brother, Cuthbert, was innocent of protest and therefore became his father's heir. Roger then applied himself to law, with special reference to the Chancery Division, and with the urgent object of upsetting his disinheritance and recovering his estate. In this he partially succeeded: acre by acre, house by house, often using nominees for secrecy, he bought back the immediate surroundings of Meols Hall, so that by the time I knew him it looked like a minor stately home which had been in the family, intact, for centuries.

This was an illusion. The Heskeths, like many families in south-west Lancashire, had been Catholic recusants. Meols Hall, surrounded by marsh, had been a safe house for Catholics, with the obligatory priest's hole.* Spirits, on the other hand did not hide: they found the place conducive to their goings-on. One evening Lady Mary saw smoke coming from halfway up the wall by her bed and had Roger unbrick the wall. All that was revealed was an old fireplace. This phenomenon was one of many over the years – havoc with electricity, bedclothes pulled off, handshakes with flesh 'like a skinned rabbit' – indicating a poltergeist, who appeared indifferent and superior to exorcism. The story seemed frighteningly similar to a book I published: that Father Stonor had died on the train on his way to an exorcism at Meols Hall and the local rector, assisting the Bishop of Lancaster, at the next exorcism, died three weeks later. Thus, on my first visit to this curious house, I was careful to keep my *tefillin* by my bedside.

One of Roger's first moves in the plan to ransom, heal and restore his house was to install a retired gilder, a Mr Burrows, who worked daily for years on cabriole legs and ornate frames until his death. Most of the furniture and the decorations were, as Lord Curzon might have said, of unexampled splendour, but every now and then there was a trick. I particularly admired a Grinling Gibbons mirror – I have always refused to say glass – above a Sheraton console: it came from Peter Jones.

Roger enjoyed being mayor of Southport in the fifties but was not so happy as its MP, in, one need hardly say, the Conservative interest. He received an enormous majority of seventeen thousand,

* Campion stayed there on his last visit to Lancashire.

attributable surely to his personal renown. He had bought *The Master Builder*, an eclectic trade magazine, and became a DIY architect, spending numerous late-night sessions making quarter-inch balsa models of extensions to Meols Hall.* Though the barn looked as if it had been built in 1753, it had actually been put up in 1953, when one was only allowed to build farm buildings. Similarly the library, which the knowledgeable would date at around 1790, built of old brick, and the garden room, with its worn black and white marble tiles, had both been created by Roger in the 1960s.

The new wing, with its blank windows, was an equally convincing addition and no one could tell that it had not been put on to the original house by an eighteenth-century Hesketh. A rose red wall, half as old as time, was Roger's present to his wife for an anniversary. Ingenuity and a capacity for taking pains, finite and thus stopping just short of genius – he was perhaps in this respect a casualty of a large income – were two of Roger's many characteristics. The new wing included a kitchen that he had himself designed. He disdained labour-saving devices: shelves were made narrow so that a pot of marmalade could not conceal one of honey. Trays were concealed in a special cupboard to be always accessible and uncluttered. For recipes he only used Escoffier's *Guide culinaire*. Laura has thirty *électroménagers* and hundreds of cookbooks but concedes her father was a better artist. We once bought him a salamander from New York, but he never used it, stating the only good ones were eighteenth century and unobtainable. He would get up in the middle of the night to satisfy himself that his partridge *quenelles* had set. Watching him make his own breakfast was enlightening. He would beard two slices of Mother's Pride with a pair of scissors, put an egg into a pan of boiling water, turn off the gas, place the two pieces of bread in the toaster (having checked the setting), and then wait. When the water was tepid he would transfer the egg into an egg cup, making sure the egg was the right way up (!), and decapitate it with a special device.

---

* These were featured in three successive issues of *Country Life* and in a smart book on English country houses.

Despite being fussy, he was a calm and tolerant traveller. I found him in his room in the Klosenberg Hotel in Galle, when he was in Sri Lanka for our wedding, quietly seething with laughter. He had asked one of the 'boys' to bring him a roll of lavatory paper. ('I say, d'you think you could possibly bring me . . .) After the usual indecent interval the man had returned with a large whisky and soda. He acknowledged that, to a Sri Lankan, a not too intelligible request from a ruddy-faced Englishman at the end of a hot day could only mean one thing.

The next morning he escorted Laura, in her bridal outfit, up the drive of our house, keeping a discreet distance from the preceding elephant, because he had learned it had diarrhoea. The Colombo Police Band, which had been hired for the occasion, played the march from *Aida*.

*　　*　　*

Roger's claim to fame was his part in Operation Fortitude, that successful piece of deception which shortened the Second World War by months if not years. His inclusion in the counter-intelligence team at MI6, with John Mills (son of Bertram), Dennis Wheatley, Johnnie Harris, Hugh Trevor-Roper and Hugh Astor, may have been partly due to his familiarity with the German mind. The purpose of Operation Fortitude was to convince the German High Command that the Normandy landing was a feint and that the real Allied invasion was to come across the Straits of Dover. Roger's own account of Operation Fortitude was blocked by the War Office and, worse, was written, though I never told him, in a style so pedestrian as to constitute a traffic hazard.*

My favourite memory of my father-in-law is of a moment during Sunday service at St Cuthbert's at the end of the drive, which he always attended, often alone, sitting in the family pew. One of the forthcoming arrangements the rector wanted to announce was the date of the beating of the parish bounds. 'Would the fourteenth be convenient for Colonel Hesketh?'

---

* It was later published as *Fortitude: The D Day Deception Campaign*.

Roger started to look for his diary. It wasn't in any of the pockets of his overcoat. It wasn't in his inside breast pocket. Surely he wouldn't have put it in a trouser pocket? The congregation, several hundred strong, waited. He couldn't have left it on his dressing-table, could he? He fumbled away. Not a *frisson* of impatience from anyone. Ah, here we are. 'What day did you say, rector?'

'The fourteenth, colonel.'

'Oh no, that's on the twelfth. Yes, the fourteenth will do.'

A collective sigh of relief.

The only time I addressed a Church of England congregation was from the pulpit of St Cuthbert's, a concession readily granted to a son-in-law of the colonel. The rector dolled me up as an Oxford MA, with white tabs, so I looked and, what is just as important, felt convincing. My address – it was not a sermon because a bishop has to license a preacher for that – had as its theme the Feast of the Circumcision on 1 January, an event bypassed in the Church of England, but once, indeed, a Feast of Obligation. Circumcision takes place within the statutory (Jewish) eight days after the birth of a male child and is celebrated even if it falls on Yom Kippur. (I reckoned they would have heard of that.) In this case, of course, it was eight days after the birth of Jesus – Christmas Day. I concluded by saying, in Hebrew, the blessing which begins 'The Lord bless you and keep you, the Lord lift up his face towards you . . . ' and then I translated it.

The expression on the faces of the congregation had been attentive but blank and this I put down to their Lancashire phlegm. I had spoken into the microphone attached to the pulpit, quietly and firmly, but had not been told the microphone was tuned into a wavelength only audible – so caring is the Church these days – to those with a certain kind of hearing-aid. I had been inaudible to everybody else. A lady in the Hesketh Arms, the pub next to the church, who had the appropriate appliance, had heard every word quite clearly. I believe my address to have been symbolic of my effect on my father-in-law and on his demesne.

CHAPTER TWENTY-SEVEN

Sri Lanka

Whilst I was languishing on the SS *Ben Cruachan*, Laura had been picked up by a couple of high-powered locals. Raja, a Tamil businessman, seemed to be on five per cent of everything, including the Mahaweli Dam; whilst his boozy and equally lecherous chum, Esmond Wickremasinghe, ran the biggest chain of newspapers and was known as the eyes and ears of the president, J. R. Jayawardene.

By way of these connections, Laura and I were introduced to Sri Lankan political society. My first encounter with one of the country's brightest political stars, Lalith Athulathmudali, ran as follows:

> LALITH: And where did you go to school?
> ANTHONY: Eton and New College . . . actually quite an old college.
> LALITH: Not as old as mine – Univ.

Lalith, I was to discover, was typical – though in fact he was exceptional – of a classically English educated member of the 'élite' (almost, like the 'masses', an official designation) in Ceylon, which they persisted in calling the island.* His social superiority was not forced or hearty, like that of upper-class – and often much richer – Indians. There have never been maharajas in Ceylon, and the caste system, never so marked, is like an inverted pyramid with the landowners, which includes the peasantry, the most numerous, at the top. Lalith was clever, privately cruel – we knew his girlfriend – and ambitious. J. R. Jayawardene once commented to me, 'He said

---

*   So tiny compared to the sub-continent of India, from which it dangles like a pearl, or a ham, depending on one's inclination.

the things we only used to think.' Ranasinghe Premadasa, JR's successor, was jealous of Lalith, and, it was thought, had him murdered.

Esmond asked us to stay in what he called his *garçonnière*, where he justified a liberal *train de vie* on the grounds that he was Hindu and not Buddhist, and therefore not racked by that cult's inhibition over drink, dancing, make-up and celibacy. We often partied with endless slugs of Chivas Regal and doubtful blonde girls. I remember one gloriously unseemly occasion with two senior citizens reeling round a railway track outside a restaurant in Mount Lavinia quarrelling about who went home with what . . .

*   *   *

My connection with Ceylon had begun in the early fifties. The British Council had asked me to take two of my authors, Simon Raven and Jennifer Dawson, to the Edinburgh Festival, together with a poet, Guy Amirthanayagam, who was also Deputy High Commissioner for Ceylon.*

We set off in my Ford Fairlane, an absurdly wonderful extravaganza and the largest production car ever built; it had a retractable hard roof that folded unbelievably into the boot, leaving enough room for a briefcase. When completely converted there was no sign that driver and passengers could be protected from the rain, so an excellent tease in a traffic jam was to wait until the first drops fell, then reverse the process and wipe the smiles off the faces of the onlookers. Jennifer Dawson was terrified of this mechanism and bored us with this fact throughout the journey.

The Edinburgh Festival, under a lord provost who was a lemonade manufacturer,† was not the giddy affair it is now. The city was not jolted out of its sourness by our arrival. I remember the indifference shown towards the drunken Ledig Rowohlt – a German publisher – as he bounded down the stone staircase of

---

*   Guy became a friend and twenty-five years later came to stay in France, with his daughter, a rich obstetrician with a vineyard in California.
†   This man was noted, even in that acerbic profession, for his philistinism.

a classy tenement full of Writers to the Signet, yelling to the stars in unaccented English, 'Tonight I am going to have a fuck with History!' We were all impressed by his command of idiom.

Guy was the first brown man to become a friend. Forty years ago there were not that many around, and the first time many of my contemporaries at Oxford ever saw a black man was in the market in 1949. Undergraduates rushed round for a gape, like Londoners, in the early eighteenth century, crowding to see Queen Anne's Indian kings in Whitehall.

Guy was a favourite fast-track civil servant of the former prime minister Mrs Bandaranaike ('Mrs B'),* a Catholic Tamil, whose family had been converted by St Francis Xavier three hundred years before. It was through Guy that Laura and I visited her, then in opposition, in her Highland-style lodge, made creepier by the dazzling pines and *bhikkhus* peering through the windows. As Prince Charles was outshone by his princess, so I was eclipsed by Laura, who chatted to Mrs B about life in women's colleges at Oxford and the spreading qualities of Kraft cheese. I did manage to ask about her role in the JVP rebellion,† which was clearly more dangerous than the world was told. She had turned to the Navy for help – 'so much more reliable than the Army' – and had arranged for the leader to be arrested – 'for his own safety'.

Guy lived with his wife and children, one of whom was autistic

---

* Mrs B had succeeded her murdered husband and became the world's first woman prime minister, presiding over the Singhalese dominance of the language and educational system. The Tamils, the sixteen-per-cent Hindu majority in the north and east, ceased to be integrated and demanded autonomy. The most intelligent had now fled to England, Canada and Australia where they flourished and were able to remit funds to finance the 'Tigers'' war.

† JVP were the initials of an anarchic political group – rarely in any sense spelled out – which was a cocktail of student Marxist idealists, jobless art students in a country which can only use vets and engineers, trigger-happy ex-policemen, deserters and young thugs. After the tragic failure of their rebellion, when many were blown up by their own handmade pipe bombs, they terrorised the south – where we lived – killing, for instance, the local sub-prefect. Now twenty-odd years later they have aged into a respectable left-wing party with seats in parliament.

and had the face of an anguished eagle, in a big, gloomy flat, which was crowded with Catholic impedimenta, near the Albert Hall. After Mrs B was booted out, and because the treatment for autism in the US was better, Guy left the diplomatic service and secured a job at the University of Hawaii. Under some special Asiatic arrangement, I published his poems, but most of the slim volumes ended up mildewing in my library. His poetry was slight, taut, self-mocking, but occasionally beautiful, as in 'To My Autistic Son, Revantha'.

When Guy moved to Hawaii he contrived the occasional visit to London. He once brought an American for a drink, whom I shall call, for he was a convinced and practising paedophile, Bill Amaretto. Bill had read a guide to the pleasures of the metropolis we had recently published called the *The New London Spy*. He was certain that I, Guy's friend, and well versed in the undergrowth of London's sexuality, could direct him to a source of willing boys to gratify his passion; this passion was, Guy assured me, as endless as his purse was deep. It was important, Guy patiently explained, that Bill should be obliged in this way because he had only come to London and rented a flat on his, Guy's, recommendation.

If there were no such provision (of boys), Bill would pack his bags and return to Chicago, or wherever, and Guy's free and comfortable billet would be lost. This Asiatic situation was spelled out in the hearing of Bill, who then took up the narrative to describe the sort of boys he was used to, and how grateful their parents were for his attentions to their children. I was not sure whether I believed him, though he looked to be a kind if selfish and self-indulgent sort of man.

I had no idea where to start on this mission. Could Bill, who was obviously quite skilful in this kind of pursuit, not try for himself? Oh yes. Bill had scored the other night, having spotted a boy gazing at a pullover in a shop in the King's Road. He bought the pullover and then, for fifty pounds, the boy. This was at a time when an upstanding young Guardsman from the other side of the King's Road could be rented for five pounds. I was shocked. Then Andrew McCall entered the room. At that time he was known to be one of the beautiful young men. Bill briefly acknowledged his presence and said immediately that, though attractive, he was far too old. I almost felt I should apologise, but was saved by Guy, who muttered that when drunk Bill was not so choosy. I never did find a boy for Bill. He nevertheless agreed to rent the flat for another month, so Guy was accommodated. Finally Bill settled in Colombo, where there really was a troop of boy scouts who asked those pleased with their efforts to sign chits to that effect for presentation to their scoutmaster.

*   *   *

When we first arrived in Sri Lanka, JR was president. He was a courteous, dry, old-fashioned gentleman, with a face like a wellington boot. He asked us to lunch, producing a small blue Smythson diary. 'When are you free?'

We had our first sniff of power when a few days later a police officer with an entourage turned up at our breakfast table, saluted and asked if Mrs Blond liked curry? (In those days one had to wait years for a telephone.) After lunch in the presidential palace, sitting next to him in the shade of an enormous tree planted by the British, and emboldened perhaps by the warm white wine, I suggested to JR that he restore Mrs B her civil rights, which he had been undignified enough to remove. I do believe he made a note in his little blue book. Anyhow, he did and I was careful enough not to tell a soul.

By this time I had become the publisher of his official biography. Financing it was no problem at all. In September 1951, as one of the small Sri Lankan delegation to the United Nations conference in San Francisco, JR had made a short speech which concluded: 'Hatred ceases not by hatred, but by love . . . We extend to Japan a hand of friendship.' According to the *San Francisco Chronicle*, this touched off a roar of acclamation that shook the very windows of the Opera House conference room. The Japanese prime minister, who had been watching the proceedings, impassive and inscrutable, burst into tears.

Soon Sri Lanka was awash with hospitals and televisions

presented by its fellow Asian state, and when, a generation later, the young diplomat became president, the Japanese created a fund for his personal use. So nothing could be more correct than a political biography by the Professor of Modern History at the University of Peredeniya, Kingsley de Silva, together with a former US ambassador to Sri Lanka, under the imprint of a London publisher, who happened to live locally.

Over the next fifteen years, JR and I met often, usually *en famille* with our wives, and always over lunch, either in his official pad or at his comfortable and chintzy family house. Eventually he learned to offer me the native *arrack*, which he had to send out for. I was even allowed to help myself to a box of cigars (a regular bonus from Fidel Castro), which he said none of his cabinet smoked.

I think he enjoyed my pleasure in his relish of English idiom. He certainly quoted the English canon as much as any nineteenth-century Westminster politician, though, unlike many of his contemporaries, he had not been to Oxford or Cambridge. He had a sharp knowledge of the vernacular. I once asked him at his populous lunch table why (on earth) he had chosen Premadasa to succeed him as president.* Looking like a toad in a black wig, JR thought for a bit, gazed at the ceiling and then said, 'There didn't seem to be anybody else around at the time.' Then, after a long pause, 'The bugger blued it!'

The last time I saw JR was nearly the last time he saw anybody. He was just off to attend one of his wife's numerous and well-connected relations – she had the money – when the police telephoned to report rumours of a possible incident at the party. He was probably in no danger but JR decided 'not to spoil their fun'. 'They'll never get me,' he remarked. And they never did. He died in his bed.

---

* Premadasa was a street-gangster politician, rather like Milo, a crook whom Cicero unsuccessfully defended in ancient Rome. In 1993, Premadasa was driven into by a Tamil Tiger suicide bomber and blown up. It was said of him that he could never become president because of his caste – laundryman, down there with the coconut pickers and the drummers.

CHAPTER TWENTY-EIGHT

New York, New York

'Many people don't know their father, but I don't know my mother. All I know is that she wore pearls. Now Eleanor Roosevelt wore pearls . . . ' His audience for this cabaret consisted of Laura and me, and David Harlech, my employer, who had dropped by for a surreptitious vodka (or two). John Hays sat on the top of the refrigerator, the dominant piece of furniture in our newly acquired loft in a condominium in Greenwich Village. The long high slot with ten windows, formerly an ink factory, gave on to (immediately) a rubbish dump, but in the distance one could make out the twin towers of the World Trade Centre and to the right the Hudson River. When the QE2 came in, she filled the view; when it was cold, the key broke in the lock; when it was hot, we sat in the breath of an industrial fan. We partitioned the space with coffins on rollers, which were filled with ficuses supplied by a Berber.*

Bohemian New Yorkers had discovered that warehouses were habitable in the 1960s. By the time we arrived the business of converting century-old, but very solid commercial buildings, had become organised, efficient and greedy; 622 Greenwich Street was

---

* Immigrants to New York in recent years have not dissolved into the melting pot of America but have retained an identity through adopting, and often dominating, certain trades. The Koreans are the greengrocers; Russian Jews, dodging the draft, as it were, to Israel, drive yellow cabs; and the most formidable gangsters in California are alleged to be Israelis. Our local 'Jewish' delicatessen was owned by a pair of Palestinian Arabs. The ficus business, charged with filling the empty spaces in the ante-chambers of the corporations, is in the hands of Berbers. A survey of the demographic movement of buskers and bums outside the Rockefeller Center over thirty years revealed that the only ethnic minority not to move on and up were blacks.

a new conversion and many units were for sale. Laura had her half of the money in cash, having sold her flat in the Fulham Road, but I had to raise my half as I still kept the house in Chester Row. Our lawyer was a brisk, nay impatient, Jewish lady, who irritably snapped pencils when frustrated. At one point, when we seemed still to be a few thousand dollars short of collateral, she asked if I couldn't think of another asset. I mentioned I had a couple of cars in Sri Lanka: a Pontiac and a Chrysler. 'Anything owing on them?' she barked. No, but they were very old. 'Ah,' she said, a gleam in her eye, 'two vintage automobiles,' and wrote down an unlikely value. The Pontiac was invalided in a garage and someone had driven the Chrysler into the Indian Ocean, or maybe the other way round. We got the loan and nobody checked any of our declarations. If Americans want to lend money to complete a deal, they are unstoppable.

Back to the cabaret. John Hays was our char, or 'domestic co-ordinator', as he preferred to style himself. He was a hard taskmaster, for he insisted on a range of household appliances from floor polishers to mahogany coat hangers, on which he ranged our wardrobe in seasonal spaces, taking care that the cotton did not conflict with the silk, nor the silk with the velvet. He was, of course, gay – straight persons in the Village then being as rare as cowslips in a hothouse – and so enthusiastic in the passive role that Laura had to pay for repairs to what he called his 'fissure'. He was always broke but quite honest; though when Laura returned from our marriage in Sri Lanka he couldn't resist her wedding dress, a simple number, which would have suited him, from Tatters. Once he bought two jerseys by mail order from, indeed, Jersey, but made us buy them from him as he decided he needed the money more. He was also, of course, an actor, and we saw him in the part of Onassis at the Sheridan Square Playhouse. Though thin, indeed emaciated, and not resembling in any way, except that they were both tyrants, that great *armateur* (with whom I had once travelled upwards in a lift in the Dorchester, near enough to notice a painful operation on his eyelids), John Hays was completely convincing in the role. I wonder if he ever made it as an actor, though if he has survived the plague it will have been a miracle.

In the early eighties, New York was full of upper-class English attracted by accessible (gay) sex and cocaine, *and* the cheap dollar. They showed off and were rather unpopular. Two of them were heirs to an earldom and a marquisate respectively, and both died of AIDS. I remember one Saturday lunch at Mortimers, with the English noisily puffing marijuana (which always makes me sick) and being so objectionable that the native New Yorkers applauded when we left. I have always been addicted to nicotine, a vice I have had to forgo after one bypass too many, and alcohol; but at that time I did sniff the odd line of cocaine, which Freud and Lionel Bart both maintained (wrongly, I fear) was not addictive. I have always agreed with an author I once published, a New York cop in the narcotics division, the only friend of Tony Godwin and the one who found him dead in his Rhode Island exile, that the way to take crime out of drugs is to legalise them. In this way they could be monitored, regulated and – why not? – taxed.

Nevertheless, we were happy enough in the Village: a friendly place with a camp Anglican church and a gay synagogue, cosy bars, neighbourhood restaurants and good jazz. And outside the Village was America.

*   *   *

We drove up and down, down and up. We stayed with Laura's aunt in Palmyra, Virginia, in an ante-bellum house in a perfect eighteenth-century little town where she kept the general store. She stocked sacks of grain, nails and an electric saw, which she sold occasionally, but always had to repossess and return to the window, each time with more wood and grass in its teeth. The store had a food counter, the only one in town, so that when the court was sitting the judge and the accused, handcuffed to a policeman, sat on the same bench eating their hamburgers. Enormous black ladies, too wide to navigate the aisles of the nearest supermarket, were Aunt Lily Serena's most loyal customers; she would scamper up a ladder for their more arcane purchases, her delicate white hands directed from below – 'Jus' a lil' to the left, Missus Wiley. There y'go!' I noticed that relations between black and white were much easier in the South than in the colder North, but then not for nothing was Aunt Lily a daughter of the Earl of Scarbrough.

One day during the Falklands War, when we were in Palmyra, a black cop, knowing I was British, drove up and asked how it was going. Like most of Middle America, and indeed of Middle England, he approved (which I could not) the British initiative. I replied without much commitment, to which he remarked, 'Ah well, you've got dat Queen Maggie Thacker!' I made sure, via David Hart, that his comment was transmitted to Downing Street and was surprised not to get a CBE for my servility.

Twice we went to Haiti, where we nearly bought an eighteenth-century house in Jacmel. I even planned a book on that unfortunate island, once the richest of all French colonies until ruined by Napoleon's brother-in-law, General Leclerc, who cut down all the teak trees. When the buzz was that AIDS came from Haitian encounters, New York publishers sniffed with distaste.

We drove across America for the annual American Booksellers' Association *tamasha* in Anaheim, California. Laura had bought a giant pot of caviare, whose dispensation enormously increased our acquaintance.

Meanwhile, if it is meanwhile, Laura, together with her partner Marianne Hinton, who had a few percentage points of one of those Wall Street banks, had moved into the high-on-the-hog catering business for parties. These parties took place in the sort of Manhattan apartment building which refused to have Mr Nixon as a tenant.

One day Laura was short of a butler for a Christmas luncheon party for middling executives of a commodity firm called Gillon Duffus in their downtown offices overlooking the Brooklyn Bridge. I volunteered; I had always rather liked the idea of being in service. As a gesture to the Irishman hosting this cosy affair, I bought some Jameson's, with the object of making the Irish coffee I had so enjoyed at No.1, Fifth Avenue. It looked and tasted great and was surely easy enough to make. One just had to slide the cream over a silver spoon into the liquored coffee, thus creating an immaculate Guinness effect certain to rejoice the Irish heart of Mr Flynn, for that was his name. The menu was shrimp, which Laura had ordered from the famous Lower East Side fishmongers, Russ & Daughters, followed by *filet mignon* and ending with proper *pêche Melba*, which Stanley Parker, an Australian of bizarre aspect at Oxford, claimed Melba had shown him how to confect. No cheese – Americans don't understand cheese. I wore black trousers, white shirt and apron, and, with a shiver of masochism, hoped to be ordered around by arrogant executives as I laid out the drinks and mixers, sprayed the table and polished the glasses. Alas, the executives were polite and nervous at being invited to a lunch in the boardroom, the normal *habitués*, Mr Flynn explained, being in the Caribbean. They were in awe of their surroundings, and, worse, of us.

I started on the Irish coffee, but no matter how carefully I slid the cream over the silver spoon the mixture became colloidal and muddy. Of course, I drank it because we couldn't serve it to the guests; and, of course, repeated failure and the alcohol made me cross, so I shouted at Laura. Mr Flynn knocked gently at the door of the tiny galley and asked if we would mind making less noise. Then I served the shrimp and accompanying dip. A further knock on the door.

Mr Flynn. 'I'm sorry to disturb you but the shrimp is raw!'

This time I flew at Laura, with slightly more justification, but was shushed by Mr Flynn.

The shrimp was palatable when heated and the *filet mignon* could hardly fail; but the middle-rank executives did not appreciate the painstaking authenticity of my *pêche Melba*, though they thanked us humbly for their meal. As we washed up, the dining-room filled up with a new lot – salesmen from the Midwest for a conference – to whom I proposed iced coffee, without mentioning the significant ingredient. The air-conditioning could not disguise the unseasonal afternoon heat but the coolth of their libations concealed the Irish whiskey – soon they were all quite drunk.

Laura collected her cheque; and we removed a yard of smoked

salmon from the refrigerator, which would only have deteriorated over the Christmas holidays. A few months later Gillon Duffus went bust.

*   *   *

Though from the Midwest, John Dodds was the complete New Yorker. Walking down Fifth Avenue, we passed a heavily made-up lady in diamonds and furs, trailing an equally dolled-up poodle.

'That,' he said 'is *McCall's** cook.'

John knew everybody on the New York scene and had a good and a bad word for them all. Alger Hiss, for instance, was a bore and unlucky: 'My dawg ate his hat.' John was briefly a literary agent, and I bought from him an interminable Civil War novel, more to oblige John than the author, called *And Wait for the Night*. And God did we have to wait. Its author was one John Corrington, an Anglophile who drove a Morgan and was a passionate Southerner, with whom I stayed in Baton Rouge. There I observed the violence of the South: the rackety houses of the blacks, so thin that bullets could pierce through and kill the neighbouring inhabitants; nine-year-old boys clutching their rifles; the practice of setting a racoon alight with petrol and laughing as it ran. My delicate hostess kept a revolver in the glove compartment of her car. The day I arrived the local radio announced that the neighbourhood baseball coach had shot his wife's lover with a rifle. Five days later it was declared an accident.

On my annual visits to New York, I had always touched base with John Dodds, a popular, amiable fellow, who commuted between publishers, not because he quarrelled with his employers but on account of his limited attention span. An overt homosexual, he married Vivian Vance, who played the lady neighbour to Lucille Ball in the *I Love Lucy* soap. They loved each other dearly. Viv looked like a hippopotamus and was a perfect foil to the *svelte* and incredibly nasty Lucille Ball, notorious for having insisted on continuing her show the day after Kennedy was shot when the

* An American magazine.

entire crew was in tears. Viv earned a large amount of money every week – though not, of course, as much as Lucille Ball – reinforced by ten thousand dollars each time she did a commercial for Maxwell House coffee, empty tins of which, one for each showing, lined the kitchen of their jetty-side weekend home in the Hamptons. Neither of the Doddses liked boats: they only bought the place, they said affably, because it cost so much. For the same reason they lived in a penthouse overlooking Central Park, near another millionaire, Alistair Cooke, the Manchester lad who had done so well explaining America to Americans.

When Viv died, and with her the income, John had to move. I suggested he follow us to the Village. 'I haven't been to visit because I can't find a tank,' he complained. I replied that the Village was now safer than midtown Manhattan: there being no blacks, no armed tramps and no delinquent children. Furthermore, I explained the inhabitants were mostly gay couples of both sexes who walked hand in hand in their leathers to St Luke's on Sundays.*

John Dodds came and saw and bought a loft a block or two down the road from us. He furbished the place and installed a young man, who left with his most valuable artefact, the mantel-piece. With Midwestern tenacity, John pursued and recovered his treasure across three states, but not the boy. There were others though.

Charlotte Dugdale, an old friend of Laura, bought an enormous loft a block away, opposite a famous homosexual club called The Mineshaft, which I longed to plumb. Apparently one could only be admitted if totally clad in leather. During a blizzard, Charlotte and Laura kitted me out and I clomped off through the snow looking like an Arctic explorer. The Mineshaft was a huge

---

* I attended a gay synagogue service in the Village, which was full of children. Unlike in Europe, churches of every denomination pullulate in America. In Memphis there are more churches than gas stations; in Livingston, Montana there are nine, all full on Sundays. In a Jewish suburb of Boston, staying with my editor, I noticed children dragging their parents off to *shul* and insisting that they walked.

over-heated upper room, where my gear, which I had thought both appropriate and fetching, appalled the clientele, whose get-up was T-shirts. Two men drinking margaritas by the bar – obviously, from their conversation, from Wall Street – were talking shop: a banal encounter until I noticed that one of them had nonchalantly exposed balls. In a corner a group was watching, without much enthusiasm, a man being fist-fucked in a hammock. Albinoni tinkled. I felt an awful fool and stomped home.

We stayed in the Village on and off for four years. The Anglophobe lesbians, who controlled the condominium where we had bought our loft, accused us of importing cockroaches – *qui est absent a tort*. I was supposed to be scouting for Frederick Muller, which, under David Harlech, had purchased Blond & Briggs. I think David only bought us out of what my father called 'k of h'. Needless to say, I didn't find much for him in New York. My scouting consisted of mooching round the Village till I thought it seemly to indulge in the first Manhattan of the day. It didn't matter much: our continual losses were listed under 'stationery' in HTV's accounts and hoovered up in a twinkling by their enormous profits. 'Our accounting,' David enjoyed saying, 'is in Welsh.'

However, during this period, in 1981, I did publish the second most significant book of my thirty years in the game. *The New Science of Life* by Dr Rupert Sheldrake made a lot of money for Blond & Briggs. Publishers may be interested to know that this came about through the number of orders received by the warehouse, at full cover price plus post and packing, from the other half of C. P. Snow's 'two cultures'; for though the book was completely ignored by the posh papers, the technical press was thrilled. Rupert had been a mate of Andrew McCall at Clare College, Cambridge. He later worked as a biologist in India, developing a tough strain of hybrid wheat, and was one of those responsible for trying to eliminate starvation from the Indian sub-continent. Although everyone agreed he was a genius, he had failed to place the *chef-d'oeuvre* which was to make him internationally famous with any British scientific publisher. Moreover, he received, not rejection slips, but often, after many months, agonised and sometimes outraged explanations for rejection. When I published *The New Science of Life*, the journal *Nature* editorialised that the book was an intolerable tract and should be burned. This rare and surely unwise outburst provoked a clattering of telegrams from scientists the world over and promoted Sheldrake as an international anti-establishment figure. Milton's *Areopagitica* was quoted: 'As good almost kill a man as kill a good book.'

I sold the American rights to Jim Wade in New York, but he gave me lunch to explain why, after all, he could not publish it: his science editor said he would resign if he did, his authors would also leave. The hostility of the regular brigade, whose organ was *Nature*, derived from their recognition that alongside Sheldrake's eccentric, if not batty, theory of 'morphic resonance'* controlling the growth of all organisms (by whom one wondered – God?), there was a palpable attack on the most sensitive element of the body of the scientific profession – their wallets. Over twenty years and several books later, Sheldrake believes in the 'English string and sealing wax' approach to science. What did Newton receive in government grants? The apple that fell from the tree was free.

While we were there, Rupert became a cult among the young in America as had, ten years before, E. F. Schumacher. Laura and I attended a conference of trendy 'heads' at Tarrytown in upstate New York, where Fritjof Capra and the man who invented the credit card (Diners) were speakers. They were applauded, but for Rupert everyone stood up.

*   *   *

* His phrase, meaning that every living thing, from crystals to human beings, are informed, guided and developed by a collective outside agency to which they are magically connected. How else, for instance, do homing pigeons home; do sheep from Montana to New Zealand suddenly learn how to cross cattle grids by tucking their legs and rolling over them; can we ride bicycles when our great-grandfathers never could; can our children master computers in minutes; did London sparrows learn to peck the tops off milk bottles in three weeks? This resumé of a complex and controversial theory is intended more to intrigue rather than inform.

John Dodds died after we left New York. He was a strong man, barrel-chested like an opera singer and in the prime of life. He could have had Kaposi's Sarcoma, before it became known as AIDS, but I never knew. Who could have told me? John was a typical New Yorker, appearing and disappearing without trace.

An early victim of what appeared to be this plague affecting only homosexuals was a gentle, discreet and handsome young man who lived in our condo and performed as Hibiscus in 'Hibiscus and the Screaming Violets'. A candle-lit vigil was held outside St Vincent's Hospital as he lay dying, and after his death our janitor sprayed his apartment with disinfectant, sealed his front door with a shield of steel and sent his family out of New York City. As Edmund White,* now the gay guru and apologist, recalls, nobody knew the origin of the infection. Should they have shaved off their moustaches or stopped popping poppers?

Promiscuity in the bathhouses of Manhattan and San Francisco had generated a *rage au corps* among homosexuals, and in these hothouses the infection spread. Among the English who came to New York to enjoy this facility was a friend, and one time invigilator of Laura at Oxford, Philip Lloyd-Bostock, a young Spanish scholar and Fellow of Wadham College. Philip pillaged Manhattan for conquests and used to come round the next day bubbling with tales of his sexcess. Even then I had a *frisson* of fear – I was sure this wasn't 'quite right' – but then I had been known at school and at Oxford to have been a prig and rather 'pi' about these matters. I could not claim never to have dipped into those waters, but not, I reassured myself, as the death-toll rose, for a long, long time. Bridget Heathcoat-Amory gave a birthday party for Philip one sunny evening in a meadow near Lansdowne Square. It was known that he had not long to live. Babies were produced for him to kiss. It was a lyrical occasion. Not long afterwards Laura went to his memorial service, where some said his parents did not know of what he had died.

---

* White calculated that between 1962 and 1982 he had sex with 3,120 'partners'.

My oldest Oxford friend, who worked for the mayor in New York, came to our house in Sri Lanka for a holiday, clearly suffering from it, but not, as was then the custom, admitting it. My American editor, who also lived in the Village and who, when he worked for me in London, had assembled *Small is Beautiful* from papers on the floor of Schumacher's study,* died of it. I received no answer when I wrote an appreciation to his parents. AIDS struck high. Three museum directors of our acquaintance, in Bath, Chicago and East London, died of it, as did the most famous and surely the nastiest of New York lawyers (denying it to the end) Roy Cohn. As did Liberace, an early victim also of palimony, whom we had met with Edward Montagu at Beaulieu. America was ashamed. The British behaved better, especially, rather surprisingly, the upper classes.

The death of Roy Cohn caused few tears because he was the most loathed and feared lawyer in New York. I remember his coming to London in the fifties, with his buddy Shine, a golden-haired hotel heir and the first in New York to have a telephone in his car, with whom both Cohn and his patron, Joe McCarthy, were in love. Their mission was to cleanse the American Embassy of 'homos' and 'commies'. The day after their press conference the *Guardian* printed an editorial so indignant that they had to leave. McCarthy died, drunk and derelict, and Cohn became a lawyer representing only the rich and powerful (e.g. Nixon).

When we were in New York, Cohn was riding high. So when Marianne Hinton announced that she had been asked to quote for catering a party Cohn was going to give in Studio 54, we were rather excited. The theme, we were told, was 'prison' (so queer). Laura found a confectioner who agreed, for a price, to make a cake in the shape of Alcatraz. I thought my black and white chequer board of 'finger food' with steak tartare (secret ingredient whiskey) on pumpernickel and cream cheese would be fine and dandy, and felt entitled to offer my Bloody Mary that had gained me the only

* Rather like my editor has done with these memoirs.

prize I had ever won.* Money was no object: Mr Cohn's beano was going to be BIG. Then we were told the theme had changed to 'heaven'. Obediently we went back to the drawing board and started work on angel cakes, angels on horseback, pies in the sky, et cetera.

Then we were told Roy Cohn had given the job to his aunt. I considered his subsequent demise was truly a JOG – Judgement of God. The episode showed how easy it was to be affected by the Bonfire of the Vanities† which is New York. As the maxim goes: 'If you want to make God laugh, tell him your future plans.'

The snakes and laddery ways of the worlds of New York and Hollywood were exemplified in the careers of our two tenants: an Englishman in the loft and an American in Chester Row. The latter was a film producer who had entertained us to dinner in his Monticello lookalike in Beverly Hills with Timothy Leary, a tall, hammer-chested man, who was no longer on the LSD he had promoted but who drank a bottle of whiskey without blinking. (His father had been among the top brass at West Point.) We had someone in common, Michael Hollingshead, whom I had commissioned to write *The Man Who Turned on the World,* which indeed he had, having introduced Tim Leary, then at Harvard, to LSD, which he had ordered from Roche in Switzerland. Originally Michael had proposed this interesting new chemical, designed to cure migraine, but with curious side effects, to Aldous Huxley. Fortunately, Huxley was only interested in natural hallucinogens, like psilocybin (the magic mushroom), and suggested Leary. The

---

* In a competition run by the *Independent*, judged admittedly by our friend, the now late and much lamented Jeremy Round.
† Tom Wolfe, the author of that book and the most decent of men, gave Laura and me dinner at the Coffee House Club, where I had been introduced by my Wasp (five per cent of the population of New York) publishing friend, Clarkson M. Potter III. The club is one of the best things about Manhattan, distinguished, casual and friendly, somewhere you can even cash a cheque. Tom Wolfe remembered, which I did not, a restaurant column I wrote, for London theatre programmes, where I introduced a rating out of ten for the welcome given to patrons coming out of the cold; the concept pleased him.

rest is history. At first LSD succeeded as a wonder drug, under supervision, turning murderers into placid short-order cooks. Its disciples, who hailed its beneficent effects as Freud had endorsed cocaine, planned to supply the Pentagon to pacify that institution too, but a conspiracy between Time Life and the CIA, according to Michael, combined to ostracise and criminalise LSD, and its purveyors were persecuted.

I remember Billy Bolitho – son of a man known as 'Pull Through Bolitho' who had invented a system whereby naval guns only fired when the vessel was level – arriving off the *QE2* with a suitcase full of the stuff and giving parties in his Pont Street flat; the drinks were spiked with LSD with disastrous results. The son of Heather Potter, wife of Stephen and inventor of the Marriage Bureau, flew out of a window to his death, high on LSD. It was a dangerous drug and should have been legalised and monitored.

The film producer's beautiful grey-eyed and, I thought, loving wife had cut the sleeves off his immaculate suits and snipped all his ties in half. In the chest of drawers in my bedroom I found scores of miniature bottles of drink. When I telephoned him in America he told me he was an alcoholic and bankrupt. We never got the rent, but I said I would pray for him. Ditto with our English friend, who had been arrested at John F. Kennedy International Airport with a suitcase full of cocaine (detected immediately by sniffer dogs) and sentenced to eight years in a prison in upstate New York (a year per kilo). In his case, he paid us his rent out of the profits of his trade as a purveyor of mineral water – more solid than cocaine, I suppose.

We sold the apartment in New York, rather well, in 1984 and bought a slice of a warehouse in London's Docklands, the size of a tennis-court, or, as some said, a small Sainsburys.

CHAPTER TWENTY-NINE

Thank You for 'Aving Me

He stood apart. The other little boys from the orphanage were flitting round the garden, hunting for the chocolate bars stuck accessibly in the branches of the frangipani trees. He was examining the motorbike, scowling at the dumb buttons and trying for a reaction. He was the smallest, and, at five, the youngest, with a pot belly bursting his tiny shorts; he was slightly bow-legged and had a determined air. Cakes were distributed. He stuffed one in each pocket and held one in each hand. When trips round the garden on the motorbike were offered to each child in turn, he was the first to clamber on to the machine, handing me one cake to look after in order to give himself a free hand. He stuck to the petrol tank with his grubby knees for all eighteen expeditions; the others did not gainsay him. He was, as Billy — who was the chief of protocol for the party — said, 'the buzzer'. (Billy was a Glasgow tearaway, recently released from Preston Gaol and currently a touring apostle for Alcoholics Anonymous in a blue suit.) There, and more or less then, Laura and I decided, no such intention having previously crystallised in our minds, to adopt him.

Of course, he had adopted us. The orphanage was in the village of Wakwella, a few miles off at the end of the road. It was recognised as a place of beauty by a nineteenth-century American traveller to Ceylon, who stayed there to recover from the social life in Galle. We used to drive there for the sunsets and to see hundreds of egrets returning to their sanctuary, fluffing on to the branches of the trees like puffballs.

Next to a temple were a schoolroom and a dormitory for eighteen little boys. Both were barren of artefacts: no toys, no books, and not always enough to eat, since the orphanage, though run by a *bhikkhu*, was not official and relied on the surrounding villages to provide food. Their diet consisted mainly of bread, since rice, of which there was a surplus in Sri Lanka, could not be cooked without fuel. The average orphan ate three slices; Ajith ate five.

Ajith had not seen a mirror till he came to stay with us; when he did, he kissed his reflection with enthusiasm. Only one of the children was a victim of the troubles. He came from Batticaloa in the east, where his father and mother had been shot by the Tamils. In contrast, the Galle district was famous for it placidity: 'a dry dull place', according to a newspaper editor. Ajith and his fellows simply lacked fathers and/or mothers.

*   *   *

Ajith's family house stood by a muddy track, in a valley where cinnamon, paddy, rubber and tea flourished side by side. They said that a walking stick grows a papaya after six weeks. But it was also one of the poorest areas on the island. The family were cinnamon peelers by profession and caste. In Ajith's immediate household his grandfather was blind, his grandmother creaky and his mother mute, leaving his aunt as the main earner.

We arrived in our forty-year-old Austin car with Ajith, whom we had collected at the orphanage, and his *bhikkhu*, our negotiator and interpreter. It was made clear that dealing could not begin in the absence of his aunt, who was working on a tea estate and had to be sent for. This took about an hour, during which time two tin tables and some rickety chairs were produced: the only furniture in the concrete bungalow, a four-roomed affair which, more elaborately furnished, would not have been out of place in Peacehaven or any other modest seaside town. Grandma found a ten-rupee note in her shrivelled bosom and warm coloured fizzy drinks were served. I signalled to Laura that she *must* partake. Time dawdled. A man showed me how to peel cinnamon.*

Ajith began in an offhand but determined way to recite a prayer –

---

* The outer skin is removed with an age-old instrument, like a tiny cheese-grater, and thrown away; the husk is hollowed out and the green stick is dried in the sun until beige and brittle.

it was his only skill — perhaps to ease the tension which had increased with the crowd. Among the villagers was a pair of youths holding hands and gazing into each other's eyes. Nobody much cared. We were in another world. His aunt arrived breathless, in a brilliant green sari, as if she had been going to a ball, rather than just walking through the fields. The *bhikkhu*, who had promised a quiet place for these intimate negotiations, moistened his lips and began to explain our intentions in a low, serious voice. The neighbours and relations listened in silence. They had heard that foreigners took children from Sri Lanka and sold their kidneys and hearts for surgery, or dropped them down the wells or staircases in their big houses to claim the insurance. These well-known facts, as the Irish say, were reiterated to Ajith's family in the ensuing weeks. It is a mistake, as Tolstoy tells us, to imagine that simple people are kind to each other.

Although his family might be persuaded otherwise, we were planning a different sort of destiny for Ajith. An observer, especially from the nationalistic and increasingly xenophobic press, taking time off from reporting Tamil atrocities in the current civil war, might have constructed the scenario thus: English 'master' and 'wife' (I was pointed out in a small hotel on the island as the 'man who sleeps with his daughter') descend on a poor cinnamon peeler's house with a tame priest and the fatherless child of a mute peasant girl in their car, an object as inaccessible to them as a helicopter to an English farm labourer. They suggest removing the child from his mother's side and placing him in an alien culture on the other side of the world, and promise to send photographs. There was nothing false in this fancy, and it might have made just such a paragraph, but the whole truth was that Ajith had never lived with his family. He had spent his four years in three different orphanages. When he was a child and we left him to go out, he would say, 'Are you coming back?'

There can be little room in an orphanage for a child to express himself, but, once removed from there, Ajith's pent up emotions were stunningly released. He was allowed to stay with us pending the adoption. On the fourth day he marched into the kitchen and asked the servants, 'Why don't you stand up when I come into the room?' The orphan boy had only been contained, not formed, by his environment.*

Unlike the family friends, his fellow orphans (he was not old enough to go to school) were pleased for and proud of him. When we shopped in Galle for seventeen pairs of shoes, socks and pants, as well as seventeen T-shirts for the children of the orphanage, people congratulated us on giving Ajith the chance to leave for, in their words, 'a better life'.

*　　*　　*

You could see a dimple when he smiled. At first he never cried; tears can't be much use in a Buddhist orphanage, where the priest and his two male helpers have to divide their mother-love between eighteen little boys. He did not even cry when he was frightened. We quickly realised his fascination for water, even for a running tap, and thus his particular interest in our swimming pool. One morning he fell in and, being quite small, sank silently beneath the surface. I waded in and fished him out. After patting him dry, I was amazed to see him resume his former perilous position, leaning over and splashing the water with his hands.

The representative of the British Council and his adventurous Swedish wife, who had crossed Africa by Land-Rover and by train, were staying in the house, so we decided on a *promenade à l'eau* in a fishing boat, rented from the beach at Unawatuna and destined for the port at Galle. Ajith had never been in a boat. The sea was in a bad mood. Nevertheless, the fishermen, fearful of losing their fee, insisted on setting out and launched their boat broadside on. A fat wave slopped over the boat and knocked Ajith down. He looked terrified but kept silent. Mrs Representative picked him up and held him in her arms throughout what had now become a voyage rather than a trip: for once we were clear of the bay, the sea grew

---

* The social workers and their textbooks stress that adopted children should be reminded of their origins. We tried, but this bored him. Even in adolescence he was not interested to discover that he is descended, like everybody else in Ceylon, from Kandyan kings.

menacing. Despite the protests of the seamen, we insisted on disembarking illegally at the Naval Maritime Academy in Galle. According to Mrs Representative, had Ajith been any older he would have strangled her because he held on so tightly.

The district minister, whom we had harnessed, like everybody else we knew on the island, to help in the process of adopting Ajith, and who had already heard that 'he was very dark but had a sweet smile', advised us that he should be wormed. We bought some pills, at sixty pais each, which, like everything else, was beyond the means of the orphanage. The next day he excreted a tapeworm nearly two feet in length. It was long, dry, stick-like and very dead.

*　　*　　*

The procedure for (legally) adopting any child, anywhere in the world, is painstaking, protracted and, for the would-be parents, painful. I saw the desperation on the pale faces of the Scandinavians, who waited anxiously in the ante-rooms of Colombo officials.

I was the publisher of the president's official biography, a citizen of the former and much respected (barely a shot fired in anger in over a hundred and fifty years) colonial power. Moreover, I married Laura in our own house near Galle, giving us a certain amount of clout locally. Nevertheless, we could not bypass the bureaucratic route prescribed for the process of adoption, though we did travel down it at a pretty smart lick. Laura's grandfather had been the last British governor of Bombay. He had jailed (impartially) both Nehru and Gandhi and was much admired by the equally diminutive foreign minister, a Moslem, who had been serving at his post for a long time. On one occasion when we were having trouble locating Ajith's identity papers I remember his telephoning the registrar general at home on a national holiday and saying, 'I want that birth certificate on my desk Monday morning.'

Returning to London to gather evidence that Anthony Blond, aged fifty-eight, and Laura, aged thirty-three, were suitable adoptive parents, I discovered that I had not led the sort of life designed to produce such evidence. My long-standing friends were drunk, dead or inaccessibly rich and grand. None of them were social workers, the required testimonial source. I hadn't *got* a family doctor. My rabbi's wife thought it wrong to tear a child from his roots in the Third World and submit him to an alien culture. (I hadn't asked her!) I called a stipendiary magistrate who had once been to dinner and asked him to provide a reference. He replied that, though he remembered our large apartment and quite impressive lifestyle, he could not in all conscience . . . Didn't the man realise we lived in a loft? Had the food and drink been *that* good?

Back in Sri Lanka, Laura had been shuffling lawyers from a creaky room in the Galle Face Hotel, a building that Ajith had twice tried to ignite. The British papers were now urgently needed for the Sri Lankan court, which was to decide the issue. But who would vouch for me? I thought of my stepsister and second cousin, a contemporary of impeccable standing and bossiness. Our relationship was cool but I bit my lip and she agreed to see me. She began writing her reference: 'I have known him well for three months . . . ' Oh dear, a strange slip. The rewrite referred more accurately to a period of thirty years.

The day of the court-hearing arrived. There was a moment when Ajith's mother appeared to want to change her mind, but the day was saved by Ajith, who, when asked by the judge to which of his mothers he wanted to go, pointed firmly to Laura-Mama. The documents were faxed by the Sri Lankan High Commission to their Foreign Office via a machine which had been installed just in time. (God was working electronically.) Ajith now became Ajith Charminda Prema Lal Blond, and Laura promised to send photographs.

*   *   *

When we returned to London, we put up at the Savoy while our pad was being decorated for the Laura Ashley catalogue. Ajith sailed in there like a baby maharajah. (What roots? what alien culture?) He discovered that buttons marked MAID, VALET and WAITER, when pressed, produced interesting results. He ran up and down corridors with Laura's cousins, who were bigger than him, but less determined. For an undernourished, under-everythinged Third World child his energy was, and is, prodigious. So too is his charm. One of his godparents – we quickly assembled a posse – gave a lunch for him to meet some children. While the grown-ups, mainly 'foodies', gorged in the ample kitchen of our hostess, the children entertained themselves next door. After a while we noticed a strange silence. They were listening to Ajith, spellbound: he was talking in Singhalese.

*   *   *

Sir Raymond Carr gave a farewell lunch for his retirement as Warden of St Antony's College, Oxford, and Laura and I were 'bidden', as Simon Raven might have said, to attend. Among the top academic brass was Martin Charteris, the Provost of Eton. With Sarah Carr's consent I fetched Ajith from the car, where he had been asleep with his minder, another Sri Lankan.

We loved to show him off: with his pearly teeth, fine eyes, uplifting smile and energy, he never failed to please. After watching Ajith for a bit, Charteris turned to Laura and said, 'Give me your address and I'll send him the papers.' So when people asked, as they quite often did, 'Oh, I suppose he's down for Eton?' I could safely say that he was. (Simon Raven was indignant, maintaining that, as a black, Ajith would never be accepted. Oh so typical of Raven to transfer his *own* middle-class mores.) In the event, Ajith entered a humbler establishment.

I was a fairly good friend (twenty-five pounds per annum) of Southwark Cathedral, though how good a friend I failed to realise until the local church school enrolled Ajith without seeing him (bless them). He picked up English pretty swiftly, but what English! I took him to the indoor pool in our block and he learnt to swim, a skill Sri Lankans mainly lack. He also learnt to ride a bicycle in minutes. His body and personality were budding. The doctors at Great Ormond Street recommended a diet of milk, butter and eggs. But he had acquired a taste for foie gras: not so difficult to procure for him since I was *Vogue*'s restaurant critic at the time. Ajith disdained the child's menu.

We found out soon enough that our son was aggressive, demanding and occasionally fell into Hitlerian rages of frustration. We reminded ourselves of his loveless, toyless, joyless childhood and the hours he had spent in the temple intoning prayers. But he also had a gentle and most endearing side to his nature. Once, when we were crossing Oxford Street, he said, quite simply, 'Thank you for 'aving me.' He displayed compassion beyond his years, but maybe he was two thousand years old. The Sri Lankan biographer of the president explained that a Buddhist would have no difficulty whatsoever relating to Ajith's success as a little human being. It was a matter of karma. When Laura and I were wondering what to do about our one property speculation – a dinky new apartment overlooking the Thames which remained empty and unsold – Ajith said, 'Why don't you give it to someone who 'asn't got a 'ome?'

PART SEVEN

Un Promeneur Anglais en France

CHAPTER THIRTY

Blond in Blond

My publishing business had gone to the wall; our flat, the size of a tennis-court, was costing an arm and a leg; the headmistress of the school attended by Ajith had resigned, leaving it in disarray; and the car had been robbed twice of its complicated radio – street value nil. London was suddenly cold, cruel and dirty. The needle swung towards the vasty fields of France. My solicitor and friend of some forty years standing, or rather lying down, because I fatally never took his advice, had bought a house in the Lot-et-Garonne and asked us to stay.

The first good meal of my life, in 1946, was in the dining-car of the wagon-lit between Paris and Lyons, as it rattled through the war-torn countryside. I remember with clarity the six courses, including the aperitif and the digestif, each signalled by a different colour of chalk on the damask tablecloth. People were hanging on to the outside of the train, but respected the privacy of the few first-class passengers. For the first time in my life I felt rich. It was that massage of sweet poison, which evaporated in later life. But at the time it was important to have money, for in old age one has fewer wants. Fortunately, forty-three years on, I had learned to cultivate what the Germans call *Bedürfnislosigkeit* – wantlessness.

On the way to the Lot-et-Garonne, Laura and I broke our journey in Bellac, a small town between Poitiers and Limoges, and a fulcrum for traffic jams and caravans. There we spent a hot, noisy and sleepless night, in the middle of which Laura noticed on the map a village called BLOND.

The next morning we rose early and drove the nine kilometres to the commune of Blond, where we visited the twelfth-century church. As we left the church Laura saw a postcard pinned to an apple tree with the words A VENDRE in rain-washed ink. It was early in the morning and no one was about; but then all French villages have that feel: as if the inhabitants have fled, anticipating panzer divisions twenty minutes down the road.

Climbing up the Monts de Blond and emerging through the forest to a view of the plain below, I was struck by the beauty and tranquillity of the place. I was also beginning to get a kick out of the name, and the thought of my correspondence being franked BLOND. Once we reached the Lot-et-Garonne, numerous telephone calls were made to the *notaire* in Bellac and finally I secured the house for sixteen thousand pounds.

* * *

Blond in Blond, needless to say, did not work out. Laura bought a much grander house in Bellac, which in the seventeenth century had a rue des Juifs and a quartier des Juifs (so I felt more at ease), and we moved there. It is in Bellac that I now spend my life – apart from a few months a year in Sri Lanka – reading and writing, as well as entertaining those who come to stay. Laura peaks at around 3 a.m., by which time I am safely in bed, and resurfaces by the time I have said my morning prayers, finished my amateur yoga, and have read whatever was in the post – so often only junk mail, but still I read it.

Our acquaintanceship here is mixed: an assortment of old English friends who live locally; newer English acquaintances who I wish didn't live locally; the French who mostly keep to themselves; and – Bellac being a fulcrum for caravans – gypsies.

When Laura and I came to live in Bellac, we thought to widen our acquaintanceship, and so got to know a family of gypsies. We enjoyed their winning ways and learned to distrust them totally and absolutely, but not to dislike them. The mother had six children, and one, Hercule, was the same age as Ajith. They went to the same school and shared the same interests: in anything violent, noisy and dangerous, on and off screen, including a little light breaking and entering.* Punishment, when it occurred,

---

* They were so incompetent they were always caught within minutes.

consisted of TIG (*travail d'intérêt général*), tasks like cutting up fallen trees – though the organisers seemed principally concerned lest their charges were not properly wrapped up against the cold.

Hercule and his friends were always congratulated on their deportment at our parties. After one such, Laura's ruby and diamond ring went AWOL. So I took a photograph of it to the caravan and told the gypsies that Interpol had a copy and anybody attempting to sell it would be instantly flung into gaol. That didn't impress, but they might have registered my offer of five hundred francs for its recovery. They all proceeded to swear 'on the body of their brother' – why this should be in any way sacred is a gypsy mystery – that they had not seen the ring. A few days later, however, Hercule arrived with the ring, which he said he had found in his brother's – another one's – box. Gladly, I paid the ransom.

A seventh child was born, and in a gesture of reconciliation I agreed to become her godfather. I had always admired the mother's style; she used to arrive at the post office with an orange plastic flower in her hair and leave her menfolk outside while she collected wads of money, which she thrust into her modest bosom.

The municipality in Bellac allows gypsies to station their caravans, mostly alas motor drawn, on sites usually adjacent to a rubbish dump, with access to water and electricity, for four years at a time, after which time they must move on to another similar site. Three years after my promise, Madame reminded me of my undertaking and urged me to see the priest and arrange a date for the baptism. It was urgent, so she said, because their term in Bellac would soon end, and they would be moving to Le Dorat, all of six miles away. She and one or other of her extended family, especially a well-developed fifteen-year-old we called 'Mademoiselle Gèle-Bête', stalked me round the little town. I relented. Since priests in France are hard to pin down, and since the family, patently unemployed, had even less on their plate than I, I told them to fix any date they could with the priest and I would attend.

Another ambush and we all poured into the *presbytère* down by the church in the old town and were invited to sit down. There were not enough chairs, so the priest, quite an old man, went to fetch some more. None of the gypsies budged. With a sweet smile he asked if any of us could write? Madame was swift to deny any such accomplishment; Mlle G.-B. said she could . . . a little . . . So I spoke up. He did not know me, and while I had known two of his predecessors (one of whom told me 'les Bellachons sont religieux mais pas très chrétiens'), I did not know him. He had ten other parishes to attend to and I was touched that such a busy man should bother to baptise yet another gipsy baby, but I suppose he was a Christian.

How had I become acquainted, he asked, as I filled in the only simple form in France.

'We are friends,' said Madame firmly.

The priest lent us a booklet on baptism and told us to choose a text for the reading. On the way back to the caravan I undertook to order the baptismal cake, big enough for twenty, and the *dragées*.

'What about the baptismal dress?' asked Madame.

The eximious George Weidenfeld has invented a phrase for this ploy, 'susceptibilité peante', meaning the capacity to exact concessions from a position of weakness, with which he characterised Israeli diplomacy.*

Madame was a brilliant player.

I reminded her that all her other children had been baptised – or so she said. What had they worn?

'They have grown out of them,' replied Madame.

I had no answer to that one and fell silent. She dealt another card. 'We must hire a place in the *mairie*; there's not enough room in the caravan for a reception.'

I had to agree but when I asked Laura if we could host the occasion she said under no circumstances whatsoever was she opening her house to that lot; an opinion endorsed by Ajith and everyone else, as it were, on the block. After more long-distance negotiations when I blocked her request for musicians (wasn't that the one thing gypsies could do?), it was agreed I should deposit the cake, and

---

* Menachem Begin insisting on a bowl of water in which to wash his hands before sitting down to lunch at Downing Street.

supply, deliver and return the baptismal party to the caravan, which in the event was beautifully spruced up for the reception.

When I arrived to collect the baptismal party they had lost the key, a supererogatory concern, I thought, as the other two caravans on the site were occupied by relations; but, no, one of the daughters had to stay behind to caravan-sit. Mlle G.-B. held the child, clad in an embroidered pillow, on the back seat, and she began to be car-sick even before I had turned the key in the ignition. The other seat was occupied by a cousin, a blonde beauty of about eighteen, who was pregnant by yet another cousin and had already two other children.

My goddaughter was, at least temporarily, the child of a one-parent family, her father having gone off with his niece, now with child by him. Ajith's friend, his second son, explained that his father was unlikely to return because, if he did, arrangements would be made for him to be lynched. We set off. I told Madame I would 'take care' of the priest and patted the envelope in my jacket pocket, where l had put a new five-hundred-franc note, together with a letter of thanks. Laura was to meet us at the church with a few other congregants from our side, as it were, including a local English antique dealer and his two sons, one of whom was the same age as one of Madame's but almost twice the size. The priest arrived on time and I waited for him to don his soutane before handing him his money. I felt for the envelope.

It wasn't there. I must have left it in the car. It wasn't there. I asked Madame if she had seen it and she pointed to the church door, where it had fallen. I picked it up. My note was there but not the money. Hold on. I looked at her expressionless face. Surely not . . . not at her own daughter's baptism . . . the money due to the officiating priest?

I gulped. What a fool I had been! I wondered what Jesus, say, would have done.

(I knew what Hitler would have done.)

I had another five-hundred-franc note, put it in the envelope and gave it to the priest. He laid the envelope on a table, then, glancing at his congregation, put it inside a book.

Anger, hate and self-pity swept over me as I struggled to
concentrate on the priest trying to explain to the polite but clearly
not *croyant* congregation the significance of the ceremony. Candles
were issued and the baptismal child was sufficiently distracted to
forget her distress at the odious comforter being removed by Laura
from her bud-like mouth. She looked quite fetching dancing
around the gothic shadows of the nave, originally the chapel of the
Comtes Bozon de la Marche, big-time feudal lords, one of whom
tried to stop the Hundred Years War and is buried in Westminster
Abbey, surrounded by enamels from Limoges.

Mlle G.-B. had chosen a poem by Charles Péguy but wasn't up
to reading it herself; and though, in the phrase of Peter Mayer, I
was, like him, 'a church-crawling Jew', I thought I had crawled far
enough on this occasion. Laura, whose family had only ceased to
be recusant on their way to Chester Gaol in 1720, would be the
more appropriate performer. Her dear, dear classic voice rose easily
to the twelfth-century roof and soothed my savage breast.

A plea from the priest that we be more responsive with our
responses provoked an argument from the expats that we did not
understand the vernacular (French) . . . but had they remained in
Latin . . . This rather iffy proposition was briskly countered by the
priest, who said that Latin might suit us, but what about Bulgarians
or Romanians? The discussion lapsed.

The baptismal child responded with dignity to the occasion and
that, with the expertise of the priest, the patent pride of the gypsies
and the genuine gothic gloom lightened by candles, made of it an
event.

On the return journey Madame had trouble lighting her thirty-
ninth cigarette. And for a moment I thought she would repeat the
gesture of the uncle in Jacques Tati's film and throw the cigar
lighter out of the window; but she managed, after fumbling, to
return it to its socket. She told me, with a sense of achievement,
that that very day the hospital had said her lungs were black.

As a riposte (retaliation?) to Madame's request for music at the
reception, I stationed the car with radio blazing outside the
caravan – ditto the headlights, to guide the rest of the party, which

seemed to have lost its way. I suppose, in the dark, one rubbish dump looks much like another. Then all twenty-two of us squeezed into the caravan and tucked into the enormous and succulent cake, washed down by fizzy peach goo and sweet champagne. After this feast we had our pictures taken. They came out well and I sent them, via her son, to Madame, who, later, telephoned. But I thought gypsies never said thank you.

*   *   *

The hospitality of certain English acquaintances in France is often dreaded, though difficult to decline. The Blundells' (for let us call them that) invitation was the most dreaded. They lived in a *département* famous for its damp and war dead, and must have bought the château on a rare and sunny day. It sat at the end of a long winding drive, colonnaded by beech trees, through which the sun, when it shone, cast a pleasing dappled shade and revealed a gentle Victorian façade, which overlooked a swimming-pool and a sloping valley. It had cost the price of a studio flat off the Fulham Road.

In winter the lawn became a marsh, the pool a tank trap and the interior of the château as cold and misty as Rannoch Moor. The vast fireplaces with their grisly logs were as useless and irrelevant as sandwiches in a nightclub, and as for the central heating, it was invoked just long enough to stop the pipes from freezing.

Unwisely I removed my overcoat. The château reeked of financial illiquidity, and Mrs B. with her first remark confirmed this impression by asking hectically: 'Did you just try and telephone? To say you were late . . . or something?'

No, we hadn't. (We were very late.)

'Oh, thank God, they haven't cut off the telephone!'

After a chilly, but not chilled, aperitif we were sate at the dining table. Quails, in packets of four, were, we knew, *en promo*. They are not very fleshy birds, and two, stuffed, are necessary to be at all palatable. On this occasion they were singular and unstuffed – so a paltry dish. They sat like two derelict hangers, each with strands of meat trailing from the roof, on plates which one was invited to encompass with mounds of (home-grown) potatoes. I observed that their child, thin with long hair and of indeterminate sex, had not been offered one.

'He/She is vegetarian,' announced Mrs B. proudly. Then with a hideous gleam in her eye she produced a bottle of wine. 'Only six francs a bottle!' Gosh, we all said. Now that was real shopping.

On our second visit – it has to be said that the English in France in their early days are thin on social intercourse, and why should we have been an exception? – the château was even colder. The Blundells had sold the Aga. But they didn't give up, like so many, appalled by the inability of the French to understand them even when they articulate English so clearly. The Blundells had been trying to sell their château almost since they bought it. They wanted to move south. The south was warmer, contained more affluent English, who might be more eager to take their counsel on stocks and shares, wood chips, horses, pottery, wholemeal loaves, swimming-pools or whatever else they wanted to peddle.

The Bundells did eventually sell their château to another English couple – well not quite English and not quite a couple. A Lithuanian Jew and a young Spaniard of great charm, in turn, sold the château for even more money to God knows whom.

As for Laura and myself, I think we shall stay. When I die all I wish for is a Jewish funeral in Blond: that my rabbi performs the *K'ria*, and that after the *K'vura* is completed, my sons say the *Kaddish*. Although buried in France, I shall remain what I am – a Jew made in England.

Index